The Devil's Derivatives

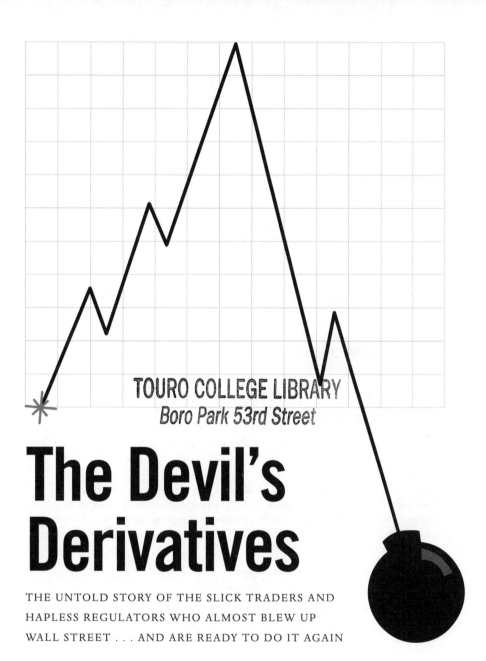

The Devil's Derivatives

THE UNTOLD STORY OF THE SLICK TRADERS AND
HAPLESS REGULATORS WHO ALMOST BLEW UP
WALL STREET . . . AND ARE READY TO DO IT AGAIN

Nicholas Dunbar

Harvard Business Review Press • Boston, Massachusetts

BP53

10 9 8 7 6 5 4 3 2 1

Library of Congress Cataloging-in-Publication Data

Dunbar, Nicholas.
    The devil's derivatives: the untold story of the slick traders and hapless regulators who almost blew up Wall Street. . . and are ready to do it again / Nicholas Dunbar.
        p. cm.
    ISBN 978-1-4221-7781-5 (alk. paper)
    1. Derivative securities—United States.   2. Finance—United States.   3. Investment advisors—United States.   4. Investment banking—United States.   5. Financial services industry—United States.   I. Title.
    HG6024.U6D86 2011
    332.640973—dc22

                                                                            2010038506

The paper used in this publication meets the requirements of the American National Standard for Permanence of Paper for Publications and Documents in Libraries and Archives Z39.48-1992.

1/18/13

For T

Contents

Foreword

What follows represents my interpretation of and commentary on events based on my long experience in the field of financial journalism. The views that I have reached and set out in this book are my own, and I have come to them based on my impressions from the people whom I have spoken to and the documents that I have reviewed.

Introduction:
The Siren Song of the Men
Who Love to Win

> It is safer to be a speculator than an investor. . . a speculator
> is one who runs risks of which he is aware and an investor
> is one who runs risks of which he is unaware.

—John Maynard Keynes

On a chilly winter's evening in 2003, I went out to an exclusive night-club in London's Knightsbridge district favored by bankers and hedge fund managers. My senses were assaulted by thumping dance music as I followed my friend who was weaving across a dance floor thronged with leggy Russian blondes and the men who love them. There were acquaintances under the strobe lights: I spotted the global head of interest rate trading at a big German bank shimmying up against a pair of microskirted brunettes who towered over him. We then went up some steps and came to the closed door of the VIP lounge—which had its own doorman. The door swung open and we continued our way to a low-ceilinged room, the VIP lounge within the VIP lounge. There, sprawled across low sofas and thick cushions were bankers celebrating their annual bacchanal, which is also known as "bonus season."

There were a few Brits and Americans there, but most of the revel-ers were continental Europeans wearing well-cut Italian suits and well-pressed dress shirts, with their Hermes ties long ago cast to the winds. They either sipped £30 whisky sours or topped off their glasses from

£400 bottles of Belvedere vodka. This was London before the smoking ban, and the glowing tips of cigarettes could be seen tracing formulas in the air as bankers sketched out the key details of their wildly successful deals for one another. I knew about some of them: there was the head of financial institutions derivatives marketing who forgot which of his Italian supercars had been towed off to the car pound. There was the head of credit structuring notorious for preying on female staff and having his corporate credit cards stolen by prostitutes. These young men—and almost all of them were young, some shockingly so—were the avant-garde of the credit derivatives boom, enjoying their first, fifth, or tenth million; outside the door of the VIP lounge, the Eastern European blondes were waiting to pounce on them.

There are many sobriquets for these young lions, but I like to think of them as the *men who love to win.*

The Moneymaking Gene

In London and New York—the twin cities of finance—the bonus season was big business for many people, and at Christmas, the streets tingled with money being splashed around. I had grown up in both cities, at a time when they were still postindustrial. In my youth, enclaves like London and New York's SoHo districts were edgy places that still had the brio of bohemian excitement, but in the past twenty years, those dingy streets had become dazzlingly clean and new. The bankers and hedge fund managers had arrived, bringing with them obscenely bloated annual bonuses, finely crafted automobiles, and their exhaustively renovated offices, homes, and wives.

In the early 1980s, the United States and the United Kingdom produced most of their wealth by manufacturing. A decade later—the financial services industry was dominant. In the United Kingdom, the sector contributed a quarter of all tax revenues and employed a million people. The business of making money was a very big business indeed. By the 1990s, the City and Wall Street had become the engines of the economy, sucking investments in from all over the world, then feeding credit to the masses and helping them pump that money through Main Street, High Street, and a million suburban shopping malls. The money thrown off by this engine did not just pay for the bankers' smart houses but benefited many other workers, such as architects, nannies, personal trainers, and chefs. The taxes skimmed off allowed politicians to claim credit for further largesse, to be enjoyed by a vast constituency of teachers, nurses, soldiers, and so on.

The transformation of New York City and London went far deeper than the upgrading of neighborhoods, the steep increase in property values, and the proliferation of boutiques stocked with overpriced merchandise. The value of financial assets held by banks, hedge funds, and other institutions had far outstripped the actual producing power of the U.S. and U.K. economies, and could be measured in multiples of gross domestic product (GDP). The nearly unfathomable wealth these people generated—and pocketed—fundamentally and irrevocably changed the world's financial system, and very nearly destroyed it.

To truly understand what brought on the great financial meltdown of 2008 requires a thorough understanding of the men who love to win, and how they came to fundamentally change not just the practices of a financial system that had been in place for centuries, but its very DNA.

This rare, often admirable, but ultimately dangerous breed of financier isn't wired like the rest of us. Normal people are constitutionally, genetically, down-to-their-bones risk averse: they hate to lose money. The pain of dropping $10 at the casino craps table far outweighs the pleasure of winning $10 on a throw of the dice. Give these people responsibility for decisions at small banks or insurance companies, and their risk-averse nature carries over quite naturally to their professional judgment. For most of its history, our financial system was built on the stolid, cautious decisions of bankers, the *men who hate to lose*. This cautious investment mind-set drove the creation of socially useful financial institutions over the last few hundred years. The anger of losing dominated their thinking. Such people are attached to the idea of certainty and stability. It took some convincing to persuade them to give that up in favor of an uncertain bet. People like that did not drive the kind of astronomical growth seen in the last two decades.

Now imagine somebody who, when confronted with uncertainty, sees not danger but opportunity. This sort of person cannot be chained to predictable, safe outcomes. This sort of person cannot be a traditional banker. For them, any uncertain bet is a chance to become unbelievably happy, and the misery of losing barely merits a moment's consideration. Such people have a very high tolerance for risk. To be more precise, they crave it. Most of us accept that risk-seeking people have an economic role to play. We need entrepreneurs and inventors. But what we don't need is for that mentality to infect the once boring and cautious job of lending and investing money.

Embracing Risk

I was granted my first look inside a modern investment bank around 1998, when I visited the trading floor of Lehman Brothers in London. What struck me was the confidence with which those traders and quants handled risk. On their computer screens were curves of rising and falling interest rates, plugged into the pricing models used to value and hedge their trading portfolio. I could see that the future behavior of these interest rate curves was uncertain, yet I listened as the traders loudly opined that their risk models were the best on the street, bar none. They ridiculed their competitors for getting things wrong. There was not a shred of self-doubt in the place.

On a later visit to the Lehman trading floor, I was introduced to the head interest rate trader, Andy Morton, a blond Midwesterner with intense, laser blue eyes. His acolytes were confident that their models had taken care of uncertainty, but Morton was like a risk-chomping crocodile. He had come out of academia having helped invent a famous interest rate pricing model, and no one on the trading floor had more reason to be assured than he was that Lehman had all its bases covered. By 2006 he was making over ten million dollars a year.

That kind of confidence—based not on bluster or bravado, but on intellectual analysis and fervent belief in markets—had crept up on the world unnoticed. I got a ringside seat onto Morton's world when I took a job at a trade magazine, editing and publishing technical papers written by quants at Lehman and the other big banks. There were debates aplenty over the risk models examined by my army of anonymous peer reviewers, but no one doubted that finance was becoming more scientific and safer, while old-fashioned prudence and caution belonged in a museum. The love-to-win mind-set was incubated and nourished within these investment banks. And the scientific gloss of the models assured you that the world outside, with its fear and inefficiencies, could be exploited to make you rich and virtuous at the same time.

The bankers and hedge fund managers celebrating their bonuses in the London nightclub had been created—and unleashed on the world— with an unnatural confidence about uncertainty that very quickly made our world a different place. And a more dangerous place.

For the Love of the Game

When I first met Osman Semerci, in January 2007, he was beaming with pleasure. It was not just the $20 million bonus he had recently been awarded that caused him to glow with self-satisfaction as he flashed million-dollar smiles while sharing a celebratory dinner with a gaggle of his tuxedo-clad colleagues. As the dapper, Turkish-born head of fixed income, currencies, and commodities at Merrill Lynch cracked jokes, he was proudly clutching a phallic, hard-plastic trophy with the logo of the trade magazine I worked for honoring his firm as "House of the Year."

By this time, my professional life had become synced with the annual cycle of the bonus season. The financial trade press could not survive by publishing technical articles or by selling subscriptions and ads. The magazines all discovered that one of the surest moneymakers was to hold an annual awards ceremony for investment bankers. Even in the toughest market conditions, the promise of winning a shiny trophy at a gala event would pry open the checkbooks to "buy" a table for the night.

Researching the yearly candidates for these various awards and rankings brought us journalists closer to the banks and the people who ran them. This was a good and bad thing. Enticed by the bait of an award, the bankers would open their kimonos and give out details of their deals and the names of their clients—information that normally was a closely guarded secret. That was good. More troubling was the fact that, somehow, the journalist entered into a complicit relationship with the institution.

This uncharacteristic openness puzzled me. Because awards season coincided with bonus season, I had assumed that the litany of client deals I was now privy to was an attempt by the head of a particular department to justify their bonuses. But I soon came to realize that the bonuses were often set before the awards were. Why, then, did these firms take these awards so seriously? I heard many stories of senior bankers pushing their underlings to work weekends—and sometimes all night—to prepare the pitch documents that would be submitted. It didn't take me long to figure out that the bankers were no longer motivated just by money. The status of a Lucite trophy had become part of their calculus of happiness, part of what drove them to do deals and concoct new products. No matter the stakes, they had to win.

This unique tribe sat at the heart of the financial system for the past decade. One of the mysteries to be solved in the following chapters is how its tolerance for risk and its blind need to win was institutionalized and disguised from the guardians of our financial system, who had such a terrible shock when things fell apart in the summer of 2007. Semerci himself was a case study in this final decadent phase, his firm racing to package and sell the most toxic financial products ever invented, until his job imploded seven months after he picked up the award and investment banks started choking on their own effluent. "Isn't your magazine responsible for some of this?" an executive director at the Bank of England asked me in early 2008, highlighting the role of the trade press as a cheerleader of destructive innovation.

With or without the assistance of magazine publishers, the love-to-win mind-set spread like a virus. With all the pixie dust—or was it filthy lucre?—these bankers sprinkled across London and New York, who could be surprised that their influence spread? First, it infected traditional bankers (and their hate-to-lose cousins at insurance companies, municipalities, and pension funds). Men and women who had been the pillars of their communities from Newcastle-upon-Tyne to Seattle, shrugged off their time-honored—boring!—roles of prudently taking deposits and offering loans, and started wanting to make "real" money. Regional bankers in turn spread it to consumers, who were encouraged to drop their "antiquated," risk-averse attitudes toward borrowing and home ownership. And thus was born the greatest wealth-generating machine the world has ever seen. It was truly awe inspiring in its raw power and avarice, and truly horrifying when it came crashing down.

There were many steps on that road to ruin. The first was the creation of the love-to-win tribe. Next came their easy seduction of traditional bankers and consumers, which led to a corruption of the ratings agencies, all of which was encouraged—either openly or through benign neglect—by the regulatory agencies charged with monitoring these people. Add several trillion dollars, and you have a recipe for disaster.

It took a final, crucial ingredient—a catalyst, an ingenious and insidious financial innovation that made it all possible. A helpful tool that upended the distinction between banking and markets. An enabler of a massive shift of power toward love-to-win traders that traditionalists barely understood despite their insistence that they too were "sophisticated." A mechanism for replicating reality and synthesizing financial robots that allowed complexity to go viral.

It's time to meet our first derivatives.

CHAPTER ONE

The Bets That Made Banking Sexy

Starting in the late 1980s, a new emphasis on shareholder value forced large banks to improve their return on capital and start acting more like traders. This sparked an innovation race between two ways of transferring credit risk: the old-fashioned "letter of credit" versus a recent invention, the credit default swap (CDS). Behind this race were two ways of looking at credit: the long-term actuarial approach versus the market approach. The champion of the market approach, Goldman Sachs, quickly moved to exploit the CDS approach and was richly rewarded for its ambition—and ruthlessness.

Something Derived from Nothing

There was a burst of tropical thunder in Singapore on the autumn night in 1997 when I met my first credit derivative traders. Earlier that day, there had been a lot of buzz in my hotel's lobby about an imminent Asian currency crisis. People were muttering about the plummeting Thai baht, Malaysian ringgit, and Korean won. Suharto's Indonesian dictatorship—only a thirty-minute boat trip away across the Singapore Strait—was lurching toward default and oblivion.

But there were also people who were planning ahead. They were the attendees of the finance conference I had come here to write about, and they were sequestered away from the tropical humidity, in the air-conditioned, windowless suites of the conference's main hotel.

They wore name tags and listened attentively to presentations on managing risk. Many of them worked for companies that imported and exported to the region, or had built factories there. You could see evidence of this globalization in the fleets of freight ships endlessly passing through the nearby Singapore Strait. As the writer Thomas Friedman put it, the people at this conference had figured out that the world was flat, and there was money to be made everywhere.

Well, maybe not quite. There were still a few bumps to pound smooth. The troubles in Thailand, Korea, and Indonesia had just injected a big dose of uncertainty into the world's markets, which the acolytes of globalization at this conference didn't want. For companies that become big and global, financial uncertainties inevitably creep in: uncertainty in foreign exchanges, the interest rate paid on debts or earned on deposits, inflation, and commodity prices of raw materials. One might accept that betting on these uncertainties is an unavoidable cost of doing business. On that day in Singapore, however, the looming Asian crisis had heightened fears to the point where most people wanted to get rid of the problem. Delivering presentations and sponsoring the exhibition booths nearby were the providers of a solution: financial products aimed at shaping, reducing, or perhaps even increasing the different flavors of financial uncertainty. These products went under the catchall name of *derivatives*.

They were called derivatives because they piggybacked on—or "derived" from—those humdrum activities that involved exchanging currencies, trading stocks and commodities, and lending money. They weren't new—in fact, they were centuries old—and they were already routine tools in many financial markets. For example, imagine trying to buy a million barrels of oil, right now, in the so-called spot market. Leaving aside the financing, a deal (and hence a price) is only feasible if you have a place to store the commodity you buy, and there is a seller storing the commodity nearby waiting to sell it to you. A *forward contract* specifying delivery in, say, a month from now, gives both sides a chance to square up the logistics.

The important thing about these contracts is not that they refer to transactions in the future—after all, all contracts do that—but that they put a price on the transaction *today*. The derivative doesn't tell you what those barrels of oil will actually cost on the spot market in a month's time, but the price that someone is willing to commit to today is useful information. And with hundreds of people trading that derivative, discovering the forward price using a market mechanism, then the value of the contracts becomes a substitute for the commodity itself: a powerful way of reducing the uncertainty faced by individual decision makers.

Thus, while *bureaux de change* might offer spot currency transactions (for exorbitant fees), big wholesale users of foreign exchange markets prefer to buy and sell their millions in the forward market. Because these buyers and sellers are willing to do that, many analysts believe the rate of sterling in dollars or of yen in euro next week is a more meaningful number than its price today.[1] Gradually, banks offering foreign exchange and commodity trading services extended the timescale of forward contracts out to several years.

For example, German airline Lufthansa might forecast its next two years' ticket revenues in different countries and the cost in dollars of buying new planes and fuel. Lufthansa, which works in euros, then uses forward contracts to strip out currency and commodity risk. The attraction of controlling uncertainty in this way created an efficient, trillion-dollar market. The derivatives market.

Yet for that audience in Singapore, forward contracts weren't quite enough to control financial uncertainty in all the ways they wanted to control it. There were presentations on *options,* which, in return for an up-front premium, gave the right, but not the obligation, to sell or buy when one needed to—a bit like an insurance policy on financial risk. And there were *swaps,* which allowed companies to exchange one type of payment for another. This last derivative, in addition to providing a price information window into the future, had a potent transformational property: the ability to synthesize new financial assets or exposures to uncertainty out of nothing.

Consider the uncertainty in how companies borrow and invest cash. A treasurer might tap short-term money markets in three-month stints, facing the uncertainty of central bank rates spiking up. Or they could use longer-term loans that tracked the interest rates paid by governments on their bonds, perhaps getting locked into a disadvantageous rate. Imagine that once you had committed yourself to one of these two financing routes, an invisible toggle switch allowed you to change your mind, canceling out the interest payments you didn't want to make in return for making the payments that you did. Thus was the interest rate swap, the world's most popular derivative, born.

Swaps first proved their value in the 1980s, when the U.S. Federal Reserve jacked up short-term interest rates to fight inflation. With swaps, you could transform this short-term risk into something less volatile by paying a longer-term rate. Swaps again proved useful in 1997, when Asian central banks used high short-term interest rates to fight currency crises. Just how heavily traded these contracts became can be gauged from the total "notional" amount of debt that was supposed to be transformed by the swaps (which is not the same as their value): by June 2008, a staggering $356 trillion of interest rate swaps had been written, according to the Bank for International Settlements.[2] As with forward contracts on currencies and commodities, the rates quoted on these swaps are considered to be a more informative way of comparing different borrowing timescales (the so-called yield curve) than the underlying government bonds or deposit rates themselves.

Derivatives—at least the simplest, most popular forms of them—functioned best by being completely neutral in purpose. The contracts don't say how you feel about the derivative and its underlying quantity. They don't specify that you are a hate-to-lose-money corporate treasurer looking to reduce uncertainty in foreign exchange or commodities. A treasurer based in Europe might have millions in forecast revenues in Thailand that he wants to hedge against a devaluation of the Thai currency. A decline in those revenues would be "hedged" by a gain on the derivative. But if there weren't any revenues (after all, forecasts are sometimes wrong), the derivative didn't care. In that case, it became a very speculative bet that would hit the jackpot if Thailand got into trouble, and would lose money if the country rebounded.

Saying a derivative is "completely neutral" in purpose is true, but misleading. The derivative doesn't care which side of the bet wins, but the person who sold the derivative certainly cares about making a profit. In the Singapore conference room that week, there were many people who didn't work for corporations but instead were employed by hedge funds engaged in currency speculation. For the community of secretive hedge fund traders, which included people like George

Soros, financial uncertainty was a great moneymaking opportunity. Governments—Malaysia's in particular—were already railing and legislating against currency speculation, but derivatives invisibly provided routes around the restrictions. A derivative didn't care whether you were a treasurer with something to hedge but then decided to use derivatives not as insurance but rather to do some unauthorized speculation. Right from the start, derivatives carried this potential for mischief.

That's why some people felt they needed to be regulated. One answer was to quarantine derivatives in a special public venue called an *exchange,* a centuries-old innovation to ensure that markets work fairly and safely. But it was too late to box derivatives in that way—by the time I attended that conference in 1997, a fast-growing alternative was already eclipsing exchange-traded derivatives. These were *over-the-counter* (OTC) derivatives traded directly and privately with large investment banks, with the interest rate swap being the most obvious example. The banks that created and traded OTC derivatives did not want to take only one side of the market, such as only buying yen or only lending money at a five-year interest rate. The derivative-dealing banks set themselves up as secretive mini-exchanges. They would seek out customers with opposing views and line them up without the other's knowledge. The bank sitting between them would not be exposed to the market's going up or down and could simply skim off a percentage from both sides, dominating the all-important pricing mechanism that was the derivatives market's big selling point. There was so much to be skimmed in this way, and so many ways to do it. But perhaps the most lucrative way of all was to invent new derivatives.

In Singapore on the night after the conference, I joined a group of conference delegates on a tour of some of the city's famed nightspots. With me were a pair of English expat bankers who worked on the emerging market bond trading desk of a Japanese bank. They told me about a derivative that had been invented two years earlier. It was called a credit default swap. Rather than being linked to currency markets, interest rates, stocks, or commodities, these derivatives were linked to unmitigated financial disaster: the default of loans or bonds. I found it hard that night to imagine who might be interested in buying such a derivative from a bank. The nonfinancial companies whose activities in the globalized economy exposed them to financial uncertainty didn't seem interested. The derivatives that were useful to them—futures, options, and swaps linked to commodities, currencies, and interest rates—had already been invented. It seemed to me as if the credit default swap was an invention searching for a real purpose. As it happened, the kind of companies that found credit default swaps most relevant were those that had lots of default risk on their books: the banks.

Losing That Hate-to-Lose-Money Mind-set

Back in the early 1990s, the world's biggest banks were still firmly rooted in an old lending culture where the priority above all else was to loan money and get paid back with interest. Like the small banks on Main Street, USA, these Wall Street banks were run by men who hated to lose money. There was just one problem with that fine sentiment: despite the vaunted conservatism of the traditional banker, money had a habit of getting lost anyway. In the 1980s, Walter Wriston, the chairman of Citibank, declared that "sovereign nations don't go bankrupt." A few years later, Mexico and a host of Latin American nations defaulted on their loans and put Citibank on its knees. By the time I flew to Singapore for that conference in 1997, the big bankers knew all too well about the dangers of emerging market lending and were looking for ways to cut their risks.

By then, the traditional banker had already become a mocked cliché on Wall Street, the cranky grandfather ranting at the Thanksgiving dinner table about "those damn kids today . . . !" And in the same way that only the neoclassical facade of an old building is saved from demolition, commercial banks like Chase or J.P. Morgan studiously gave the appearance of being powerful and prudent lenders. But behind that crumbling facade, the real business of banking was rapidly changing.

One way around the problem was to make more loans but then immediately distribute them to investors in the form of bonds. As long as the bonds didn't go bad immediately, the credit risk was now the investors' problem, not the bank's. This was the world of the securities firms: Goldman Sachs, Morgan Stanley, and Lehman Brothers. The

Glass-Steagall Act, which kept commercial banks out of securities, was about to be abolished in 1999 and was becoming increasingly irrelevant anyway: by using new products like derivatives, or by basing subsidiaries outside the United States, American banks could do as much underwriting and trading as they liked.

And yet, the Goldman Sachs model of underwriting securities and selling them to investors was no panacea: market appetite for bonds could dry up, and in some areas, like Europe, companies preferred to borrow from banks rather than use the bond market. So as the new breed of multinational bank took shape and branched out into new businesses, the credit losses kept coming. In early 1999, I flew from London to New York City to interview Marc Shapiro, the vice chairman at Chase Manhattan. He was a lanky Texan whose off-the-rack suits and homespun manner personified the hate-to-lose commercial banker. After we'd talked, I was taken to meet the bank's chief credit officer, Robert Strong, who talked about his memories of the 1970s recession and how cautious he was about lending. I knew why Chase was selling me this line so hard. A few months earlier, it had lent about $500 million to the massive hedge fund Long-Term Capital Management (LTCM), which was on the brink of bankruptcy and threatened to bring much of Wall Street down with it until a consortium of banks (including Chase) bailed it out. At the time, Chase was mocked for being so careless with its money, and Shapiro was keen to signal that this had been a one-off.

That same trip, I went to J.P. Morgan's headquarters on Wall Street, where it had been based for a century. The tall Englishman with a high forehead who greeted me in a mahogany-paneled room reminded me of the head of a university science department. Peter Hancock was the chief financial officer (CFO) of J.P. Morgan, but his aura of sophistication and analytical intelligence was the complete opposite of Shapiro's. Despite the sharp contrast in styles, Hancock's bank had also embarrassed itself with imprudent lending. The difference was that the lending took place through the fast-growing OTC derivative markets. A Korean bank had signed a swap contract with J.P. Morgan that, on the face of it, looked like a reasonable exchange of cash flows intended to reduce uncertainty. But it also amounted to a bet that a local-currency devaluation wouldn't take place. When the Korean won was devalued against the dollar at the end of 1997, the Korean bank suddenly owed J.P. Morgan hundreds of millions of dollars, and it was unable to pay. J.P. Morgan had to write that off as a bad loan and was now suing to recover the money. This was embarrassing, not because the contract didn't say the money was owed (it did, and this was confirmed by a court), but because J.P. Morgan had not anticipated the amount's becoming so large and had not checked to see whether its Korean client was good for the money.

Although the nature of the losses was different, the challenge for Chase Manhattan and J.P. Morgan was the same: they had had to ratchet up credit exposure in order to compete, and now they had to find ways of cutting it back again without jeopardizing revenues. Shapiro explained that this pressure came from the fashionable doctrine of *shareholder value added* (SVA). Invented in the 1980s and associated with General Electric CEO Jack Welch, SVA argued that nonfinancial companies should ditch low-growth businesses that tied up shareholder capital, and produce a bigger return for shareholders. But how did it apply to banks, whose primary business was lending money?

The problem with bank lending as a profit generator is simple: no business is hungrier for capital than the one that hands out money to borrowers and then waits to get paid back. Add in the capital reserve for bad loans and the regulatory cushion to protect depositors, and the income for shareholders is modest. That is the price shareholders once paid—happily—for investing in a boring but safe business. However, SVA made traditional bank lending look unattractive compared with other kinds of banking that didn't tie up all that expensive capital. Chase and J.P. Morgan attacked the problem in fundamentally different ways: one embracing the new innovation of credit derivatives, and the other following a more traditional approach. The success and pitfalls of these two routes would reveal just how subversive the new innovation was to the way banking worked.

All the Disasters of the World . . .

How do financial institutions justify taking credit risk? Given that banks are by design hate-to-lose institutions, conditioned to avoid bad lending whenever possible, how do they come to terms with the uncertainty surrounding their borrowers? And if you don't want this kind of uncertainty, whom do you pay to protect against it? And how much should you pay?

In the late 1990s, the way most bond investors and lending banks looked at credit was reminiscent of how insurance companies work. This safety-in-numbers actuarial approach went back three hundred years, to a financial breakthrough that transformed the way people dealt with misfortune: the birth of modern life insurance. The early life insurance companies were based on the work of Edmund Halley, who published the first usable mortality tables, based on parish records for the Polish-German city of Breslau, in 1693, showing that about one in thirty inhabitants of the city died each year. Armed with these figures, a company could use the one-thirtieth fraction to set prices for life insurance policies and annuities. Policyholders were members of a population subject to patterns of death and disease that could be measured, averaged, and thus risk-managed. Thus, wrote Daniel Defoe, "all the Disasters of the World might be prevented."[3]

If a life insurance company brought together a large enough pool of policyholders, individual uncertainty was almost magically eliminated . . . so long as the actuary did his math correctly. The actuarial neutering of uncertainty takes us to the statistical extreme of probability theory—the premise that counting data reveals an objective reality. By analogy, bankruptcy and default are the financial equivalent of death, and are subject to a statistical predictability over long periods of time. A bank with a loan portfolio is equivalent to a life insurance company bringing together policyholders to pool mortality risks. In other words, owning a portfolio of bonds might alleviate some of the anxiety of lending.

Of course, this doesn't absolve the bank or investor of the need to do due diligence, in the same way that an insurer might require proof of age or a health check of someone seeking a life insurance policy. In bank lending or bond investing, there are "credit police" ready to help. This might be the credit officer at a bank or, more ubiquitously, a credit ratings agency paid by the borrower to provide them with a "health certificate." Instead of an actuary counting deaths, lenders can turn to a ratings agency to count defaults and crunch the numbers. For smaller banks, and insurance companies and pension funds lacking the resources and data of big banks, there was no other way to go.

The world's first modern-day credit policeman-for-hire came on the scene over a century ago. He was a financial journalist called John Moody, and he became particularly interested in American railroads. Moody was writing for an audience of investors based in the growing financial centers of New York and Chicago, and he wanted to explain to them how this confusing but booming industry worked and which pitfalls to avoid. Around 1909, he saw an opening for his analytical skills. He set up an eponymous business selling expert opinions to hate-to-lose investors considering an uncertain bet on a company's bonds. Moody's independent experts would drill down into a company's accounts and scour public records to find out what a company really owned and how its assets were performing.

Moody already had well-established competitors, notably Henry Varnum Poor's company, which had been doing the same thing for fifty years. With a flash of marketing inspiration, Moody decided to distinguish himself by lumping opinions about different companies into common categories, depending on creditworthiness. The categories were labeled alphabetically. Three As, or triple A, was the very best category, equivalent to the credit standing of the mighty United States itself. Then came double A, single A, then on to B (subdivided in turn), next C, and finally D, for default. Bonds above the Ba rating would be called *investment grade,* and the ones below it *speculative grade*. It was a clever branding idea, and within a decade, several competitors in the business of selling financial research—the Standard Statistics Company and Poor's firm (which later merged to become Standard & Poor's), and Fitch Ratings—began doing the same thing.[4]

At first, Moody sold his bond ratings to investors via a subscription newsletter, similar to financial trade publications today. Those who trusted his opinions didn't have much more to go on than the sheer skill of Moody's analysis and insights. But over time, the business model evolved. Moody began counting bond defaults—there were thirty-three in 1920 and thirty-one the following year—and used the data as a way of monitoring his analysts' performance. Hate-to-lose investors who relied on Moody's expert opinion to validate bond-buying decisions were heartened to see that the proportion of investment grade bonds defaulting was much lower than speculative grade, a sign that Moody was indeed sorting the sheep from the goats. By the end of the twentieth century, Moody's and the other ratings agencies had counted thousands of corporate defaults, and their influence as credit police was unparalleled.

If you assume that statistics have indeed tamed the uncertainty of default, how much should you expect to lose? A portfolio of bonds of a particular grade would need to pay an annual spread higher than that of a risk-free cash investment, to compensate for the average default rate for bonds. In the same way that life insurance premiums vary according to the age of the policyholder, there is a credit spread for a particular rating of bond—so, for example, bonds rated *Baa* by Moody's should pay about a quarter of a percentage point in additional interest to make up for expected defaults over time.[5]

If you make it your business to lend money to a large number of *Baa*-rated companies, then on average, over time, your business will theoretically break even—so long as you charge these companies at least a quarter of a percent more a year than the loan rate enjoyed by the government. "Healthy" (investment grade) companies are happy to pay this "insurance premium" in return for borrowing money, and the spread earned on corporate bonds or loans is typically a multiple of the statistical default loss rate.

Back in 1997, most credit investors followed this actuarial approach to owning bonds or loans. Even today, there are still plenty of investors like this around—two of Britain's biggest life insurers, Legal & General (L&G) and Prudential, proudly trace a lineage back to the Victorian era. L&G said that for bonds used to back its annuity liabilities, the long-term historical default rate was 0.30 percent, while Prudential stuck to its figure of 0.65 percent. Both companies insisted that over a thirty-year span, they would be vindicated. Thirty years. This actuarial approach only works if you keep a steady hand and don't give up on your investments prematurely. The year-to-year default rate can jump all over the place, even if the long-term average remains stable. Taking a long-term view means being able to ride out a recession by waiting for the good loans in your portfolio to balance out the losses over time.

Moody's Investor Service and Standard & Poor's and Fitch set themselves up as the guardians of this actuarial approach. The ratings agencies used the term *through the cycle* to describe their ratings, a reassuring phrase that implied that the actuarial approach was recession-proof.

The Grim Repo Man

By 2002, Moody's was being pushed to incorporate a very different way of rating loans and bonds. Call it the *Goldman Sachs*, or *market*, *approach*, which is what the people manning the trading desks of investment banks and hedge funds call it. With this approach, buying a bond or making a loan means holding an asset in a *trading book*. Like the loan or *banking book* of a bank, the trading book is leveraged. Unlike the banking book, it is financed not with customer deposits, but with another form of short-term lending, called *repo*.

Repo is a bit like a very short-term mortgage—a lender advances you the cash to buy your house on condition that they keep the title deed as collateral. Like a mortgage, repo lending is collateralized, and if a trader can't repay the loan, the lender "repossesses" it and can sell it, like a foreclosed house. However, there are key differences. One is that while mortgage lending operates over years, repo lending typically functions with a horizon of a week or even a day. More important, repo lenders watch the value of their collateral very carefully. If the value declines sufficiently, the hate-to-lose-money repo lender sends out a *margin call*—a demand for instant cash to make up for that loss in collateral value. If the margin call is not met, the bond can be liquidated or sold. Margin calls acutely concentrate the minds of traders, which makes their lives fundamentally different from those of traditional lenders or insurance company executives who see the world through long-term spectacles. The discipline imposed by short-term collateral funding gives investment bankers a profound respect for market valuation. They are equally likely to inflict margin calls on others (such as hedge funds) as they are to be on the receiving end of one. They live by the sword of market value or die by it.

Think about owning a bond or loan in this new world. The idea of patiently waiting for years to be proved right by long-term statistics becomes almost absurdly antiquated, even laughable. The uncertainty of market prices now rules. The market is likely to sniff out problems before a ratings agency chalks up another default, and margin calls will quickly force people to sell. Default or bankruptcy is still going to be a problem if you own a bond, but rather than waiting to record a loss the way an insurance company does, the question is whether you can afford to stay in the game.

In this price-driven environment, the spread (the return above risk-free rates) paid by a bond or loan is no longer an actuarial insurance premium for long-term default risk. Instead, it is compensation for price risk, which changes to reflect the day-to-day opinion of the market. Suppose that after you have relied upon the ratings agency "health check" and made a large investment in a company, the market turns against the company so much that no one will buy its bonds. The price, which is an agreement between buyers and sellers, drops to a level commensurate with default. It won't even matter that there might not actually be a default—if you are a forced seller in such a situation, it will have the same effect on you and your portfolio.

The Billion-Dollar Swap Meet

These two approaches to taking credit risk—the actuarial and the market approach—have created two distinct cultures in finance: the long-term world of lending banks, insurance companies, and pension funds, and the short-term world of trading firms and hedge funds.

This cultural divide was hardwired into the system via accounting rules and regulations. Lending banks and insurers have typically recorded their holdings of loans and bonds at *book value,* which is the amount originally lent out, with some allowance for interest accruals. Book value could only be written down when a borrower had defaulted or was clearly in difficulty. Investment banks (including the parts of lending banks that trade), mutual funds, and hedge funds use *fair value* accounting. This is typically the market price, and if the market doesn't like a particular borrower or its loans, this immediately lands on the balance sheets of its creditors.

These two civilizations of credit, each with trillions of dollars of assets, have kept a wary eye on each other for a long time. Lenders and insurers argued that economic growth and stability depended on a patient, long-term view of credit. Trading firms responded that book valuation lets banks or insurers conceal problems and let them fester (such as the savings and loan, or S&L, crisis of the 1980s), problems that would be sniffed out quickly by the market.

Back in the late 1990s, such back-and-forths may have been good fodder for academic debate but didn't seem to matter much in the real world. But business pressures suddenly put the two worlds at odds. There was the pressure on senior bankers such as Chase's Marc Shapiro and J.P. Morgan's Peter Hancock to shift credit risk off their balance sheets, and the pressure on investment banks to respond to the threat of commercial banks' breaking into the securities business. But what really rocked both of these worlds was a radical financial innovation: credit derivatives.

Imagine a bank looking to make corporate loans or to own bonds—but without the credit risk. How does it strip out the risk? Easy: think of the loan as two separate parts. Pretend the loan is made to a borrower as safe as the government, which will repay the money without fail, and pays a "risk-free" rate of interest in compensation. Then there is an "insurance policy" or indemnity, for which the risky borrower pays an additional premium to compensate the lender for the possibility of not repaying the loan (although they might have to hand over some collateral). Bundled together, the risk-free loan plus the insurance policy amount to a risky corporate bond or loan. For a bank that wants to hold on to its loans, shedding the credit risk can be done by unbundling that package. Instead of keeping the "indemnity payments," the bank passes them on to someone else, who takes the hit if the customer defaults. At this stage, it becomes a question of how such a credit risk insurance contract might be designed, and who would provide the coverage.

It turned out that providers could be found in both financial camps. If you wanted to deal with people who lived according to the actuarial approach, then there was a centuries-old method of hedging credit risk by transferring it to a third party: banks that would sell you contracts, which they called a *letter of credit*. And of course, there were bona fide insurance companies that would agree to underwrite the credit risk of bonds and loans with policies they called *wraps, surety bonds,* and other names. It was a well-established business, with some insurance companies, called *monolines,* specializing in offering the policies.

At Chase Manhattan, Marc Shapiro decided to work with insurance companies and banks that provided letters of credit. An example of how this worked was in a niche lending market: Hollywood. Independent filmmaking is glamorous but risky, with fickle audiences determining whether financiers get repaid. But Chase's global entertainment group in Los Angeles wanted a piece of it, so in the late 1990s, the bank's loan officers loaned some $600 million to producers of films, including *The Truman Show,* by persuading an executive working for French insurance giant AXA to write policies against poor box office results.

Now suppose you preferred to work with people who swore by the market approach to credit, as Peter Hancock did. The credit default swap was the trading world's modern solution. This industry had already created a thriving business enabling clients to protect themselves from—or speculate on—fluctuating interest rates, currencies, and commodity risk using derivatives. Why not expand the innovation to handle credit? For instance, if Hancock had been able to buy a derivative that hedged J.P. Morgan against clients' defaulting, the bank would have been spared the embarrassment of its Korean swap fiasco.

Like foreign exchange options, credit default swaps could be easily detached from any underlying exposure that might "justify" their existence as a hedge. Like those currency speculators in the 1997 Asian crisis, you could use them to place bets on disasters: in this case, the death of a company. It was a bit like buying a life insurance policy on someone else's life. With foreign exchange, however, the underlying market was already there, trading billions per day. With credit risk, it was fragmented between the actuarial approach and the market approach, and the invention of the CDS provided the market approach with a significant advantage.

Using over-the-counter contracts with banks, you could trade bets on corporate deaths in complete secrecy, in as big a volume as the banks would allow. You could even sell protection on a company's going bust, without setting up an insurance company (like all derivative contracts, a CDS didn't care who the buyer or the seller was). What started out as an academic-sounding exercise—stripping out the credit risk element of a loan or bond and passing it on to someone else—spawned a market. That cost of protection from risk now had a quantifiable price that could be traded every day.

In the late '90s, I spoke to several London bankers about these new CDS contracts, which still seemed impossibly obscure to me. No one could even agree on what to call them: Merrill Lynch called them *credit default options* because—as with options on equities and other assets—the new-fangled credit derivatives involved a fairly modest premium payment up front and potentially a much bigger payout down the line. J.P. Morgan and Credit Suisse First Boston, thinking of them more as a bit of financial-risk alchemy that could secretly sit alongside a bond or loan, called them credit default swaps. Rather than make the premium payment up front, you could pay it in installments and receive protection against default in return, a sort of continuous exchange that justified the term *swap*.

There were also debates about how to define the terms of the contracts, particularly when there were actual defaults. For example, if you read a newspaper report saying that the Indonesian government had decided not to repay a loan, did that trigger a payment on the contract, or did the actual bond you were exposed to have to go down in value first? Early on, the bankers had realized that contractual niggles like these would not build confidence in credit derivatives. The International Swaps & Derivatives Association (ISDA) had been set up by the dealers in the 1980s, and enlisted panels of traders and high-powered lawyers to thrash out a consensus. By 1999 they agreed on the definitions of a default, and people were able to hedge on not only the perception of future default but the event itself. J.P. Morgan won the argument to call them CDSs when its chief lobbyist pointed out that "options" were regulated by U.S. commodities and securities agencies, while swaps were specifically excluded from such oversight, an exemption approved by Congress in 2000. Calling them swaps would ensure that CDSs would remain off the regulatory radar for a decade.

The Bank That Outsmarted Itself

Although J.P. Morgan was ostensibly a commercial bank in the late '90s, it saw itself as an international financial titan shrewdly using derivatives to leapfrog into the top ranks of investment banks, alongside Goldman Sachs and Morgan Stanley. By 1999, derivatives trading accounted for over a third of the bank's revenues. Yet for regulatory purposes it was lumped together with the giant banks that really were still committed to the actuarial approach, such as Citigroup, Chase, and Bank of America. With a smaller balance sheet than those banks, J.P. Morgan could get away with having a smaller capital base—but only if its enormous derivatives portfolio stayed off its balance sheet.

Banking regulators had already noticed something troubling. According to one measure, J.P. Morgan had a potential credit exposure to derivatives counterparties of over 800 percent of its capital—a ratio twice the size of its closest competitor, Chase, and probably an underestimate.[6] J.P. Morgan's credit exposure to derivatives counterparties and "legacy loans" in its back book was like owning a bond that it wanted to sell but couldn't openly sell, because its derivatives deals and loans were part of long-term investment banking relationships that were very lucrative. As Morgan's CFO, Hancock had to do something to keep the machine turning, but rather than use insurance contracts, as Chase was doing, he used derivatives.

Hancock was already a convert to the market approach. When I met him in 1999, he spoke in clipped, minute detail about how the bank was using patterns in currency options markets as an early warning signal to spot derivative counterparty problems. He sounded more like a trader than a hate-to-lose-money bank CFO, and he was acting like one as well. After he had to write down his Korean derivatives, he responded not by trading fewer derivatives, but by trading more. For Hancock, derivatives were not just hedging or speculative tools; they were part of a radar system he was building. Naturally he gravitated to the market approach to pricing credit risk, looking for a way of using credit derivatives to transfer the derivative and loan default risk off his firm's balance sheet. Starting in early 1998, Hancock began transferring credit risk off J.P. Morgan's balance sheet. His view of default risk was increasingly colored by market prices. If his complex early warning system suggested trouble ahead, Hancock was happy to pay the market price of default protection. However, this ability to listen to the market had an effect on J.P. Morgan's balance sheet that his shareholders didn't like.

By 2000, J.P. Morgan had hedged some $40 billion of loans and derivative counterparty exposure using default swaps, and Hancock was such a believer in market pricing that he used the cost of buying protection to indicate whether loans were profitable. Chase, on the other hand, used the traditional actuarial approach for evaluating the profitability of loans (in the sense of exceeding the cost of capital). The result was that Chase's lending appeared to be profitable, while J.P. Morgan's didn't.

The outcome was predictable: board members of J.P. Morgan were under pressure to improve performance, and Hancock was ousted. By the end of 2000, Chase Manhattan and J.P. Morgan merged into JPMorgan Chase (JPMC). It was the end of Peter Hancock's experiment with running a commercial bank as if it were a credit derivative trading desk.

That led to Chase's management taking the key positions in the merged firm.

Getting Greeced

On the other side of the divide, one investment bank in particular had a vision. It went far beyond the commercial banking notion of shedding credit risk from the balance sheet, toward using derivatives as a means of seizing control of the loan market.

Around the same time that I met Shapiro and Hancock, I was invited to a press party on London's Fleet Street. It took place in the sumptuous art deco lobby of what had once been the headquarters of the United Kingdom's *Daily Express* newspaper. After the exodus of print publishing from Fleet Street, the Express building had been purchased by Goldman Sachs. Most of the journalists present still thought of the investment bank in terms of its stellar reputation for advising companies and governments on privatizations and takeovers, but I was introduced to a man lurking on the sidelines, a rising star at the firm. Michael Sherwood had just become European head of FICC (fixed income, currencies, and commodities), perhaps Goldman's least understood but most profitable division. Trading—derivatives in particular—was his forte.

When credit derivatives were invented in the mid-1990s, Goldman held back. But once the utility of the new tools had been demonstrated, Sherwood became the firm's leading default swap visionary. The newly invented tool was going to lead to the "derivatization of credit," he would tell colleagues. He believed the market approach to buying, selling, and owning corporate bonds had a massive disadvantage to the much more transparent markets in equities. If you like the prospects of a company, say, Walmart, an equity trader only has to look at one type of security: Walmart's stock. In fixed income, a company might have hundreds of different bonds in the market, repayable in different currencies, and with myriad maturity dates and interest payment profiles. Which one should you buy or sell? You had to be a geek to figure it out.

With credit default swaps, all that detail could be stripped away. As with equities, there was a single "reference entity" or "name," Walmart Inc., whose potential for default drove the price of the swap contract. Better still, the default swap distilled this crucial credit information out of the hundreds of Walmart bonds. And for Sherwood, information was power. He realized that by combining trading in credit default swaps and corporate bonds on the same desk, Goldman would have its finger on the pulse of the world's biggest corporate borrowers: not only could Goldman control its own exposure, but it would control its clients' access to the market for credit.

Having "broken down the walls" in this way in 1999, Sherwood duly paved the way for his firm's FICC division to power to the top, taking him to the level of vice-chairman. But to Sherwood's irritation, his management innovation would reveal itself early on, with a huge but highly controversial deal that stunned competitors.[7] The deal was hatched back in 2000 by Sherwood and his head of sales, Addy Loudi-adis. Rather than a corporate borrower, the deal involved a spendthrift nation that wanted to fiddle the membership rules of an exclusive club of high-performing countries: the Eurozone. As Citibank discovered in the late 1980s, and Peter Hancock learned through J.P. Morgan's Korean bank difficulties, a currency crisis can have the same impact on foreign lenders as a corporate default. That is why weakening foreign exchange rates are a good early warning system that a country and its banking institutions might be unable to repay their debts.

When the strong economies of northern Europe created a single currency in the 1990s, they threw out this market-based warning system for detecting spendthrifts. Instead, the Maastricht Treaty that created Europe's single currency contained strict rules designed to prevent countries that sought to enjoy the currency's benefits from overspending. And these benefits were substantial: the possibility of borrowing money at virtually the same cheap rate as that paragon of fiscal rectitude, Germany.

Just as investors in private companies depend on accountants to verify corporate borrowing and expenditure, the European Union (EU) created Eurostat, a Brussels-based statistical agency whose job it was to check national accounts. But for countries where deficit spending is everyday political expediency, rules are made to be broken. And fatally for the EU, the feel-good nature of monetary union was not backed up with credible enforcement.

Visiting a government ministry in Athens can feel like a trip back in time. Offices without air-conditioning have windows flung open to the sounds and smells of gridlocked streets below. Chain-smoking bureaucrats are hunched behind desks, their in-boxes overflowing as they struggle with long-obsolete computers. Even the Greeks have a hard time tracking state expenditures, as Eurostat memos plaintively acknowledged.[8] In 2000, Greece was in breach of the Maastricht rules, but Brussels chose to show the newest incoming member of the Eurozone a degree of indulgence if its government produced budget forecasts projecting that debt and deficit ratios would steadily decline over the next four years. Forecasting those numbers was easy enough; hitting them was close to impossible. It would be politically toxic for the Greek government to cut pension entitlements or raise taxes.[9] Fortunately, with Goldman Sachs's help, a solution presented itself.

The deal started with a quite humdrum derivative that was given a dramatic, Goldman-style tweak. The starting point was the €30 billion or so in foreign currency–denominated debt that Greece had outstanding in 2000. The humdrum derivative that Greece already was using was called a *cross-currency swap*. For large national or corporate borrowers, foreign currency borrowing is a matter of finding a broader investor base for their debt and thus lowering their funding costs. Cross-currency swaps allow them to do this without taking any foreign exchange risk. There is nothing particularly dramatic about this derivative. In the same way that a bureau de change allows you to exchange a sum of foreign currency into domestic currency, the cross-currency swap lets big borrowers do the same thing for the repayments on their foreign currency bonds. Just as owning foreign currency is risky because rates can go against you, owing foreign currency is also risky because of exchange rates. In both cases, a transaction gets rid of the problem.

Suppose you were based in the Eurozone and borrowed $10 billion at a time when one dollar was equal to one euro. If the dollar strengthened to the level of one dollar equaling two euros, the amount of debt in euros would double. Fortunately, with a cross-currency swap you don't have to worry about that because everything is locked in at the one-euro-per-dollar rate. What Sherwood and his team cooked up for the Greek government starting in December 2000 worked slightly differently. Imagine you had a thousand dollars that you wanted to change into euros. A bureau de change proposes a special deal. Instead of the one-euro-per-dollar rate (before fees) displayed on the wall of the booth, the teller offers a contract paying you double that rate. Perplexed, you ask, "Are you giving away a thousand euros?" "Of course not," replies the teller. "Actually, I'm lending you the money, and you'll have to pay it back, with interest. But that's our little secret. No one will know because the slip of paper I'm giving you makes it look like you've got 'free' money."

In its deal for Greece, Goldman did something equivalent to this mythical bureau de change. It cooked up a cross-currency swap, and in the blank space marked "exchange rate," it wrote a wildly incorrect figure. By using this derivative, Greece had magically reduced its debt by almost €3 billion, but this paper gain would have to be balanced out later by a series of swap payments to Goldman. Over the ten or so years that the swap was to last, the value of these payments amounted to several billion euros. In other words, Goldman was secretly lending the Greek government money and getting paid back over time.

Incredibly, Eurostat's loophole-ridden debt-accounting rules allowed the Greek government to do exactly that, and thus "demonstrate" to Brussels that it was sticking to its budget targets. In fairness to Greece and Goldman, they were not the first partnership of spendthrift country and bank that fiddled the system in this way: Italy is said to have used the same trick to join the single currency in 1998. According to sources familiar with the deal, Eurostat even gave advance approval of Goldman's contract with Greece (six years later, the agency would deny any knowledge). Of course, transparency was precisely what the

Greek government was not interested in, and Goldman was happy to oblige, for a price.

When my sources first told me about the deal in May 2003, two years after it had been completed, the price seemed shockingly high—some €500 million in return for concealing several billions in debt. It was not an explicit price in the sense of a negotiated fee, but rather an implicit spread on top of the swap payments that Goldman had calculated as being necessary to balance out the off-market value of the swap. Given that the transaction costs for standard, market-priced cross-currency swaps were a hundredth of this amount, it was not surprising that people were shocked when I published a story exposing the deal, and that Goldman and its public relations machine were anxious not to see the €500 million number in print.

From Goldman's perspective, the CDS was necessary because, like the "wrong" exchange rate transaction offered by the mythical bureau de change, the swap with Greece amounted to a secret loan from Goldman. While the likes of J.P. Morgan or Chase Manhattan may have been comfortable with putting such a loan on its balance sheet (albeit a diminishing one), Goldman was not. Or as Sherwood explained it to me, "We're generally conservative on credit risk. We like to take credit risk at a point where we can lay it off."

Had Greece chosen to raise a billion euros of debt for twenty years by issuing bonds, it could have placed the debt with actuarially minded investors like Prudential. The prices of Greek bonds in 2001 suggested that such investors would have been prepared to accept a spread over ultrasafe German government bonds amounting to about €60 million over twenty years. But the Greek government was desperate to avoid public debt markets, because its borrowing was already well over the Maastricht limits. By using Goldman to raise the money, Greece had to accept the bank's subjective view of its credit risk expressed as a CDS premium—the €300 million price at which Sherwood thought he could "lay it off" in the market.

It took a change of Greek government for the facts of the Goldman swap to be officially acknowledged, although this revelation did not seem to harm Greece's relationship with Goldman, which made over $100 million from the deal.[10] Finding a borrower prepared to pay €300 million in default risk premium when a traditional actuarially driven investor would have required $60 million seemed to electrify the firm's bankers. Just as Sherwood had envisaged, Goldman had "derivatized" credit.

There was only one obstacle now to Goldman's dreams of world domination: apart from the likes of Greece, for which desperation or secrecy made it willing to pay for a CDS, why would any sane borrower not stick to the actuarial system, where loans were much cheaper? If Goldman were going to dominate credit markets as Sherwood wanted, it would have to undermine the rival system, forcing corporate and sovereign loan rates to be pegged to CDS prices. That led Goldman to publicly campaign against the guardians of traditional lending: the big banks.

So Cheap It Hurts

In 1999, Glass-Steagall was abolished, and U.S. commercial banks were now free to offer investment bank services. With their new, share-holder-driven philosophy, some of these banks were crowding into Goldman territory, pitching for business such as advising on takeovers. What most enraged Goldman was how banks such as the newly merged JPMC, Citigroup, and Bank of America were poaching blue-chip clients by dangling the prospect of actuarially driven cheap loans as a sweetener. For those that depended on traditional credit investors to lend them money, the historical pricing of default risk kept their loans cheap because they were still using accounting rules that kept the value of loans frozen at book value. This made their loans "cheaper" than those based on the CDS market—if JPMC lent $1 billion to a big customer, and the credit derivative market implied that the loan was now worth only $800 million, then so much the worse for credit derivatives.

Without the ability to freeze the value of loans on its balance sheet, Goldman had to either sell loans at the secondary market price or buy credit derivative protection. That meant if customers wanted to borrow money from Goldman, they would have to pay a lot more for it, as Greece had done. So Goldman went on the offensive. In April 2001 the firm wrote to the U.S. Financial Accounting Standards Board (FASB), requesting that a type of loan facility very popular with large borrowers be treated like credit derivatives: in other words, the loans should be recorded at market value on bank balance sheets.

The commercial banks instantly saw the threat here and fought back.[11] Goldman's campaign was merely sour grapes about its loss of market share, they said. But Goldman's argument that the market pricing of credit derivatives was more "fair" than loan pricing demanded a more substantial rebuttal. The banks pointed out that a large percentage of their new loans were *syndicated*—farmed out to hate-to-lose investors, typically medium-size regional banks. And because these investors accepted the pricing of the big banks that originated the loans, this was "fair value," which had been established in a market.

Goldman rolled out Princeton finance professor Jose Scheinkman, who argued that this claim by commercial banks was intellectually flawed and anti–free market. The banks then pointed to the benefits of low borrowing costs to their customers. Dina Dublon, then CFO of JPMC, told me, "If I was Goldman, I'd be careful about arguing that *their* clients ought to be financed at higher rates. You can say banks are 'dumb,' but they have a staying power, and a market cap that, as an industry, is significantly larger than that of securities firms."[12]

Goldman lost the argument, and the FASB ruled against its proposal. JPMC was allowed to keep its actuarial measuring stick (based on the evidence of syndication to other banks). But Goldman didn't give up on the "cheap-loan" war, because time was on its side. With shareholders continuing to demand that commercial banks improve returns on capital, the need for places to dump credit risk off the balance sheet was greater than the loan syndication market could support. And by the start of 2002, it was clear that the credit default swap was the best tool for the job.

The Sad, Strange Death of Hate-to-Lose Banking

The takeover of J.P. Morgan by Chase had one ironic twist: it turned out that Peter Hancock was a much better credit risk manager than his successors at the top of the firm, such as Chase's head of risk, Marc Shapiro. Recall that Chase preferred the actuarial method to offset credit risk, and now deployed it for its biggest and most lucrative client: the fast-growing energy company, Enron. Shapiro had known Enron's chairman Ken Lay since his old Texas banking days, and the company paid Chase tens of millions annually in fees.[13] Much like Greece, Enron could only sustain itself by fraudulent borrowing and was enabled by banks bending over backward to skirt the boundaries of legality.

What Enron's CFO Andy Fastow invited Chase to do in the late 1990s was typical of the complex secret borrowing that would eventually land him and Enron CEO Jeff Skilling in jail and get Chase slapped down by the Securities and Exchange Commission (SEC) with a $135 million fine. Like Goldman and Greece, Chase and Enron started out doing something that appeared routine, trading "prepay" forward contracts, a kind of derivative based on natural gas. However, the derivatives were a red herring. As with Goldman's deal in Greece, the derivatives were set up to carefully balance out leaving behind a $2.6 billion loan from Chase to Enron. As a condition for extending this secret loan, Chase bought default protection. Rather than using a default swap as Goldman did, it bought traditional-style protection from ten insurance companies, including Allianz, Travelers, and The Hartford, that provided $950 million in protection using surety bonds. A remaining $165 million in protection came as a letter of credit from the German bank WestLB. To keep things secret, they did this through a shell company called Mahonia, which Chase controlled.

The last bit of credit insurance was bought in September 2001. A month later, Enron's fraud was finally coming to light, and Chase's bankers learned that their favorite client had borrowed much more than they realized. "$5B in prepays!!!!!" e-mailed one Chase banker to another when he heard the news; "shutup and delete this email [sic]," came the immediate reply.[14]

In December 2001, Enron filed for bankruptcy. The ten insurers and WestLB argued that they had signed up to insure the credit risk of bona fide natural gas payments, not secret loans, and the discovery of fraud at Enron meant that they didn't have to pay.

Early in 2002, I visited Enron's bankruptcy auction in London. There was a palpable sense of shock at Chase that its risk neutralization hadn't worked out as planned. The stress of dealing with the recalcitrant insurers was enough to give one of Shapiro's minions, a credit officer named Jim Biello, a heart attack. He was invalided out of the bank into early retirement. The man who replaced Biello, David

Pflug, paid tribute to him in what would serve as an epitaph of the hate-to-lose banker: "They killed themselves trying to save it and then they killed themselves trying to collect it."[15]

A couple of years later, Chase managed to secure in court about 60 percent of the $1 billion pledged by the insurers, but by then was facing prosecution for abetting Enron's fraud. It settled those charges by paying that $135 million SEC fine, and Shapiro apologized to Manhattan District Attorney Robert Morgenthau: "We have made mistakes," he said in 2004. "We cannot undo what has been done but we can express genuine regret and learn from the past."

One of the many things Shapiro no doubt regretted was depending on a flawed risk management strategy. Using insurance policies to protect against default was obviously a risky move. But that was a problem with the strategy, based as it was on the insurance tradition of demonstrating loss ex post and checking for fraud. Meanwhile, the market approach to hedging credit risk passed the Enron test with ease. Unlike with surety bonds or letters of credit, it was hard to argue with the ISDA's definitions of the events that triggered credit default swaps.[16] You couldn't argue, as Chase's surety bond counterparties did, that fraud somehow voided the contracts. Even insurance companies on the other side of default swap contracts had to pay up. Federal Reserve chairman Alan Greenspan spoke warmly about how default swaps made banking safer as a result.

With this apparent certainty that providers of credit protection would have to pay up, traditional loan-based banking was now a love-to-win game. The only remaining obstacle was price. If the price of credit derivative protection was higher than what borrowers expected to pay on a loan, the big dealers resolved to find some other way to get that protection at a lower price. After all, actuarially driven credit investors still were willing to accept a lower return on bonds that passed the ratings agency health check. Using tricks developed at J.P. Morgan and elsewhere, the market-based world would soon figure out how to play these gatekeepers to get money at the price they wanted . . . and then use that to reap astounding profits. And in the process, they used credit default swaps to subvert—and nearly destroy—the financial system.

CHAPTER TWO

Going to the Mattresses

*In 1994, a new model for measuring risk—value at risk (VAR)—
convinced large segments of the financial world that they were being
too cautious in their investing. Another new financial tool, over-the-
counter derivatives, seemed to cancel out unwanted risks by transferring them elsewhere. Thanks to VAR and OTC derivatives, the trading
positions and profits of banks grew exponentially. In 1998, the fatal
flaw of this paradigm was exposed by the collapse of LTCM, but
traders and regulators learned the wrong lesson from that near-death
experience, setting the financial world up for an even bigger cataclysm.*

The Sweet Bliss of Know-Nothing Regulators

Early in 1994, Peter Fisher was head of foreign exchange in the New
York Federal Reserve's markets division, where he helped conduct the
auctions for U.S. Treasury bonds by so-called primary dealers, including
the big securities firms such as Goldman Sachs. The division also borrowed from and lent to those private sector banks that had access to the
Fed's discount window, and it could, if necessary, buy or sell dollars in
foreign exchange markets, which was Fisher's main responsibility.
He was a tall, patrician New Englander, a clever man some colleagues
considered to be a bit arrogant. He would shake his head condescend-
ingly at behavior that displeased him: "It's a muddle," he would say
sorrowfully.

That spring, the financial world seemed to be one giant muddle as a
rise in rates for federal funds rocked the markets. The commercial banks

the Fed regulated could borrow directly from America's central bank—the lender of last resort—because of their vital role in taking deposits from and extending loans to individuals. With the U.S. taxpayer potentially standing behind them, the banks decided to take more risks. The more ambitious New York–based banks—notably J.P. Morgan and Bankers Trust—had branched out into trading derivatives and emerging market loans. The securities firms that participated in the auctions would take enormous bets on the Treasury bond market, and sometimes their aggressive behavior got them into trouble. In 1991, Salomon Brothers almost went out of business after the Fed caught it rigging the primary-dealer auctions. That same year, Citibank's stock price had dropped to $3 a share because of its exposure to Mexico and Latin America. Now, in spring 1994, investment bank trading desks and hedge funds were losing a fortune on bonds and currency swings.

Fed regulators fretted that it was impossible for them to effectively do their job if they didn't know the risks commercial banks were putting on their trading books, and the banks were now taking on a lot more risk through derivatives. Sixty years earlier, Congress tried to answer that question with the Glass-Steagall Act, which forbade banks from trading and issuing securities. But Senator Glass and Representative Steagall hadn't anticipated that banks would get around this restriction by trading derivatives. Nor did they anticipate the growth of an offshore dollar market and how U.S. banks (at holding company level) could enter the securities business by setting up subsidiaries in Europe.[1]

These banks were tightly regulated because taxpayers were on the hook if they failed, but now that they had figured out how to legally circumvent the Glass-Steagall Act, they were taking more risks, sometimes huge ones. The banks argued that their new trading activity not only increased profits, but helped clients and the economy. What was the Fed supposed to do? How could it accurately gauge the risk its banks were now taking on? And the folks at the Fed were vexed by an even more fundamental question: how and why had bankers suddenly transformed from cautious stewards to seemingly reckless traders?

Historically, bankers have been cautious. That was a fundamental requirement for their job, but also part of their nature. A fundamental part of all our natures, in fact. Behavioral economics research shows that most people are highly risk averse. Send the average person to Las Vegas, and the sting of losing $100 at the craps table far outweighs the joy of winning $100. Take away the ability to calculate odds with dice and cards, and the risk aversion increases even more. We are hardwired to avoid uncertainty as much as we can. In our primal brains, ambiguity equals danger.[2]

A sense of imminent danger seemed to have gripped Fisher's previous boss, New York Fed president E. Gerald Corrigan. Before he resigned in 1993, Corrigan had presided over the Salomon bond scandal and in 1992 persuaded Congress to provide emergency authority to the Fed to lend to securities firms. That same year he delivered a coruscating speech aimed at those banks plunging into the new derivatives market and building up positions in the trillions. He said, "Bankers had better take a very, very hard look at off–balance sheet activities," and he concluded, "If that sounds like a warning, it's because it is."[3]

His completely reasonable—and very human—risk-averse response might have suited the Federal Reserve regulators who worked for him, but the rich and powerful men running the big banks wanted to make even more money trading in financial markets. They argued that they could not afford—literally—to be hobbled by such a reflex against risk. Even the most mundane, market-making aspect of trading requires risk taking—buyers and sellers are not always present at the same time and place, so competing for business involves holding on to an inventory of assets that change constantly in price. But where does this ability to be comfortable taking big risks come from? It comes naturally to some in the financial world, and to the rest, it is taught.

Investment banks deploy special training techniques to make their employees fear resistant. In a meeting room in London's Canary Wharf, a senior trader at Morgan Stanley demonstrated a simple psychological ploy used to inure junior staff to the natural fear associated with big gambles. He called it "the mattress." "Suppose the spot price for a stock is $100," the senior trader explained. "You give one trader a position at $100 and say, 'Go trade.' Then you do the identical thing with another trader but give that person the position at $98. In that case, the mattress is $2. You then compare the behavior of the two traders, who started with the same position but initiated their trading at different levels.

"The trader who got the position at $100 might make money, but he will probably want to cut his position very quickly on the upside, and on the downside too. Whereas the other one will say, 'I have some room. As long as the price is not below $98, I'm still making money.' So he has a mattress on the downside and will also let his profits run more on the upside. In most cases, the trader with the mattress is much more profitable. The comfort you gave the trader initially, 'the mattress,' gives him some confidence that he doesn't have if he's just at the market."

Like an astute circus trainer, the senior trader only uses the mattress as a confidence-building tool. If the stock's position ends up at $100, the junior trader doesn't keep the $2 mattress he was given as personal profit—the senior trader takes it away before bonus time. But compared with a mattress-free colleague, the second junior trader is more likely to earn a bonus because his additional confidence will have allowed him to profitably hold on to the stock in a risky market rather than bail out for the certainty of cash. The mattress is just a trick—the $100 stock is not really worth $98 when the trader starts trading it, and eventually he or she is let in on the joke—but it can dramatically change the way a trader handles risk.

Now go back to the problem faced by Gerald Corrigan and the New York Fed in the early 1990s. New financial innovations such as interest rate swaps and securitization had whittled away the Glass-Steagall barrier. Was there a "mattress" that could make Fed regulators comfortable with the trading risks now being taken by the big commercial banks? After all, the senior management of J.P. Morgan and other big commercial banks had also been in the dark about trading derivatives, but they got over those qualms and poured money into this new market.

In March 1994, rumors were circulating that Corrigan's nightmare was about to become reality. Bankers Trust had supposedly been wiped out by the rise in federal funds rates, and its stock would be suspended. In a phrase that Corrigan had recently invented, Bankers Trust was "too big to fail"—the Fed would have to bail it out. Peter Fisher, one of the few New York Fed staffers who knew about the new derivatives markets, called up Steve Thieke, a former New York Fed colleague who now worked at J.P. Morgan. Hearing the worry in his voice, Thieke let Fisher in on the secret. He and a handful of executives at Bankers Trust and Citibank had decided to look at the problem scientifically.

The 5 Percent Solution

John Arbuthnot, a genial Scottish physician who was friends with both Alexander Pope and Jonathan Swift, introduced the word *probability* into the English language. Arbuthnot asked how likely it was that the (presumed) fifty-fifty chance of a birth producing a boy could be reconciled to the fact that London's population in 1710 had a ratio of 18 to 17 in favor of boys. Deploying the recently invented mathematics of probability, Arbuthnot argued that since this was a statistical "impossibility," God must have set the 18-to-17 birth ratio.[4]

Much like Arbuthnot, Thieke and the J.P. Morgan risk managers began with an assumption about how changes in share prices, currencies, and interest rates should affect their positions, and tested it against what they had observed. Rather than the birthrates of girls and boys, they were concerned about whether their bank's trading desk made or lost money. And, like Arbuthnot, one might start out assuming that making or losing money was equally likely (like tossing a coin), and then be pleasantly surprised to see that one actually made money on eighteen days, while losing on seventeen. Of course, there was a bit more to it than that. J.P. Morgan was not thinking about binary outcomes, but a range, or distribution, of daily trading performance figures from the very good to the very bad. From a senior management perspective, it was important for J.P. Morgan to understand how bad "bad" could be, so that it could manage its risk successfully. While Arbuthnot had started out assuming that predicting the birth of boys or girls was like tossing a coin, Thieke and his fellow risk managers at J.P. Morgan looked at the recent history of the market and statistically sifted out the worst fraction of outcomes—say, the bottom 5 percent.

Applying that bottom 5 percent of market outcomes to the bank's current trading position gave them a number—value at risk (VAR)—which could serve as an assumption to be tested in the market. A day in which the performance was worse than VAR was called an "exception."

If the bank suffered through too many exceptions—a substantially greater fraction of days than one in twenty in which its performance was worse than VAR—then their assumptions about the markets were wrong. Armed with this scientific evidence, senior bankers could then step in and order their traders to cut positions.

When Thieke told Fisher about VAR in early 1994, a mystery was suddenly solved. Seemingly unconnected events that spring—a jump in the dollar–yen exchange rate, a plunge in German bunds, and the March sell-off in Treasuries—were invisibly linked by the VAR models the banks were using. As the worst-case assumptions were breached in one market, banks would cut positions right across their portfolios to protect themselves from further losses.

Since no one outside the banks (including the Fed) understood this, the new risk management cognoscenti were making money by second-guessing the market. Fisher learned how Heinz Riehl, a Citibank risk manager, made a killing by purchasing Bankers Trust stock because he understood the way his competitor's VAR model operated. Despite the rumors, it was simply impossible for Bankers Trust to have been crushed by the rise in federal funds rates, because its VAR model would have prohibited such a one-sided bet on the direction of bond prices. When Fisher explained all of this to William McDonough, who had replaced Corrigan atop the New York Fed, McDonough was so impressed that he immediately made Fisher head of the markets division.

Enthralled by this powerful new tool, VAR, Fisher wanted to spread the gospel. Surely this scientific approach was better than the climate of fear and secrecy that made the markets a volatile and dangerous place for banks. Knowing the level of the banks' VAR would give regulators some idea of how much risk they really were taking on. Even better, Fisher argued that disclosing VAR would also reassure banks about each other's exposures and would serve as a governor on their control of risk. Of course, it was not enough to confine VAR to the United States. With U.S. bank trading subsidiaries already sprawling across Europe and Asia, Fisher needed an international forum for his vision.

He was already chairman of a Euro-currency working group of central bankers affiliated with the Basel-based Bank for International Settlements (BIS). In September 1994, that group produced a report recommending that "regulated and unregulated financial intermediaries" be required to disclose information about their VAR. Fisher got his way, and the report prompted international banks to start revealing VAR numbers in their annual accounts. Indeed, J.P. Morgan had already begun doing so and was so proud of its VAR that it published the methodology behind it that October and spun off the unit that implemented it as a consulting business, RiskMetrics.

International bank regulators not only adopted the VAR model, they went much further than even Fisher had hoped. They already knew how to inspect bank loan books and require a capital cushion to be held against them to protect depositors. Now, here was a ready-made mechanism for doing the same with fast-growing derivatives trading portfolios. The idea was not new.

On the other side of the Glass-Steagall divide, the Securities and Exchange Commission (SEC), the regulator for Wall Street securities firms, had imposed what it called a *net capital rule* in the 1980s. Firms like Goldman or Lehman—which then were still partnerships—had to put up their own money to back bets they had taken on, enough to cover a one-in-twenty worst-case scenario. However, the rule only applied to securities (it ignored derivatives), so it wasn't much use because it failed to reflect the idea that a hedged position—a security plus a derivative—should have a lower risk.

By 1994, this ad hoc system now had a quasi-scientific gloss. By holding an amount of shareholder capital related to a multiple of VAR, banks were supposedly protected against trading losses up to whatever degree regulators wanted. For regulatory agencies that could never pay investment bank salaries, the idea of the banks doing the hard work of building their own VAR models and then having regulators simply check their numbers was especially appealing. The VAR model appealed to bankers and regulators because it expressed knowledge about trading uncertainty across many separate markets in the form of a single, easily understood number. As behavioral economists would put it, the VAR, once it was calculated, was an "anchor" that defined what bad news amounted to in a trading business. If you had the VAR figure in dollars as a bundle of cash in your back pocket, or even better a multiple of VAR (say, three times the number), then you had a cushion against losses. Your instinctive risk aversion would diminish. You had a mattress.

Even with the best of intentions, assuming that like John Arbuthnot and his birth ratios, you really could assess financial markets from an objective standpoint, this mattress had tricky foundations. Sifting through recent market data wasn't enough to anticipate what happened once you crossed into the one-in-twenty danger zone. To do that, you had to include extreme market moves, or "fat tails," in your VAR calculation, but by definition these were the rarest events of all, those that pushed the statistics to the limit. Yet the advantages of VAR—shining a light into dark corners of trading books—seemed to justify these technical challenges.

By 1995, the BIS began turning VAR disclosure into a trading book capital rule for banks, in what would become known as the *1996 market risk amendment*. The United States, United Kingdom, and other BIS members agreed to implement the amendment as part of their national banking law. The mattress had done its job—it had given international regulators the confidence to sign off as commercial banks built up their trading businesses.

Betting—and Beating—the Spread

Now return to the trading floor, to the people regulators and bank senior management need to police. Although they are taught to overcome risk aversion, traders continue to look for a mattress everywhere, in the form of "free lunches." But do they use statistical modeling to identify a mattress, and make money? If you talk to traders, the answer tends to be no. Listen to the warning of a senior Morgan Stanley equities trader who I interviewed in 2009: "You can compare to theoretical or historic value. But these forms of trading are probably a bit dangerous." While regulators and senior bankers may have embraced VAR, traders themselves have always been skeptical.

Instead, traders at market-making firms stay on safer ground. For example, they prefer to exploit their position to set buy (or bid) and sell (or offer) prices for the securities they trade. Just like the currency rates on the walls of consumer bureaux de change, the bid is always lower than the offer, and the difference (called the spread) can be taken as profit. As that senior Morgan Stanley trader who explained the mattress to me puts it, "Be a market maker—try to buy and sell very quickly, and take benefits from the spread between the bid and offer."

Another popular technique is to exploit the middleman's advantage to learn what everyone else is doing or thinking and ride the wave, along the lines of the famous "beauty contest" metaphor used by John Maynard Keynes. According to the Morgan Stanley trader, "You study the perception of the market: I buy this because the next tick will be on the upside, or I sell because the next tick will be on the downside. This is probably based on the observations of your peers and so on. If you look purely at the anticipation of the price, that's a way to make money in trading."

One reason traders don't tend to make outright bets on the basis of statistical modeling is that capital rules such as VAR discourage it. The capital required to be set aside by VAR scales up with the size of the positions and the degree of worst-case scenario projected by the statistics. For volatile markets like equities, that restriction takes a big bite out of potential profit since trading firms must borrow to invest.[5] On the other hand, short-term, opportunistic trading (which might be less profitable) slips under the VAR radar because the positions never stay on the books for very long. In markets for fundamental traded assets such as stocks, commodities, currencies, and government bonds, VAR initially did what it was supposed to do. It protected shareholders—and, ultimately, U.S. taxpayers—of regulated banks from trader recklessness, while permitting market makers to serve their clients who wanted to buy and sell. VAR also provided a common language for talking about risk that enabled markets with very different cultures to be viewed through a common lens.

For the freewheeling Wall Street securities firms, that common language was a welcome restraint. An investment bank such as Goldman Sachs faced a perennial problem of strong personalities on the trading floor risking too much of the firm's money. Bankers Trust may have escaped trouble in early 1994, but Goldman lost so much money in the U.S. Treasury market that it was forced to raise emergency capital from the Japanese bank Sumitomo. By introducing the analogue of white-coated lab experts to adjudicate—its so-called firmwide risk department with its VAR estimates—Goldman partly neutralized this danger. Motivated to find the balance between collective and individual greed, with little prompting by regulators, Goldman managed to get the governance right.

If markets didn't evolve and financial innovation didn't take place, that might be the end of the story—a happy ending provided by VAR models. But this story does not have a happy ending. VAR quickly became dangerous not so much because of technical pitfalls like "black swans" or "fat tails," but because it was used as an incentive rather than as a restraint. Suppose that a way could be found to stop scrabbling around as a middleman and earn big money instead by making bets—but without the risk. And suppose that the VAR system—the policing mechanism keeping the firm safe—said that the bet had low VAR and didn't require much capital.

Think for a moment about the relationship between traders and those who provide them with capital. As in any business, different traders compete for this capital by trying to offer the best risk-return proposition. If the bottleneck is a mechanism that defines how questions of risk should be addressed, then the winner in the struggle for capital will be the one who best plays that mechanism to their advantage. Presented with this incentive, traders gave statistics and economic theory a much warmer welcome on the trading floor. The smarter traders figured out how to game the scientific governance mechanism. They learned how mathematical economics could be manipulated to make a much "cushier" mattress, reducing VAR and giving them the confidence to expand their businesses to the scale of trillions of dollars. And the tool that enabled them to do it was financial innovation—in particular the new market in derivatives.

The False Apostles of Rationality

In April 1998, I traveled from London to the United States to interview several economics and finance professors. It was during this trip that I learned how derivatives had broken down the wall of skepticism between Wall Street and academia. My trip started at the University of Chicago, whose economists had become famous for their theories about market rationality. They argued that markets were supposed to reach *equilibrium,* which means that everyone makes an informed judgment about the risk associated with different assets, and the market adjusts so that the risk is correctly compensated for by returns. Also, markets are supposed to be *efficient*—all pertinent information about a security, such as a stock, is already factored into its price.

At the university's Quadrangle Club, I enjoyed a pleasant lunch with Merton Miller, a professor whose work with Franco Modigliani in the 1950s had won him a Nobel Prize for showing that companies could not create value by changing their mix of debt and equity.[6] A key aspect of Miller-Modigliani (as economists call the theory) was that if a change in the debt-equity mix did influence stock prices, traders could build a money machine by buying and shorting (borrowing a stock or bond to sell it and then buying it back later) in order to gain a free lunch. Although the theory was plagued with unrealistic assumptions, the idea that traders might build a mechanism like this was prescient.

Miller had a profound impact on the current financial world in three ways. He:

1. Mentored academics who further developed his theoretical mechanism, called *arbitrage.*

2. Created the tools that made the mechanism feasible.

3. Trained many of the people who went to Wall Street and implemented it.

One of the MBA students who studied under Miller in the 1970s was John Meriwether, who went to work for the Wall Street firm Salomon Brothers. By the end of that decade, he had put into practice what Miller only theorized about, creating a trading desk at Salomon specifically aimed at profiting from arbitrage opportunities in the bond markets. Meriwether and his Salomon traders, together with a handful of other market-making firms, used the new futures contracts to find a mattress in securities markets that otherwise would have been too dangerous to trade in. Meanwhile, Miller and other academics associated with the University of Chicago had been advising that city's long-established futures exchanges on creating new contracts linked to interest rates, stock market indexes, and foreign exchange markets.

The idea of arbitrage is an old one, dating back to the nineteenth century, when disparities in the price of gold in different cities motivated some speculators (including Nathan Rothschild, founder of the Rothschild financial dynasty) to buy it where it was cheap and then ship it and sell it where it was more expensive. But in the volatile markets of the late 1970s, futures seemed to provide something genuinely different and exciting, bringing together temporally and geographically disparate aspects of buying and selling into bundles of transactions. Buy a basket of stocks reflecting an index, and sell an index future. Buy a Treasury bond, and sell a Treasury bond future. It was only the difference between the fundamental asset (called an *underlying asset*) and its derivative that mattered, not the statistics or economic theories that supposedly provided a benchmark for market prices.

In the world Merton Miller lived in, the world of the futures exchanges (he was chairman emeritus of the Chicago Mercantile Exchange when I met him), they knew they needed speculators like Meriwether. Spotting arbitrage opportunities between underlying markets and derivatives enticed the likes of Salomon to come in and trade on that exchange. That provided liquidity to risk-averse people who wanted to use the exchange for hedging purposes. And if markets were efficient—in other words, if people like Meriwether did their job—then the prices of futures contracts should be mathematically related to the underlying asset using "no-arbitrage" principles.

Bending Reality to Match the Textbook

The next leg of my U.S. trip took me to Boston and Connecticut. There I met two more Nobel-winning finance professors—Robert Merton and Myron Scholes—who took Miller's idea to its logical conclusion at a hedge fund called Long-Term Capital Management (LTCM). Scholes had benefited directly from Miller's mentorship as a University of Chicago PhD candidate, while Merton had studied under Paul Samuelson at MIT. What made Merton and Scholes famous (with the late Fischer Black) was their contemporaneous discovery of a formula for pricing options on stocks and other securities.

Again, the key idea was based on arbitrage, but this time the formula was much more complicated. The premise: A future or forward contract is very similar (although not identical) to the underlying security, which is why one can be used to synthesize exposure to the other. An option contract, on the other hand, is asymmetrical. It lops off the upside or downside of the security's performance—it is "nonlinear" in mathematical terms. Think about selling options in the same way as manufacturing a product, like a car. How many components do you need? To manufacture a stock option using a single purchase of underlying stock is impossible because the linearity of the latter can't keep up with the nonlinearity of the former. Finding the answer to the manufacturing problem meant breaking up the lifetime of an option into lots of little bits, in the same way that calculus helps people work out the trajectory of a tennis ball in flight. The difference is that stock prices zigzag in a way that looks random, requiring a special kind of calculus that Merton was particularly good at. The math gave a recipe for smoothly tracking the option by buying and selling varying amounts of the underlying stock over time. Because the replication recipe played catch-up with the moves in the underlying market (Black, Scholes, and Merton didn't claim to be fortune-tellers), it cost money to execute. In other words you can safely manufacture this nonlinear financial product called an option, but you have to spend a certain amount of money trading in the market in order to do so. But why believe the math?

The breakthrough came next. Imagine that the option factory is up and running and selling its products in the market. By assuming that smart, aggressive traders like Meriwether would snap up any mispriced options and build their own factory to pick them apart again using the mathematical recipe, Black, Scholes, and Merton followed in Miller's footsteps with a no-arbitrage rule. In other words, you'd better believe the math because, otherwise, traders will use it against you. That was how the famous Black-Scholes formula entered finance.

When the formula was first published in the *Journal of Political Economy* in 1973, it was far from obvious that anyone would actually try to use its hedging recipe to extract money from arbitrage, although the Chicago Board Options Exchange (CBOE) did start offering equity option contracts that year. However, there was now an added incentive to play the arbitrage game because Black, Scholes, and Merton had shown that (subject to some assumptions) their formula exorcised the uncertainty in the returns on underlying assets.

Over the following twenty-five years, the outside world would catch up with the eggheads in the ivory tower. Finance academics who had clustered around Merton at MIT (and elsewhere) moved to Wall Street. Trained to spot and replicate mispriced options across all financial markets, they became trading superstars. By the time Meriwether left Salomon in 1992, its proprietary trading group was bringing in revenues of over $1 billion a year. He set up his own highly lucrative hedge fund, LTCM, which made $5 billion from 1994 to 1997, earning annual returns of over 40 percent. By April 1998, Merton and Scholes were partners at LTCM and making millions of dollars per year, a nice bump from a professor's salary.

By the late 1990s, investment banks were supplanting exchanges as the favored market-making institution for options and other derivatives, but LTCM worked with both. The original mathematics behind the Black-Scholes formula had gone through several generations of upgrades and refinements since 1973 and was gathering acolytes daily.

According to Black-Scholes, the cost of manufacturing options increased with market volatility. Traders learned to use the option price as a kind of "fear gauge," measuring what the market expected future volatility to be. (In 2005 the CBOE would adopt this fear gauge in the form of a new index called the VIX.) What started out as a valuation recipe for obscure contracts became a crucial tool for generating information that allowed traders to make risk management or investment decisions.

It is hard to overemphasize the impact of this financial revolution. The neoclassical economic paradigm of equilibrium, efficiency, and rational expectations may have reeled under the weight of unrealistic assumptions and assaults of behavioral economics. But here was the classic "show me the money" riposte. A race of superhumans had emerged at hedge funds and investment banks whose rational self-interest made the theory come true and earned them billions in the process.

If there was a high priest behind this, it had to be Merton, who in a 1990 speech talked about "blueprints" and "production technologies" that could be used for "synthesizing an otherwise nonexistent derivative security."[7] He wrote of a "spiral of innovation," wherein the existence of markets in simpler derivatives would serve as a platform for the invention of new ones. As he saw his prescience validated, Merton would increasingly adopt a utopian tone, arguing that derivatives contracts created by large financial institutions could solve the risk management needs of both families and emerging market nations. To see the spiral in action, consider an over-the-counter derivative offered by investment banks from 2005 onward: an option on the VIX index. If for some reason you were financially exposed to the fear gauge, such a contract would protect you against it. The new option would be dynamically hedged by the bank, using VIX futures, providing liquidity to the CBOE contract. In turn, that would prompt arbitrage between the VIX and the S&P 500 options used to calculate it, ultimately leading to trading in the S&P 500 index itself.

As this example demonstrates, Merton's spiral was profitable in the sense that every time a new derivative product was created, an attendant retinue of simpler derivatives or underlying securities needed to be traded in order to replicate it. Remember, for market makers, volume normally equates to profit. For the people whose job it was to trade the simpler building blocks—the "flow" derivatives or cash products used to manufacture more complex products—this amounted to a safe opportunity to make money—or in other words, a mattress. In some markets, the replication recipe book would create more volume than the fundamental sources of supply and demand in that market.

The banks started aggressively recruiting talent that could handle the arcane, complicated mathematical formulas needed to identify and evaluate these financial replication opportunities. Many of these quantitative analysts—quants—were refugees from academic physics. During the 1990s, research in fundamental physics was beset by cutbacks in government funding and a feeling that after the heroic age of unified theories and successful particle experiments, the field was entering a barren period. Wall Street and its remunerative rewards were just too tempting to pass up. Because the real-world uncertainty was supposedly eliminated by replication, quants did not need to make the qualitative judgments required of traditional securities analysts. What they were paid to get right was the industrial problem of derivative production: working out the optimal replication recipe that would pass the no-arbitrage test. Solving these problems was an ample test of PhD-level math skills.

On the final leg of my trip in April 1998, I went to New York, where I had brunch with Nassim Taleb, an option trader at the French bank Paribas (now part of BNP Paribas). Not yet the fiery, best-selling intellectual he subsequently became (author of 2007's *The Black Swan*), Taleb had already attacked VAR in a 1997 magazine interview as "charlatanism," but he was in no doubt about how options theory had changed the world. "Merton had the premonition," Taleb said admiringly. "One needs arbitrageurs to make markets efficient, and option markets provide attractive opportunities for replicators. We are indeed lucky . . . the world of finance has agreed to resemble the textbook, in order to operate better."[8]

Although Taleb would subsequently change his views about how well the world matched up with Merton's textbook, the tidal wave of money churned up by derivatives in free market economics carried most people along in its wake.[9] People in the regulatory community found it hard to resist this intellectual juggernaut. After all, many of them had studied economics or business, where equilibrium and efficiency were at the heart of the syllabus. Confronted with the evidence of derivatives market efficiency and informational advantages, why should they stand in the way?

Sleeping Through Your Wake-up Call

Six months after my meetings with Merton, Scholes, and the others, in September 1998, LTCM was on the brink of collapse and threatened to take down a big chunk of Wall Street with it. As in 1994, the crisis appeared as a series of apparently unconnected events. Russia defaulted on its bonds. Interest rate swaps went haywire. Equity option prices—the fear gauge—soared. How could arbitrage trades that were immunized from swings in fundamental markets such as equities or interest rates lose $4 billion in a matter of months? How come VAR, the tool that LTCM and all other big trading banks used to control their exposures, broke down, when it had worked like a dream in 1994?

These trades were supposedly safe bets because of the no-arbitrage principle. For example, the Black-Scholes formula suggested that buyers of options were being overcharged compared with the replication cost over time (which tracked underlying market volatility). So

LTCM sold options and paid the replication costs, earning a profit as the option price converged on the replication cost, as the quants' calculations said it would. Because of smart organizations like LTCM (and the fund attracted lots of imitators) the "ought" would become the "is." The bait that instilled confidence was no-arbitrage pricing. One question is, how much of a mattress is enough? Two dollars might be sufficient, but perhaps two cents wouldn't be. The problem that LTCM faced from the outset was that potential profits in the arbitrage or relative value opportunities it identified were small compared with the size of the two-way bets that were needed to make them work. As Scholes himself put it, the fund was in the business of "hoovering up nickels." In order to make the profits that its partners and investors expected, LTCM had to put a lot more money on the table. In other words, it deployed enormous leverage. As Fisher at the New York Fed discovered when he visited the stricken fund in Greenwich, Connecticut, that September, it had borrowed $25 for every $1 of investor capital, and even more if you counted the fund's derivatives positions.

This leverage shouldn't necessarily have been a problem, so long as LTCM could hold on to its positions until the contracts matured. That was an important caveat because there is nothing to say that the price of a derivative and the underlying security used to manufacture it couldn't diverge wildly during the interim due to short-term blips in the market. LTCM's partners had built their VAR model to understand the effect of these blips, and convinced themselves (and hence their investors) that their impact was negligible. What LTCM's VAR model missed was that the hedge fund's enormous size meant that it now *was* the market, more so than the S&P 500 index or the thirty-year Treasury bond yield that LTCM was supposedly hedged against.

In a nutshell, that is the problem with VAR as an incentive. LTCM used it not as a scientific testing tool, but rather as a mechanism to win the competition for capital from investors. Because LTCM obtained so much leverage, and had so many imitators, its assumptions based on how markets behaved were bound to be disproved. In other words, LTCM could no longer "game" the market because it *was* the market. Once the perception that the trades were a mattress vanished, LTCM became the object of speculation, and the hedge fund didn't stand a chance. Worse still, its creditors—the major banks and securities firms—were now also in trouble. For them, VAR became a conduit of contagion—it transmitted the heightened volatility of LTCM trades into increased capital requirements for trading firms everywhere, which forced the cutting of unrelated positions in the market.

VAR had become so entrenched across trading businesses that the selling pressure triggered by everyone failing the one-in-twenty test at once made assets impossible to sell. Without buyers willing to relieve trading desks of their positions, there was now a liquidity crisis for regulated banks. Peter Fisher brought them together in a New York Fed boardroom and negotiated a bailout of LTCM that averted a much bigger collapse, and set up an orderly wind-down of that fund.

Almost dragged under by trading losses related to LTCM-type trades, Barclays, UBS, Merrill Lynch, and J.P. Morgan sharply curtailed their risk taking. Some firms, notably Goldman and Credit Suisse, hung in there for another year, until another batch of losses in the sterling market changed their outlook as well. But how much had they learned?

One reason for this sudden prudence was the regulatory scrutiny that followed the LTCM meltdown. The banks did not want an invasion by regulators into their unsupervised domain of over-the-counter derivatives, so a new script was written. The Wall Street spin on the LTCM disaster: derivatives and risk technology was not dangerous; LTCM had been the threat because it was an offshore hedge fund that had poor risk management and grew too big. The banks that lent money to hedge funds solemnly promised the Fed and other regulators that they would not make this mistake again.[10]

Yes, Wall Street proclaimed, derivatives markets had seized up temporarily in September 1998, and Alan Greenspan had been forced to cut the federal funds rate by an emergency three-quarters of a percentage point to get them started again. But the positive, information-transmitting qualities of new derivatives markets had not gone away. In the same way that implied volatility from option prices became a useful fear gauge for the market, transparency and consensus about more complex derivatives pricing would bring in new radar signals, as well as an assurance that the markets were safe.

To allay fears that their secret webs of over-the-counter derivatives had increased the uncertainty in the market, the dealers took several measures. One idea was called *netting*. If two dealer counterparties had lots of derivative contracts between them, they could put in place a mechanism for canceling out exposures that offset one another. That would reduce a bank's gross exposure—the amount the counterparty owed that bank on all its derivatives—to a small fraction.

The next tweak by derivatives dealers was to beef up what was called *collateralization*. This amounted to building a cash plumbing system between counterparties. Periodically, perhaps daily, the derivative would be priced at market value (as laid down in the contract), and collateral (typically cash or a very safe asset like Treasury bonds) would flow through the pipes, depending on who owed money to whom. The idea was that if one party defaulted, the other could keep the collateral. Combined with netting, that reduced the net exposure even further.

Regulators were thrilled that the banks had seemingly done their work for them. Fed head Alan Greenspan repeatedly praised netting and collateralization for making the system safer. That was not yet proved to be true, but what was undoubtedly true was that netting and collateralization made derivatives trading more expensive to run, with banks now devoting whole floors or even entire buildings to housing their large trade operations staffs, checking hundreds of thousands of valuations and payments daily. Subtly, this huge new overhead encouraged consolidation by megadealers and reduced competition.

And finally, how about the VAR methodology that regulators had approved for banks only two years before LTCM? It seemed to have suffered a serious blow to its credibility. Even Goldman Sachs warned about how in 1998 VAR had created a herd mentality.[11] Perhaps it wasn't so safe to have trading businesses sitting next to old-fashioned loan-driven banking after all. But again, the banks offered a palliative, called *stress testing*, which amounted to identifying unusual events—such as an LTCM-type meltdown—and holding extra capital against them.

All these measures by the banks did the trick—the regulators left the old (new) system in place.[12] Symbolically, even Gerald Corrigan took a job at Goldman Sachs. That isn't to say that there wasn't some humility in the short term. For the next few years, hedge funds and proprietary desks in banks found themselves greatly restrained in both the amount of investor capital they could use to take LTCM-style bets, and the amount of borrowing available to leverage those bets.

Perhaps the most important lesson derivative dealers took from LTCM was that they stopped counting on dynamic replication to earn money—that was too risky. So if a market maker sold an option, rather than construct it by trading the underlying asset according to some mathematical recipe, the bank would have to find a way of buying an option back from somewhere else. This was known as running a *matched book*. However, without a big hedge fund like LTCM selling the options (the fund had gained the nickname "the central bank of volatility"), the bank would need to be more resourceful about finding the other side of the trade.

Meanwhile, the banks also needed to replace their old arbitrage profits. After all, the billions of dollars already spent in building up trading back-office and technology infrastructure to support derivatives bets could not be written off. The upshot of this was that banks looked outward, finding ways to get clients outside the circle of finance theory cognoscenti to trade derivatives. That played well with regulators, who were receptive to the idea of financial innovation being deployed in the real economy. However, these new clients did not have the understanding of derivatives that the dealers or hedge funds did. And this gave enormous power—and wealth—to the derivatives salespeople and marketers who dealt with those naive clients.

A Derivatives-Shaped Hole in Your Life

When I interviewed Merton Miller in 1998, I asked him about selling derivatives to retail customers. "As a member of the Merc board for so many years, I have a long experience of the marketing of these kinds of things," he said. And Miller had grown concerned that selling options like toothpaste, where Madison Avenue convinces customers that a product costing ten cents is a brand worth two dollars, was dangerous when applied to financial products with long-term risk and return characteristics.

For Miller, market value was sacrosanct, and he felt that consumers should not be lured into paying over the odds, because that implied a misjudgment about risk. "If you're buying from a dealer, what makes you think the dealer knows less than you do? It's like buying second-hand cars. These fancy products—I understand their appeal to buyers, but the fact is, unless they're mispriced, you're getting exactly what you paid for." Miller was making a reference to the so-called lemons problem identified by another Nobel-winning economist, George Akerlof. In the same way that buyers of second-hand cars face a disadvantage against dealers trying to sell them lemons, nonspecialist buyers of derivatives have less information about those hard-to-understand products than the banks that create them.

Akerlof's work highlighted a flaw in the free market: that competition will inevitably tease out all pertinent information about a product and lead to fair pricing. Although he was an unabashed advocate of derivatives, Merton Miller preferred to work with exchanges because of mechanisms that attempted to redress these failures. To be successfully exchange traded, contracts must be simple and standardized, leveling the playing field somewhat. Unlike the bespoke derivatives designed by dealers, pricing takes place in public, in a regulated venue that brings together buyers and sellers.

Think of derivatives from a dealer's perspective. Many bankers start out with an idealistic view: that they are helping build Merton's innovation spiral. "I like to think of these future derivatives products as nice consumer devices like mobile phones," the head of Paribas's derivatives research department once told me. "So well designed, so easy and simple to use, with so much technology behind them." And many bankers insist that their "structured products," where derivatives are sculpted inside bondlike investments to match customer desires, conform to this vision.

But then step back and consider how competition between bankers, and the demands of shareholders, can undermine this idealism. The fact that a derivative is bespoke means by definition it is not standardized or traded on an organized market, such as an exchange. Pricing can be dictated by the bank's trading desk to cover the cost of replicating the contract using simpler instruments, a calculation that might require an advanced degree in mathematics. Without standardization, it can be hard to understand what goes into such a calculation, or to compare one product with similar offerings.

Such dangers are well understood in consumer financial markets.[13] Where customers are confused about their buying decisions, they can fall prey to "rent seeking" by sophisticated vendors, who extract outsized profits without delivering real value for their customers. With bespoke over-the-counter derivatives and structured products, opaque pricing allows dealers to build hefty margins into the transaction. This means that the difference between the true manufacturing cost and what the customer actually pays can be earned as "rent" by the dealer over the life of the trade.

So long as the customer feels that they are getting a good deal, such rent seeking can be extremely profitable for large financial institutions. Take the most common type of retail structured product, a low-risk bond coupled with equity options. As Miller said, buyers of these products are getting exactly what they pay for, minus a margin—return of their capital at maturity (without interest and potentially with default risk), combined with the expected payoff of a derivative. By branding their products and selling them like toothpaste, the dealers fulfilled Miller's fears. Since the late 1990s, financial institutions have earned billions annually in rent by selling these structured products to price-indifferent consumers and hedging their exposure over time.[14]

At first glance, institutional derivative customers would seem to offer fewer opportunities for rent seeking by banks. Shareholders require and reward managers to avoid the fog of confusion that makes consumers easy victims of rent seeking. The managers, in turn, expect the bankers that compete for their business to genuinely act in their best interest and not try to pull the wool over their eyes. "Our best relationship banks think intensively about our capital structure and hedging strategy," is how the head of corporate finance at Lufthansa expresses it.

This requires a certain kind of skill among derivatives salespeople. Often they are former accountants or consultants who understand and empathize with their client's business. Derivative contracts—those mirror images of corporate cash flows that transform one kind of interest payment into another and so on—appear to such a banker as a *solution*. Listening to the banker talk, many corporate treasurers or finance directors will be bombarded with high-powered analyses of the problems their company has with financial market uncertainty. But a *solution* is sitting there to take the problem away.

Guglielmo Sartori di Borgoricco, the top salesman at Barclays Capital, once gave me a run-through of his sales pitch. A dapper man with a technocratic air, he started off sounding like a humble facilitator of basic services: "I'm a true overall service provider. I'll give you perfect execution in swaps and bonds."[15] What he meant was that if a client wanted to use Barclays like an exchange, trading a standardized product with minimal transaction costs, then he would make that possible. Having thus established rapport with his client, Sartori then steered the pitch into more sophisticated territory. "But I also understand what you're doing and what you're trying to achieve." While any successful salesperson must have empathy for the client, the derivatives masters like Sartori di Borgoricco, and his equivalents at J.P. Morgan, took things to a completely different level.

With CEOs encouraged to be visionaries, it isn't hard to imagine how clever derivatives salespeople can find a foothold.[16] Suppose your dream is to begin a major project in a few years' time, which will involve raising new debt. This was exactly the position of Harvard University in 2005, when its then president, Lawrence Summers, announced a multibillion-dollar building project stretching decades into the future. At which point do the uncertainties regarding such projects become real enough to hedge?

If you are ambitious enough, even the most unlikely dreams can feel like today's reality. A good derivatives salesman can devise a contract that locks away this potential uncertainty today, so that you can enjoy the fantasy properly. Before you know it, the salesman has sold you a hedge against your own daydreams. For the salesman, it is the client's dreams, fears, and aspirations that need to be understood and replicated with a specially designed derivative contract. "I understand your business," Sartori would tell a client. "Can we talk about what's on your mind and what's stopping you from becoming number one? What's your strategy?" He told me, "That's what I love to ask clients— 'I look at your balance sheet and I know what I see, but maybe there's something you're trying in particular to achieve?'"

Experienced corporate users of derivatives are wary of this kind of sales talk. Once the conversation turns from the immediate needs of the company—which might be addressed with a standardized hedging product—toward the aspirations of its management, then the nature of the solution can become dangerously bespoke and opaque. But not everyone is so cautious, so impervious to flattery and dreams.

Something Rotten in the House of Morgan

What happens when derivatives salespeople go too far in their creativity to help institutional clients? What happens when the governance mechanisms fail? When corporate managers fail to steer clear of the psychological pitfalls that bedevil consumers, and when bankers gamble with their firms' reputations for easy profit?

When I first started writing about derivatives in 1997, the industry was still recovering from a series of scandals involving respected U.S. companies such as Procter & Gamble and Gibson Greetings that had lost heavily in complex derivatives deals.[17] The bank at the center of these scandals, Bankers Trust, had to sell itself to Deutsche Bank in 1998 in order to survive. From the mid-1990s on, derivative salespeople kept their heads down while U.S. companies reformed their governance practices.

By the end of 1998, however, the banks had identified fertile new territory for selling derivatives: the corporations, financial institutions, and public sector bodies of continental Europe. Here was a market with a hunger for financial solutions to its problems, but with governance standards that lagged those of the United States and Britain. One institution that was particularly well placed for this opportunity was J.P. Morgan.

Its driving figure in Europe was Bill Winters, a J.P. Morgan veteran who lived in London. Possessed of good looks and easy charm, he had started out as a J.P. Morgan salesman in the 1980s, selling derivatives to sophisticated clients such as Harvard's endowment fund. At a time when most banks were happy to sell bonds, and salesmen were hired on the basis of sporting and drinking prowess, Winters learned to see the world through "derivatives eyes"—as a series of replicated cash flows. Eventually his talent would make him co-CEO of JPMorgan Chase's investment bank franchise.

The derivatives sales team Winters nurtured in London in the late 1990s became known as "Team Italia," because some of his best "players" were Italians. J.P. Morgan by now was one of the world's leading derivative dealers, employing diligent advisory staff praised by clients. Yet Team Italia soon stood out, making deals that had an increasingly complex flavor and were particularly profitable for the bank. What was it about the Italian clients that made them so receptive to complex products?

Ideally, the treasury of a company is a *cost center*: it leaves the risk taking and profit generating to the core parts of the business and focuses on reducing financing costs. With about €2 billion of debt, there was a routine reason for the treasury of Poste Italiane—the Italian post office—to be using interest rate swaps. The derivatives would transform its cost of borrowing into a lower, shorter-term benchmark rate that closely tracked European Central Bank rates.

Although interest rate swaps are not standardized instruments that trade on an exchange, they are heavily traded by banks, hedge funds, and corporate end users in a highly competitive market. In such markets, bid-offer spreads are tight. For a standardized, vanilla interest rate swap, the spread was as low as one basis point (a hundredth of a percentage point) of the underlying debt transformed with the derivative. For a swap on $1 billion of debt lasting ten years, that means the bank makes about $1 million in revenue.

Massimo Catasta, the finance director of Poste Italiane, wanted to reduce his borrowing costs even further. By selling options linked to interest rates, Catasta could use the premium received in return to make Poste Italiane's debt costs appear much lower than the benchmark. However, there was a downside: the options could go against the company and make its debt costs rocket upward. In other words, the short-term positive performance from selling options was effectively an illusion: Catasta appeared to be speculating with Poste Italiane's money.

He was hardly alone in doing this; a host of Italian companies were engaging in such trades with leading investment banks. Corporate treasurers from companies like Mondadori and Wind Communications would proudly tell me how they had made derivatives bets of various kinds and closed them out at a profit. Without any disclosure in corporate accounts, shareholders were unaware of the risks being taken. And with the trading revenues from such bets much higher than for vanilla hedging transactions, J.P. Morgan and other banks would happily cash in on their clients' weak governance.

Starting around 2000, one of Winters's salesmen, Antonio Polverino, sold Catasta a sequence of swap deals that contained a remarkable feature: not only was Poste Italiane selling options to reduce its funding costs, but the options were linked to dollar interest rates. By this mechanism, a company whose business activity, staffing, and capital provision were purely Europe based became heavily exposed to fluctuations in the U.S. Treasury bond market.

On the other side of the Atlantic Ocean, J.P. Morgan had plenty of clients, such as mortgage agency Freddie Mac, that were worried about rising U.S. interest rates and would buy options from the bank to protect themselves. In the pre-LTCM era, dealers might have hedged those options dynamically or bought them from a leveraged hedge fund like LTCM. Thanks to the salesmanship of Polverino and others, J.P. Morgan now had a handy and apparently safe supply of as many dollar options as it wanted.

Had Catasta chosen to speculate in a cost-effective and transparent way, he might have sold U.S. dollar options directly to an American counterparty through a broker. He would have avoided the complex structure that J.P. Morgan sold him in over-the-counter form. The bells and whistles attached to this derivative made it much more costly to trade than a standardized product, enough to justify a bid-offer spread in the region of fifty basis points. On a single transaction that reached $250 million in size, that meant J.P. Morgan could book a profit of over $10 million. One might say that there was no value being created here for Poste Italiane, just rent seeking by J.P. Morgan.

If this wasn't sufficient evidence of his lack of competence, Catasta made things worse by adjusting his derivatives, exposing himself to more trading costs and even more rent seeking. According to sources at the company, Catasta would periodically dismantle older deals and replace them with new ones, until July 2003. This last tweak—possibly a result of an earlier bet's losing money—alone cost Poste Italiane €50 million.

This was bad news for Catasta, but Polverino quickly became a star within J.P. Morgan. People who know Polverino say that he did not personally encourage risky speculation. But although he and his fellow salesmen may have sincerely believed they were helping Poste Italiane's finance director achieve his goals, in the wider scheme of things it could be said to amount to profitable rent seeking from institutional clients. And in the caveat emptor world of the wholesale derivative market, there was no rule that said J.P. Morgan should act as a nanny to its stupider customers.

No rule, but J.P. Morgan made a great fuss about how assiduously it advised its clients about risk management. All the praise that the bank accumulated from satisfied clients—and there were many—added up to "reputational capital" the bank could use to squeeze out competitors. By permitting his salesmen to facilitate speculation by clients with poor governance, Bill Winters was exposing J.P. Morgan—unwittingly or otherwise—to reputational risk.

The gamble would pay off so long as the governance flaws that allowed Catasta and his ilk to operate freely weren't checked. Given the corporate culture in Italy around 2000, that was a fairly safe bet. However, reform of governance practices was about to be imposed from the outside, by the gatekeepers of corporate conduct: the accounting profession. As a result of the Bankers Trust scandals, U.S. accountants in 2000 brought in a rule—fought by derivatives industry lobbyists—forcing American companies to apply "fair value" to their derivatives positions. Aside from very simple derivatives that demonstrably hedged existing cash flows, any changes in the market value of derivatives would be reflected in quarterly earnings statements.

By 2004, the rest of the world caught up. The International Accounting Standards Board (IASB) brought in fair value derivatives accounting for companies outside the United States. It was the application of these new rules by Poste Italiane's auditors in early 2004 that exposed the company's €104 million of derivatives losses. In July that year, Poste Italiane's management fired Catasta, closed out the contract at a loss, and sued J.P. Morgan to recover the money.[18]

The mini-boom in corporate derivatives rent seeking fizzled out, and the salesmen found new targets, particularly regional governments and municipalities in Europe and America whose accounting rules were usefully murky and where governance was weak. Trading divisions of banks could carry on calculating their capital and trading in unregulated over-the-counter derivatives markets. With these incentives in place, dry brushwood was in place that only needed two more things to catch fire: credit derivatives and securitization.

CHAPTER THREE

A Free Lunch . . . with Processed Food

A pioneering pack of very clever and ambitious traders—aided by some mathematical wizardry—figured out how to bundle risky investments into packages that carried triple-A ratings. This incredibly lucrative new market in collateralized debt obligations (CDOs), which was propped up by the ratings agencies, swept across Europe, as cautious banks sought new ways to diversify without taking on too much risk.

The Too-Perfect Investment

Like the grain of sand lodged in an oyster's shell, an irritant sometimes drives what is—and should always be—an introspective, conservative company to outsize ambitions. This is what happened to Landesbank (LB) Kiel, along with its regional sibling, Hamburgische Landesbank, in which it had a 49 percent equity stake. The two banks seem to have been institutionally programmed to stay local—their supervisory boards were dominated by local politicians (each bank was about 25 percent state owned); their core mission was local: lending money to north German small businesses, real estate projects, and shipping, which was a big regional industry.

On the sylvan shores of Lake Maggiore in the foothills of the Italian Alps was another firm with outsize ambitions. Banca Popolare di Intra (BPI), based in the town of Verbania, with total assets of €3.4 billion, had sixty branches dotted around northern Italy, catering to local businesses and individuals—many of them wealthy retirees. BPI made good money providing banking services to this rich corner of Italy, and there seemed to be no good reason for it to change.

For LB Kiel, the "grain of sand" was the lack of opportunity in Germany's overcrowded banking sector. German consumers traditionally preferred to save rather than borrow, and renting was preferred to buying a home. Corporate lending was safe, but it paid very low rates of interest, and those clients who did want to borrow were often in what had been East Germany, where home prices were dropping and unemployment was high. Starting in the mid-1990s, LB Kiel had built up a corporate finance and leasing business across Scandinavia and the Baltic states, making itself the sixth-biggest bank in Denmark. It then started making commercial real estate loans in the United States and financing ship owners worldwide. By the end of 1999, a third of its €115 billion balance sheet was invested outside Europe.

But LB Kiel and its Hamburg sibling wanted to do more, wanted to be bigger. They wanted to be major players in the financial world, and thanks to a regional government guarantee that amounted to a subsidy, they had deep pockets.[1] And so LB Kiel found itself receiving visitors from London, the hotbed of financial innovation across the North Sea. A former executive at LB Kiel says, "We had capital to invest but didn't have enough clients. We talked to investment banks and said, 'We have excess capital; do you have a product for us?' And two of them said, 'Yes.'"

Down in Verbania, BPI's irritant was the purchase of a small brokerage network in 1999 that catered to wealthy investors. It should have been straightforward: the brokers recommended investments for clients, and BPI skimmed off a layer of fees without taking any risks. But after completing its purchase, BPI discovered that the brokers had stuffed their clients' accounts with structured products that were underwater. If those clients found out, they would flee BPI, and the brokerage network would be worth much less than what BPI had paid for it. Desperately looking to avoid a brutal write-down, BPI's boss, Giovanni Brumana, needed to find an investment that could be quietly slipped into the accounts of those clients and make up for the losses. Word got out about BPI's dilemma, and in early 2000, the bank received a call from a Swiss broker called A.B. Finn. "Barclays has a solution for you," the broker told BPI staffers.[2]

A Pearl of Great Price

The Barclays salesmen from London who called on LB Kiel and BPI were closer to the culture of Wall Street than the traditions of a venerable U.K. high-street clearing bank, but Barclays had long nurtured global ambitions. Like other growth-obsessed banks, it had bulked up its securities and trading business in the late 1990s, boosting leverage in search of profits. Then, in 1998, the bank's shareholders received a nasty shock: Barclays lost £335 million from Long-Term Capital Management–style proprietary bets and loans to Russia. It was also forced to join the Fed-orchestrated bailout of LTCM to protect its derivatives positions.

The problem was a familiar one for banks: making loans swallowed up shareholder capital, so it was tempting to underwrite and sell bonds instead, in addition to making trading bets. But as 1998 showed, default risk could be equally problematic. To expand in bond underwriting, Barclays would have to lend to riskier borrowers, whose bonds would have attracted a speculative-grade rating. These bonds were hard to sell to hate-to-lose types (such as insurance companies) that were the biggest bond investors. In other words, in order to grow, Barclays would need to hold a lot of risky debt on its balance sheet that had the potential to lose the bank money. But the ferociously ambitious Bob Diamond, hired to bring U.S. financial innovation to the stodgy British commercial bank, had a plan.[3] He assigned Oka Usi, an equally ambitious trader, to manage what he called the "risk finance group." By using the latest techniques, Usi would transform and shift the risk of bonds held on Barclays' balance sheet to outside investors, freeing up Diamond's investment bankers to underwrite more debt and break into new markets.

Usi had been toying with credit derivatives since the mid-1990s and had mastered the basic tricks. He could take one of Barclays' risky assets—for example, a peso-denominated loan to a company in Mexico—and buy credit default swap (CDS) protection on it from an investor client.[4] From Barclays' perspective, that amounted to unbundling the two parts of a risky loan. There was a default-free part that Barclays kept and the additional default risk premium or compensation that the CDS invisibly transferred to the investor, who was on the hook if the borrower went bust. From the client's perspective, the swap was a weird and unfamiliar derivative. To make it more appealing, Usi would package it into a kind of structured product called a *credit-linked note*. Imagine that the Mexican loan is a red ball on a table hidden under a cup labeled "Barclays," and Usi had—without lifting the cup—made the red ball appear in the client's pocket.

However, while such cleverness might have removed a bit of risk from Barclays' balance sheet, they were not a perfect solution. When lending to risky ventures like Mexican companies, Barclays—like any bank—would demand a high interest rate as danger money—a risk premium. An investor in one of Usi's credit-linked notes would also expect a high yield for taking on that exposure, even with the local Mexican currency risk hedged out. To truly free up Barclays' balance sheet would mean shifting loans in amounts of $10 billion or more. But volume like that would require selling to the hate-to-lose heartland of regional banks, insurance companies, and pension funds that demanded investment-grade ratings. If Usi had tried to sell his risky Mexican corporate loans to these kinds of people, the credit police would have hit their sirens and blocked his way.

Fortunately for Usi, other bankers had already confronted the problem head-on. They figured out how to turn risky assets into something that appeared safe enough for even the hate-to-lose types. While the most potent use of this trick involved credit derivatives, it has been around for several decades.

The Debt and Equity Morality Play

Corporate finance often boils down to a kind of morality play about the control of corporate assets. Equity holders effectively hold the keys to the assets and can drive them around at will. They might prove to be disciplined, responsible owners who appoint tough, independent directors to keep management in check. Or they might give carte blanche to megalomaniac CEOs such as Enron's Jeff Skilling, who build ever-swelling empires until their companies collapse.

Bondholders and lenders have advantages of their own: they get paid before the equity holders do, and if the cash dries up, they have a right to cut off payments such as dividends that equity holders depend on. In extremis, they have a right to seize and liquidate assets in bankruptcy and leave the equity holders with nothing, but that amounts to a nuclear option that lenders prefer not to exercise. Do hate-to-lose lenders trust the equity holders and company management not to run the assets off the road?

If the answer is no, then the result is an impasse: the return on investment demanded by lenders is so high that from the equity owners' perspective, it isn't worth owning the assets. Securitization was invented as a sort of negotiated compromise to this impasse. With the help of bankers and lawyers, equity owners and lenders agree to create a special company, or *special-purpose vehicle* (SPV), purely for the purpose of buying and owning those assets. The lenders advance cash to the SPV in return for IOUs or bonds, while the equity holders are appointed as managers by the new company to look after the assets. Parked safely in the SPV, the assets cannot be redeployed as collateral for an irresponsible buying spree. If the equity holders find new sources of debt capital for their plans and subsequently go bankrupt, the assets are legally shielded from any claims by the new creditors. Armed with this assurance, hate-to-lose investors can be persuaded to lend money to the SPV, even if they had been unwilling to lend to the original equity holders.

In the old-fashioned world of real companies, the resolution of the morality play comes through the trust and governance involving loan bankers and board members. In the brave new world of securitization, that human element gets replaced with an engineered financial machine or structure, and for this reason is often known as *structured finance*. Unlike in a real company, where assets, revenues, and debt payments all involve real people and endless debate, the SPV doppelganger is an android, programmed by a lawyer-crafted set of rules to mechanically transfer cash between various Cayman Islands mailboxes (in this world, the taxman is just another unpredictable creditor, best kept at bay by using a tax haven).

To bring Barclays Capital and cautious investors like LB Kiel together, it was not enough for Usi to simply transfer risky assets such as Mexican loans to an SPV and ask hate-to-lose investors to lend it money. After all, they would only have to take a peek at the assets inside and ask for the same compensation they would have demanded if they had bought the assets separately. The solution depends on taking the bondholder–equity holder pecking order in a real-world company and wiring it into the heart of an SPV android. In a real-world company, assets generate revenues. Lenders have a first claim on this money, and whatever is left over trickles down to equity holders. Starting in the 1980s, bankers created SPVs that were doppelgangers of this age-old system.

As in a real company, the SPV raises capital from bondholders and shareholders. As in a real company, the bondholders get paid first, and they might have their own subdivisions of seniority and order of payment. Once the bondholders take their predefined cut, the shareholders get what's left. There the similarities end. There are no annual general meetings or proxy votes, just the cash flowing through the SPV plumbing according to the rules. The only humans involved here sit outside as hired overseers: "trustees" who check the plumbing and take a fee for their trouble. The system works best when things start to go wrong, and the assets stop producing the revenues they were supposed to. Instead of the messiness and uncertainty of bankruptcy, the rules tell the corporate robot exactly what to do: as the cash dries up, the spigot leading to the equity holders gets cut off first, followed by bondholders, in order of increasing seniority.

Although the cash plumbing rules can be subject to mind-bogglingly complex variations, the basic idea is simple. In return for getting most of the upside when things are rosy, the equity holders (or low-ranking creditors) get punished first when things go bad. From the lenders' perspective, that fact is a big source of comfort and can be quantified according to the size of the equity cushion that has to be wiped out before the lenders take a hit.

The size of the cushion is described by a variety of names. For those who see holders of equity and debt in Manichaean conflict, there is the term *subordination*. For a more positive gloss, some say *credit enhancement*. The greater the degree of uncertainty that the lenders attach to the assets, the more subordination they will want to protect themselves. Putting it another way, the proportion of equity compared to debt determines how leveraged the SPV is, just as in a normal company.

Instead of getting paid a risk premium on each loan to cushion them against uncertainty, the lenders agree to a single cushion of equity on the entire package, which would have to be wiped out before the lenders' investments were put at risk. In other words, it works kind of like a "mattress" that steels the nerves of traders. Would this cushion be enough of a cushion for Barclays to sell a bundle of risky loans to a hate-to-lose investor such as LB Kiel?

Creating the Corporate Android

Consider a $1 billion collection of risky loans—in other words, obligations of borrowers who have promised to repay their loans at some point in the future. We can imagine them sitting on the balance sheet of a bank such as Barclays, but they equally well could be securities available on the market that the bank's traders want to purchase and repackage for a profit. No one knows whether the borrowers will repay the money, so a price is put on this uncertainty by the market—thousands of investors mull over the choice of betting on these risky loans and the certainty of risk-free government bonds. To make them indifferent to the uncertainty these loans carry, potential investors require a bribe in the form of a 20 percent discount to face value. If none of the loans default, investors stand to earn a 25 percent return.[5] A good deal for lucky investors, but a dilemma for the bank, which does not want to sell the loans at a 20 percent discount and report a loss.

Now imagine that instead of selling the loans at their market price of $800 million, the bank sells them to an SPV that pays face value of $1 billion. Their 20 percent loss just disappeared. And how is such a miracle possible? The SPV has to raise $1 billion in order to buy the loans from the bank. The hate-to-lose lenders in the SPV will only want to put up $800 million against such risky collateral. The $200 million shortfall will have to be made up somehow. The bank pitches in $200 million as an equity investment so the SPV has enough money to buy the $1 billion of loans. The bank has only made $800 million after all—and it suddenly doesn't seem like such a miracle.

However, there is one catch: the lenders no longer expect to receive $1 billion—or a 25 percent return—in compensation for putting up the $800 million. The SPV payout structure guarantees that the $200 million difference between face value and market value will be absorbed by the bank—which means that they are willing to treat the $800 million investment as almost risk-free (assume for now that the market has estimated the risk correctly, and those assets aren't going to plunge all the way to zero). Even though the bank has to plow $200 million back into the SPV—as a kind of hostage against the loans' going bad—from a bank chief executive's perspective, this might be better than selling the loans at an outright $200 million loss. Like the traditional securitizations that resolve debt and equity conflicts, it is a deal that reconciles two opposing views: the market suspicion that those bank assets are somehow impaired or "toxic," and the bank's faith that its loans will eventually pay something close to their face value.[6]

One can argue that this is a virtuous form of finance. By redeploying the markdown it would have been forced to take on selling those loans in the market as subordination, or an equity stake in the CDO, the bank has a chance of getting its discount back. Even better, the bank has an incentive to look after its assets—to lend responsibly and ensure that the loans get repaid—which it wouldn't have if it sold them outright. Meanwhile, society benefits because beneficial lending takes place.

However, this virtue was not quite enough of a reward for the new breed of trader and investment banker that emerged at banks like Barclays in the late 1990s. Sure, the bank didn't have to take an immediate haircut on the bonds it wanted to sell. But locking the same amount of money up in an SPV for the decade or more that it would take for all the loans to be paid back was equally bad. For the love-to-win banker, not getting paid today is unacceptable. He wants to find a way to sell the loans at a high price without having to lock up the bank's money.

It turned out that there was a way. Recall how insurance companies, which owned portfolios of bonds on a long-term actuarial basis, were happy to value them as if they were portfolios of life policies. Instead of the high returns that would compensate them for the individual default rate set by market prices, they required their portfolios of bonds to pay only a modest premium above the average statistical default rate because of safety in numbers. Perhaps, the reasoning went, an SPV could be treated in the same manner. After all, it was set up to hold on to its portfolio of assets until they matured—there was no other reason for its existence. Like an insurance company, shouldn't the SPV be happy with lower returns on its portfolio? Of course, an

SPV was not really an insurance company. It was a corporate android, a financial machine crafted by bankers, lawyers, and accountants, and it could not be "happy" about anything.

But the reasoning was not intended to sway the android; rather it was directed toward the hate-to-lose lenders who were needed to provide the SPV with capital. Suppose they could be convinced that the portfolio of loans held by this android was not expected to lose as much money as the 10 or 20 percent uncertainty discounts attached to the loans. If so, would the lenders accept a smaller amount of subordination while still being prepared to make what they saw as a virtually risk-free bet?

With the help of some simplistic actuarial thinking, this is how the multitrillion CDO market was created. The bankers did not convince the hate-to-lose community on their own. For that, they turned to the ratings agencies. And by what could be described as mathematical alchemy, the ratings agencies became rich.

The Doctrine of Chances

The roots of this apparent alchemy by the ratings agencies go back to early eighteenth-century London. It was an era of aristocratic gamblers, lottery players, and insurance entrepreneurs who were prepared to pay for information that gave them an edge in the various bets they were making. Scurrying to satisfy this demand were mathematicians versed in the newly invented mathematics of probability, which seemed to tame uncertainty.

Abraham de Moivre, a penniless Huguenot expelled from Louis XIV's France, had befriended Sir Isaac Newton and was recognized by the Royal Society for his skills in mathematics, but none of that paid the bills. So de Moivre put his services up for sale in London's Covent Garden, where a corner of Slaughter's coffeehouse served as his makeshift office. There, he was sought out by gamblers such as Francis Robartes, the Earl of Radnor, a denizen of the card and dice tables in London's high-end gambling clubs. Robartes was different from most of his fellow gamblers, who saw gaming as a drink-fueled, all-night sport. He took this "sport" seriously and was determined to win. He had procured a French text that calculated odds for some of the simpler games, but it couldn't handle the more complex bets he wanted to make. Tired of laboriously doing his own calculations, Robartes was impressed to see de Moivre make short work of his problems using calculus. De Moivre had already shared some of these techniques with his learned brethren of the Royal Society, but it was Robartes (and other gamblers keen on replicating the success he had at the gaming tables using de Moivre's calculations) who persuaded the Frenchman to write a book and generously underwrote the cost of its printing. *The Doctrine of Chances,* published in 1718, was a success, perhaps because de Moivre took care to make it as much a gamblers' handbook as it was a mathematical monograph. "There being in the world several inquisitive persons who are desirous to know what foundation they go upon when they engage in play," he wrote in the preface. "I have endeavoured to deduce from the algebraical calculation several practical rules . . . which may be very useful to those who have contented themselves to learn only common Arithmetick."

Central to the *Doctrine* was de Moivre's argument that luck had no place in discussions about uncertainty. As he patiently explained, games and lotteries could all be reduced to simple problems of counting: somebody always had to win or lose. Dice or coins did not remember the outcome of previous games; throws of the dice were independent of each other and were governed by identical laws of probability. (Here de Moivre was building on the work of earlier mathematicians, including Fermat and Huygens.) Key to de Moivre's analysis was the binomial theorem, discovered by Newton, which de Moivre used to mathematically unlock the probabilities of successive independent events such as dice throws. It provided a formula for counting the ways that a particular combination of events could occur, and hence determining their probability. Much of *The Doctrine of Chances* involves de Moivre's applying this formula to different situations. He also showed that as the number of games or events becomes larger and larger, probability becomes dominated by averages that can be charted in a predictable way. Although he did not fully describe this famous graph, his was the first mention of what would later be known as the Gaussian, normal distribution, or bell curve.

De Moivre's dazzling use of mathematics to enlighten a formerly superstition-ridden corner of human activity was enough to impress the poet Alexander Pope, whose early work referencing the gaming tables abounded with fortune-bearing zephyrs and spirits. Presumably introduced to Pope by Robartes, his neighbor in Twickenham, the mathematician was commemorated in Pope's *Essay on Man* as a model for a scientific deity, "who made the spider parallels design, sure as de Moivre, without rule or line." Perhaps Pope was referring to the more profound passages of *The Doctrine of Chances,* where de Moivre showcases the ideas of Swiss mathematician Jakob Bernoulli. No longer was the aim to merely calculate the odds of dice throws but rather to use dice or lotteries as a mathematical model for the cruel uncertainties of life, such as the probability of death or the birth of a boy or a girl. The idea of individual life expectancy as a hidden lottery with fixed odds had obvious social value (and implications)—combining thousands of such "lottery tickets" within a life insurance company could reduce risk by spreading it around a large population. In using this new mathematics to ask how likely such events were, Bernoulli and de Moivre laid the foundations for statistical testing and, ultimately, value at risk (VAR).

Driven as ever by financial insecurity, de Moivre seized on the commercial applications of this theory for the next thirty years. Later editions of the *Doctrine* included pages of annuity and life insurance calculations, prompted by the need to update Edmund Halley's famous mortality tables. He continued revising the book until, by the final edition, he was too blind to proofread it.[7] He might have been too blind to read, but he could see that his book was having a negative impact on society. By demystifying chance, he realized that he was helping to undermine the moral strictures that kept some people away from the gaming tables. In a preface to a later edition, he insisted that "this doctrine is so far from encouraging play that it is rather a guard against it by setting it in a clear light." By the time finance seized on mathematics at the end of the twentieth century, such caution was long forgotten.

A Moody Elevator

When John Moody invented bond ratings in 1909, he was offering himself to investors as a guardian against the kinds of corporate irresponsibility that could drive their bonds into default. Over the next ninety years, Moody's and its rival, Standard & Poor's (S&P), built such stellar reputations that they were given what amounted to a sinecure by U.S. regulators. Starting in the 1930s, banks, insurance companies, and pension funds were forbidden to hold bonds unless they had an investment-grade credit rating.

Many would say that the fabled integrity of these raters was in doubt from the moment in the early 1970s when they switched from charging investors for their services to charging issuers. After all, can you really trust a policeman paid by those he is supposed to police? That said, until the 1990s, the agencies remained aloof from their paying customers, and none more so than Moody's. Its analysts were renowned for sphinxlike announcements based on secret conversations with the companies they rated. What separated investment-grade from speculative-grade bonds—the crucial sheep-from-goats distinction—was not so much a Coca Cola–style secret formula as it was a hermetic judgment by a shadowy brotherhood. Given that institutional disdain for the client, one wonders what John Moody would have made of a report his agency published in December 1996, titled *The Binomial Expansion Method Applied to CBO/CLO Analysis.*[8] It represented a profound departure for the firm, the low-key start of a dramatic realignment toward commercial imperatives that was mirrored at S&P. The report amounted to a recipe book for banks that wanted to repackage speculative-grade assets into the investment-grade gold: highly rated CDO debt that could be purchased by hate-to-lose investors. In sharp contrast to the famously cryptic dialogues Moody's typically had with corporate or sovereign bond issuers, the agency was now subtly drumming up business.

Recall the problem faced by banks trying to securitize their assets into CDO form and get their deal approved by the credit police. Suppose Moody's judged that the chance of default for each asset was like a single throw of the dice—a speculative bet with a one-in-six chance of going sour. Weighting the good and bad outcomes of the dice throw by what one stood to win or lose resulted in an expected loss of about 16 percent on one's investment. That would be labeled a "fail" by the credit police hired to approve hate-to-lose investments.

Now consider what happens when a bundle of these risky assets gets transferred into the robotic clutches of an SPV. Putting a layer of subordination at the bottom of the SPV would help cushion the projected losses, but not by much. A ratings agency would be able to check the SPV cash flow system and ensure that the reserve for debt holders was sufficient. Indeed, for early securitizations involving mortgages, this was pretty much all that ratings agencies had to do. However, even for the most leakproof plumbing system, a huge amount of subordination would be needed if the assets were risky.

The crucial thing was the safety-in-numbers effect, along the same lines as what was the basis for life insurance. Surely, dividing your investment among twenty of those one-in-six speculative bets was better than putting all your eggs in one basket. But how much better? What Moody's did with its 1996 report was to invent a mathematical model for calculating just how much the bundling of loans could reduce the risk, by inventing a "hypothetical pool of uncorrelated and homogeneous assets."[7] In other words, in rating CDOs, Moody's was proposing to model an uncertain, hard-to-understand bundle of loans by treating them in the same way that Francis Robartes wanted to calculate the odds of a certain number of coin tosses or dice throws in his London club. Armed with this assumption, the recipe book deployed the same binomial mathematics that de Moivre had used to calculate gambling odds some 250 years earlier. And the impact was stunning.

Suppose Moody's convinced itself that a CDO had spread its lending across a range of industries so diverse that it was equivalent to rolling twenty dice independently. The chance of throwing twenty successive sixes becomes very small (although not zero, as de Moivre repeatedly pointed out). The wonder of the binomial theorem, with its humped probability distribution curve, irons out the extremes, so much so that the expected loss plunges to a few hundredths of a percent. In a table helpfully provided in its 1996 report, Moody's shows how that could lead to a coveted double-A rating. Knowing that regional banks, insurance companies, and pension funds are restricted to buying such high-grade bonds, the aspiring CDO-builder now spies a pot of gold practically begging to be scooped up. But how did Moody's get from the twenty speculative-grade assets bundled up by a bank to twenty independent dice throws? The answer was something called a *diversity score,* a grand-sounding phrase for what amounted to looking at real-world assets and translating them into dice or coins. If the CDO contained loans to Ford, McDonald's, and BAE Systems, that could be modeled as three dice labeled "automotive," "food and beverages," and "aerospace and defense." De Moivre's mathematics, combined with the usual SPV cash flow plumbing, immediately produced a default probability. Moody's then could read off which proportion of its ninety-year database of corporate bonds defaulted at that rate, and come up with a rating. The more categories Moody's could identify, the higher the chance a bundle of assets would have "diversity," and thus the higher its rating.

This was the first step down a treacherously slippery—but lucrative—slope: in addition to doing its credit police job of checking the securitization cash flow plumbing, Moody's was now selling a probability model based on its own ratings. In other words, with the binomial expansion technique (BET), Moody's was recycling its existing product into something new. This made the banks very happy, because it helped them convince hate-to-lose investors that a CDO containing a portfolio of risky assets could be much less risky than the individual assets themselves. That meant there could be less of a subordination cushion or less equity placed inside the SPV by a bank as a "hostage" against the assets', collectively, going bad. And in turn, that meant banks could quickly extract more value from risky assets on their books, which was great news for the love-to-win bankers, who could now get paid and move on to their next deal.

If You're So Smart, Why Can't You Do the Same?

While few thought back in 1996 that Moody's initiative would snowball into a trillion-dollar market, some banks quickly seized upon it. J.P. Morgan leaned heavily on Moody's services from 1997 on, when it launched a series of "balance sheet synthetic" CDOs called BISTRO (Broad Index Secured Trust Offering). BISTRO stood out for its use of the nascent credit derivatives contracts to shift the default risk of its loans and currency swaps without selling them or losing clients. By 2000, the bank had shifted $20 billion of default risk in this way and proudly announced that it had reduced the capital it held against loans and derivatives by $406 million—money it could now pay out to shareholders. This project was instigated by Peter Hancock, the CFO at J.P. Morgan we met in chapter 1. His big innovation was in combining the securitization mechanism with credit derivatives, into what became dubbed *synthetic securitization*. Rather than selling loans outright to a Cayman Islands SPV it created, J.P. Morgan bought default protection on the loans from the SPV. In the same way that Usi transformed a Mexican highway loan into a credit-linked note, Hancock and his team appeared to spirit a portfolio of loans out of J.P. Morgan's balance sheet into the Cayman android.

With ratings agency assistance, what came next could be described as a feat of alchemy that even Usi hadn't thought of. Rather than the much higher amount of subordination the assets would have required on their own, J.P. Morgan deployed the Moody's diversity score to get away with an equity layer of 1 percent of the $20 billion of balance sheet credit risk it hedged in this way.[10]

Over at Barclays, Usi was watching all this carefully. Rather than just repackaging the odd Mexican corporate loan in a high-yielding note, he had the tool he had been waiting for. He could now subtly shift the credit risk of speculative-grade debt into a form palatable to hate-to-lose investors. By straddling the market and the actuarial world of credit, Usi could do even more: he could buy bonds or loans cheaply in the secondary market and use what could be described as Moody's water-into-wine mathematics to resell them at higher prices, in CDO form. Usi realized this could be a money machine: he would earn the difference between the market rate of return and the much lower return that investment-grade CDO investors required (remember that prices of bonds are inverse to their returns or yields).

The emergence of buyers for highly rated CDO notes allowed banks to set up a pipeline of newly purchased risky bonds to feed into it. Since this amounted to earning free money by using credit ratings, these transactions became known as *arbitrage CDOs*. The only bottleneck was the need to find specialist investors to buy the crucial equity layer: the little tank of cash providing protection for the hate-to-lose investors. But Usi saw himself as a proprietary trader running a credit hedge fund for his boss, Bob Diamond, so he was happy to invest in that equity layer on Barclays' behalf. His first attempt was a BISTRO imitation launched in the summer of 1999 called BarCLO Finance, which transferred the risks of loans held on Barclays' balance sheet. Trying to copy the lucrative formula J.P. Morgan had used on BISTRO, Usi brought in Moody's to rate the deal. But back in the late 1990s, the venerable ratings agency saw itself as the elite branch of the credit police, and it did not respond well to Usi's in-your-face manner. He complained to his Barclays colleagues that Moody's analysts were dismissive. They essentially told him, "Get in line, we're so busy, you're a trader, not a banker—why don't you suck up to us?" Usi was enraged; he felt his prized CDO rating was being delayed for petty reasons.

If that wasn't bad enough, he was getting pounded by his boss for not having kept up with the innovations of their competitors. The idea of running the CDO money machine like a proprietary trading desk was being implemented at UBS. "Why are they making all this money?" Diamond railed. "Why can't you do the same thing? Everyone tells me you're smart, but maybe you're not." Fortunately for Usi, the commercial pressure he was under to close deals was now being felt in the ratings agency world, and a new player was going to give him some game.

Moody's and S&P were the two grand oligarchs of credit ratings, but since the 1920s, a third, lesser player had been snapping at their heels. Fitch lacked the establishment aura of the big two, and most corporate and sovereign bond issuers did not bother paying for its ratings. Fitch fought back by giving unsolicited ratings and by swallowing up smaller ratings agencies. But most important, Fitch played to its niche status by focusing on structured finance, the catch-all expression for various types of securitization. It was already working with Usi's hated rivals at UBS, but its door was open for Barclays too. What Fitch offered Usi was similar to what Moody's could offer, but friendlier and cheaper: a diversity-type ratings model for CDOs that could perform the requisite magic with Barclays' bundles of risky bonds or loans.

By the end of 1999, Usi's plan was taking shape. A series of Cayman androids—or vehicles, as he called them—would be built to extract the arbitrage profit that spreads in the market and the Fitch diversity model said was there for the taking. Based in New York, Usi would look after the big picture. The specific design of the CDOs would depend on the appetite of prospective investors, and Usi delegated this task to a pair of structuring teams, one in New York and one in London. The London-based structurer was a bright banker named Manish Chandra. Managing relationships with investors fell to the Barclays Capital regional sales team—people who were not credit derivatives experts, but were experts on the dreams and schemes of their clients. It was their job to find clients, and find deals those clients would like. In the spring of 2000, the Barclays salesman in Germany, Christian Stoiber, brought Chandra to meet a pair of eager clients: LB Kiel and its sibling, Hamburgische Landesbank.

Diversification, Motherhood, and Apple Pie

A former LB Kiel executive summed up the bank's strategy at the time succinctly: "What we were aiming for was diversification, which is a normal way if you manage your portfolio actively. We utilized our credit investment business to diversify our risks away." In other words, follow the strategy advised by investment professionals everywhere. Doubting the benefit of diversification is the financial equivalent of doubting the goodness of motherhood and apple pie. But what do bankers actually mean by *diversification*? It turns out that there are three distinct types.

The first type can be called *actuarial diversification* and applies to situations in which investments turn out either good or bad over a long-time horizon. That's how traditional banks use insurance-type pooling to make loans at modest rates of interest. It's also how Moody's could justify awarding investment-grade ratings for CDOs containing speculative-grade bonds using its BET model. As long as the crucial assumption that risks are independent—as with dice—holds true, then adding new risks always makes the portfolio safer.

The second type, *market diversification*, covers situations where the risk involves traded investments that can go down in price (and give poor returns) rather than either surviving or defaulting. The theory behind market diversification dates back to 1952, when Harry Markowitz, a PhD student at the University of Chicago, published a seminal paper, "Portfolio Selection," which showed that if the prices of assets behaved independently, increasing the number of investments would always reduce the variance of returns. If you argued that variance (the degree to which investment returns fluctuated around their average) was a bad thing, then adding more investments—or *diversifying* your portfolio—was unquestionably a good thing. Or as Markowitz put it, "A rule of behavior which does not imply the superiority of diversification must be rejected as a hypothesis and a maxim."[11] Expressed even more simply, if variance was "risk," then Markowitz proved that diversification was "risk management." Since this flavor of diversification protects against falls in prices, justifying it requires plenty of historical price data and deft use of statistics.[12]

Then there is a third type of diversification, the joker in the pack. Behavioral economists call it *naive diversification,* in part because it seems to be hardwired into the human psyche. Psychological experiments show that when people are not restricted to a single choice on a menu, they will spread their allocation across whatever is available. For example, in an experiment cited by Cass Sunstein and Richard Thaler in their book *Nudge,* children who are offered multiple brands of chocolate will almost always divide their picks so that they can taste all the chocolates rather than sticking with a single brand.[13] In the same way, and with no more justification for doing so, investors who are offered a menu of different retirement funds blindly split their allocations across the menu, even when it is not in their interests to do so. In other words, humans instinctively spread risk—and even possible reward—around, even if there is no good reason for doing so.

So which type of diversification was the board of LB Kiel pursuing? Reading reports and talking to former executives at the bank make it seem clear that in 2000, LB Kiel was firmly in actuarial mode, taking long-term credit risks and hoping to get paid back. And its initial strategy of diversifying out of Germany and making commercial real estate loans in America and elsewhere was sound. Assuming that the performance of a long-term loan in New York is independent of a similar loan in northern Germany is a reasonable premise.

Of course, LB Kiel wasn't diversifying simply to reduce risk. The bank's board was under pressure to increase returns, but chasing higher returns meant accepting more risk on investments. However, market diversification reduced the overall level of risk. That's why many finance experts say that for long-term investors, diversification is the closest thing to a free lunch. The problem for LB Kiel was that finding new lending opportunities across the world—the equivalent of additional coins or dice that were independent of what happened in Germany—was intensive, time-consuming work. It involved a lot of due diligence to avoid the seductive trap of naive diversification. That's why what Barclays offered them seemed so appetizing—it had already done the hard work of scouring the globe and assembling a smorgasbord of hard-to-access assets. How convenient it would be for LB Kiel to get its financial free lunch in processed form, like a TV dinner ready for the microwave.

Perhaps by buying some of the structured products Barclays was peddling, LB Kiel could get some instant diversification. The only drawback was that the $15 billion portfolio that Usi managed on Barclays' behalf was mostly speculative grade, ranging from double- to triple-*B* in quality. That earned his proprietary trading desk a nice yield of around 2 or 3 percent above government bonds, but it was too risky for the Germans. However, if they could get access to Barclays' assets but have them "sanctified" with a Fitch investment-grade rating, that would be just right. And so, in the summer of 2000, the LB Kiel board listened to a presentation by Barclays, offering a structured product with a lifetime of thirty years. Similar sales pitches had already been given in Hamburg. In both cities, the Barclays crew was very persuasive—seductive, even. As a former LB Kiel executive recalls, "[The board] had a very simplistic view of the world. It was old-style German banking. They saw in structured credit nothing else but a well-rated credit which paid more spread than others and which was managed by a good institution and was going to protect them from default."

Recall that the device of subordination creates a "mattress" that helps an investor overcome the risk-aversion impulse. For LB Kiel, the idea of accessing risky assets through the comforting wrapper of a Barclays CDO seemed magical. From being hypercautious, the Germans became hyperconfident about choosing how their shiny new android would invest. With Barclays acting as a go-between, what followed were a series of conversations between LB Kiel and Usi in New York about the deal specifications and the yield the Germans would get. A member of the Barclays team recalls the discussions. "They were used to double-*A* assets earning fifty basis points (or half a percentage point) above their borrowing rate. When we increased that to seventy-five or perhaps a hundred, they would just take it. The stupid thing is that they would call you—'What can you give us? What can you do?' My God, they just went crazy." Usi's team was amazed at how eager LB Kiel was to lock up its money with Barclays, which for an investment of $100 million, would only pay an additional million per year above the return paid on a risk-free investment.

With twenty-eight separate corporate borrower industry categories in Fitch's classification scheme, one might think that there would be plenty of diversity in the assets available for Usi to put inside the CDOs, enough to get a high rating. However, those twenty-eight traditional categories could not be bought by Usi's trading desk at a price that would give LB Kiel even the modest returns it was panting over. The emerging market loans that Barclays held on its balance sheet and that Usi had already securitized in CDO form weren't good enough either.[14] But what did seem to do the trick were bonds issued by other securitization vehicles—for example, leases backed by aircraft, or U.S. trailer parks. These were offering high coupons, and although Barclays was not yet originating loans in these categories, they could be purchased cheaply in the secondary market. So Usi used these kinds of assets instead, and Fitch added fifteen categories of securitizations, treated as coins or dice being independently rolled in a binomial model. One of these new categories included other CDOs, turning Usi's creation into an early example of what would become known as a *CDO-squared*.

As with the additives in the small print on the packaging of a microwave dinner, it was easy for the investor to miss details like this—and potentially lethal. At least the additives in Moody's BET recipe were corporate bonds or loans, for which it had a default database going back to the 1920s. In 2000, the securitization categories Fitch added willy-nilly to its CDO rating model had only been in existence for a few years. But Fitch was relying on its categories' independence to support an investment-grade rating projecting thirty years into the future. To onlookers it appeared as if the credit police were allowing Usi to write himself a winning lottery ticket whenever he liked: he now had a two-way arbitrage machine doing for credit what John Meriwether had done for interest rates. Barclays' trading book could now invest in assets that paid a full percentage point more than what Usi needed to pay out on the CDOs. For a $15 billion portfolio, that suggested profits in excess of $150 million per year.

Usi now had to name his creations. During his English boarding school childhood, he had been assigned Latin texts by Cicero, Tacitus, and Livy and had fallen in love with ancient Rome. Since he saw his Cayman Islands vehicles as invisible servants, fanning out like legionnaires conquering foreign lands—such as Germany and the United States—for his arbitrage profit, he gave them Roman names: the vehicle for Hamburgische Landesbank would be called Nerva, and LB Kiel's CDO would be named Corvus. And these arbitrage machines were refined in how they borrowed money. Corvus had a pecking order of capital involving no fewer than eight separate tanks, or *tranches*, for cash to flow through.

In the summer of 2000, LB Kiel's sibling, Hamburgische Landesbank, made a €100 million investment in Nerva. A few months later, LB Kiel was so bullish about what Barclays and Fitch had come up with that it agreed to buy not just the triple-*A* tranche of Corvus, but five of them, all the way down to the tranche that had a triple-*B* rating. Its total investment was €150 million.

Legionnaires' Disease

By December 2000, the two German banks were so excited about their investment that they complained when Barclays sold part of Nerva to another European bank. Emboldened by this success, Usi's team began preparing a dozen more Roman-named androids. But replicating his success wasn't as easy as he had anticipated. If you think of Corvus as a billion-dollar wall built to protect Usi's trading book against a flood inundating the assets it was exposed to, even after LB Kiel's investment, there were still some bricks missing at the top and bottom of the wall. At the top of the wall was the layer that was protected by all the bricks sitting below it—the so-called super-senior tranche. This top layer was enormous—$500 million thick—but the magic of the newly applied binomial mathematics made super-senior tranches appear almost risk-free. Usi didn't believe this, but with the Fitch model predicting that this layer was even safer than the triple-*A*-rated layer just beneath it, the returns weren't enticing enough for LB Kiel to invest in it. So Usi persuaded two insurance companies, AXA and Chubb, to write default swap protection in return for a tiny premium.

More problematic was a much riskier layer near the bottom of the "wall." It wasn't the riskiest—that was the equity tranche, which Usi bought in order to lock in for Barclays all the excess returns on the assets it was exposed to. But just above that was the $25 million–thick

E tranche, which Fitch had given a speculative-grade rating of double-B. That made it a tough sell.

By December 2000, most of this E tranche was in the books of Banca Popolare di Intra (BPI), on the shores of Lake Maggiore. How it got there is a tortuous tale that hinged upon Usi's uneasy relationship with the Barclays Capital sales force. In Christian Stoiber and Manish Chandra, Usi was fortunate to have a team that could find the right kind of investors and translate the unfamiliarity of CDOs into language that they could relate to. However, this kind of sales skill was the exception at Barclays. More typical of the bank's sales force was Stefano Silocchi, a former bond salesman who had just become a junior member of a London-based Barclays team called "investor solutions." Back then, according to people who know Silocchi, members of this team were "client-centered" generalists who might be selling interest rate swaps one day and convertible bonds the next—whatever the clients wanted, they would figure out a way for Barclays to provide it.

After talking to a Swiss broker, A.B. Finn, Silocchi learned that this hitherto conservative client was interested in something unusual. A member of BPI's finance department laid out some simple requirements. He wanted a bond that couldn't lose BPI's brokerage clients any more money, but over fifteen or more years would give them more upside than a risk-free government bond would pay. There was no way for Silocchi to know that BPI was seeking to make up for the losses on securities in its newly acquired brokerage clients' accounts. It is also possible that the broker did not accurately convey information between BPI and Barclays. However, it should have been obvious that this client was asking for a financial impossibility. But for whatever reason, Barclays allowed BPI to become fixated on a very dangerous idea: while a single credit-linked note involving debt from Mexico or other emerging market countries would not achieve their "impossible dream," perhaps a bundle of assets accessed via credit derivatives might.

Like any salesman in a competitive business, Silocchi was under pressure, with revenue targets to meet. In early 2000, there was a buzz at Barclays about what Usi and his team were doing. For Silocchi, who barely understood the new innovations, CDOs must have seemed miraculous. And for BPI, the concept of a machine for creating an instant low-risk, diversification-based free lunch was irresistible. In its

2000 annual report, BPI stated, "In order to improve yields, customers intensified investment diversification." When Silocchi approached Usi's team for help in meeting BPI's goals, the abrasive trader had little patience for the Italian salesman. "I don't do retail, it's bad for business," Usi snapped. "And small banks are retail." Never mind that BPI's management was running a $4 billion balance sheet—Usi felt that the little bank was not sophisticated enough to be buying CDOs.

Other people at Barclays had felt the same way about clients like BPI. When Silocchi had put in place the introduction agreement with the broker A.B. Finn, Barclays' compliance department had insisted that only the simplest, plain-vanilla products be sold to such clients. According to e-mails disclosed in court, Silocchi pushed back, fighting for the right to sell them more complex products with greater profit opportunity for Barclays, and ultimately got his way.[15] (Communicating via his lawyer, Silocchi says that my reconstruction of his actions is "highly unreliable.")

Usi's risk finance group was supposed to operate according to a *Policies and Procedures Manual,* which stressed the importance of the "highest ethical standards." According to the manual, "When clients are unsophisticated, client-serving personnel should take additional steps to ensure that they adequately disclose the risks . . . client-serving personnel should not make any representations to the effectiveness of or the potential returns associated with any product being marketed . . . or create the misleading impression that Barclays will assume advisory responsibilities."[16] But the only product that would deliver what BPI wanted was one that was much riskier than BPI was prepared to accept—how could you "disclose" that? No wonder Usi was wary.

A trail of e-mails bounced around the bank's infrastructure. Usi was told not to be "unhelpful." Finally, Usi relented. After all, he needed to plug that gap in the bottom of his "wall" somehow: according to one Barclays calculation, as much as $7 million in profit was on the table if BPI bought a CDO. "Take it to compliance," he told Silocchi. "If compliance says you can do it, that's between you and compliance."

Barclays' compliance department created a *derivatives risk disclosure document* for BPI's chief financial officer to sign. In it, BPI was asked to declare that it would seek independent advice about the investment, that it knew Barclays was an "arm's-length counterparty" that wasn't providing advice, and that it waived its right to sue Barclays. Implicit in the document was that this relationship would be governed by U.K. law, rather than by investor-friendly Italian law. Barclays now had two valuable weapons: the actual transaction BPI wanted and the derivatives risk disclosure document.

Barclays cobbled together a complicated, one-off product for BPI that had a lifetime of eighteen years. Packaged with an investment-grade corporate bond to repay the initial capital at maturity, the extra large return intended to recover the underwater investments consisted in part of a $20 million CDO-style investment that Barclays referred to as a *first-loss note*. Linked to a portfolio of thirty-seven junk bonds, this note was highly risky, something that should have been obvious to a professional investor. As Barclays would later point out, BPI made little effort to heed Barclays' warning about risk and to learn more about what it was buying.

After signing the disclosure document, BPI purchased Barclays' product in February 2000 for $36 million. Barclays would later book a more modest profit of $3.6 million, 10 percent of the transaction's value.[17] Armed with a piece of paper saying that Barclays was a sophisticated, arm's-length counterparty, and after a few follow-up calls by Silocchi, Usi and his London-based trader Grant Lovett would then effectively turn the BPI portfolio into the E tranche of Corvus and other Barclays CDOs. It would find its way in through Usi's main innovation: the idea of tweaking the CDO portfolio after it had been created.

The very first CDOs, such as J.P. Morgan's, were static: once one had created a portfolio of assets in the SPV or synthesized one using credit derivatives, the portfolio was fixed for the rest of its life. From the investors' perspective, if there were some particularly bad loans lurking in there, there was nothing they could do about it. To better understand this crucial performance issue, compare CDOs with stock funds—for example, those that invest in the S&P 500. A static CDO resembles a portfolio of stocks picked at a single point in time and then left untouched. One of the reasons active funds are popular is because of their managers' touted ability to pick stocks or bonds that will outperform over time. There is a lot of debate over whether this ability is genuine or not, but there is no question that investors like to believe it exists, even if they pay a lot for that often blind faith. It was exactly this kind of reassurance that Usi intended to provide in the "managed

CDOs" he created for Barclays. Of course, there was an obvious contrast with the world of equities—in 2000, there was no credit equivalent of a standardized index like the S&P 500 against which to compare performance. The only sure reference point Usi had was the assets he controlled in Barclays' trading book, and so the proposition he made to investors (via the sales force) was that assets he placed in the CDOs should outperform whatever he owned. This may sound like a generous guarantee, but in legal terms it was no such thing. Remember the staggering margins he had built into Nerva and Corvus, which would net Barclays revenues as much as ten times what was being paid to the CDO investors, including LB Kiel and BPI. But what might be described as rent seeking—or profiteering—didn't trouble Usi's investors, given the apparent reassurance that Barclays would look after them better than it looked after itself, in addition to the benefits they were getting from subordination and CDO plumbing.

The most naive and trusting of them all, BPI, would later insist that it had been reassured that "Barclays will protect the coupon." (Barclays would later dispute this account.) When Grant Lovett, along with Silocchi, phoned BPI employee Marco Tudisco in July 2000 and asked to renegotiate part of the deal to allow Barclays to substitute large quantities of unsold Barclays CDOs into the portfolio, Tudisco assumed that Barclays was living up to its "promise." In fact, once BPI had signed the crucial document, Usi began urging Lovett to place the riskiest but most profitable assets (for Barclays, not BPI) in the CDO portfolio. When Tudisco agreed that up to 50 percent of the portfolio could be Barclays CDOs, Usi congratulated Lovett by e-mail: "Well done . . . you totally beat me to the front."

For its part, LB Kiel was a little sharper, but not much. Sure, the Germans knew that Usi's group wasn't selling them this CDO for humanitarian reasons. "My personal judgment is that when they set up and sold [Corvus], their intention was to do the job they were asked to do," says a former LB Kiel executive. "That is, make a profit on it. More than they should. But profit making is not illegitimate." However, there is a crucial reason investors trust traditional fund managers: their legal status as *fiduciaries,* which means they have a duty to always protect their customers' interests when they pick investments on their behalf. A bank arranging a CDO has no such legal duty. In fact, the derivatives documentation behind credit default swaps precludes such relationships. And if the Barclays credit trading book started to perform badly, the bank had every incentive to be disloyal to its investors. Barclays had a legal right (but not the obligation) to dump its worst-performing assets into the clients' CDOs, while cherry-picking the best assets for its own benefit. This is what derivatives cognoscenti call a *worst-of option*. It can be extremely valuable to the person or institution holding it. The only legal protection BPI and LB Kiel had was language in their contracts pledging that substituted assets would always be "of equal or better credit quality," as measured by a credit rating test, not the Barclays trading desk. Given that ratings agencies are typically behind the curve when it comes to flagging problematic credits, that was scant reassurance. Usi had essentially built a big red ejector-seat button for Barclays' trading desk, and while he might have insisted to colleagues that pressing the button was "amoral," others sitting in his seat later on did not feel the same way.

Sue the Asshole

In early 2001, Usi's securitization pipeline was on track to issue $15 billion of CDOs by the end of that year. But there were some troubling headwinds. With the bursting of the dot-com equity market bubble, investors were growing skittish. But Usi was becoming more dependent than ever on Barclays' weak sales force to sell his Roman androids in order to lock in his profits.

Meanwhile, Barclays' infrastructure had failed to keep up with the rising complexity of Usi's deals. Agreements by the sales force with shady brokers like A.B. Finn (which subsequently went out of business) to bring in unsophisticated clients raised warning flags. According to a regulatory examination of the risk finance group by the Federal Reserve Bank of New York in December 2000, there were "significant accounting and control weaknesses in the Group's structured products activities."[18] In response to that examination, Barclays set up an oversight group to keep an eye on Usi's business, which by 2001 accounted for a quarter of the firm's U.S. investment banking profits. Despite these cautionary steps, there would have been strong temptations within Barclays to use Usi's CDOs as a captive buyer of assets the bank was originating elsewhere. Usi may have felt under pressure from all sides to help out other Barclays divisions by shifting their unpalatable assets into his CDOs, but the evidence suggests that he said no.

Perhaps it was this lack of team spirit—and Usi's trademark abrasiveness—that turned Diamond against him. In the post-LTCM world, powerful and publicity-shy proprietary traders like Usi were becoming unfashionable figures at investment banks. At firms like J.P. Morgan and Deutsche Bank, the entire credit derivatives business was becoming harnessed toward selling CDOs to clients, and salespeople were the new top dogs. Traders could no longer count on the mystique of their own "market knowledge" in the face of pressure from accountants to prove that structured products were profitable: "Product control are threatening the viability of my business," Usi complained fruitlessly in an e-mail. Meanwhile, the freewheeling reputation of his team was reinforced by unwelcome press coverage of an evening when Usi and some of his colleagues spent £44,000 ($68,000) on vintage wine at a top London restaurant. That summer, plans began to be laid for a future of credit derivatives at Barclays, one that didn't involve Oka Usi. A team of bankers was hired away from Deutsche Bank to run the firm's credit business. Realizing that there was no future for him at Barclays, Usi jumped before he was pushed. He leveraged the $100 million profit his group was forecast to make that year into a $10 million payoff.

On August 3, 2001, Barclays announced that Vince Balducci was replacing Oka Usi. With scant experience in credit (he had previously traded interest rate derivatives at Merrill Lynch and Deutsche Bank), Balducci had inherited Usi's $15 billion portfolio of hard-to-trade assets and a pipeline of Latinate CDOs, which needed to be sold to investors. Without a decent sales force, and with key expertise gone, how would Balducci deliver the profits that Diamond expected? The answer came from that report on infrastructure improvements in response to the New York Fed examination; it said, "All existing transactions should be supported by fully approved valuation models." As a sharp young trader on Balducci's team noticed, that meant Usi's stated intent to deliver outperformance for his CDO investors was meaningless. The worst-of option to stuff clients' portfolios with junk was what counted. It isn't clear what role was played by the oversight working group or Bob Diamond personally (a Barclays spokesman denies that he chaired the working group). However, subsequent events prove that around October 2001, three months after Usi's departure, Barclays decided to hit the red eject button.[19]

What happened next was ugly. Perfectly good assets sitting inside client CDO portfolios were replaced by chunks of unsold CDOs with the same credit rating. The unsold CDOs would have other unsold CDOs already lurking inside them, which in turn contained more unsold CDOs, so that the Barclays deals started to resemble Russian dolls. Toxic Russian dolls.

The important point here was that the good assets that the new Barclays team removed from the portfolios could be sold in the market, while the unsold CDO pieces could not—which in trading terms defines them as bad assets. In making the substitutions, Barclays was arguably turning bad assets into cash, at the expense of its clients. Even the September 11 terrorist attacks were exploited—Corvus and Nerva CDOs were stuffed with aircraft lease securitizations, which were now doomed to default. Barclays would subsequently deny consciously putting any toxic assets into Corvus and the other CDOs, and insisted that it "shared the pain" of its investors.

By the end of the third quarter of 2001, 90 percent of the Corvus portfolio had been swapped out in this way. At this point, the changes were invisible to the investors. The bad assets and interlinked CDOs now clogging up the portfolio did not trade, by definition. There was no independent evidence from brokers indicating their value in the market. Only Barclays was willing to price them. And in e-mails to LB Kiel and other investors at the year end, Barclays insisted that all was well and its CDOs were still worth 100 cents on the dollar.

LB Kiel didn't smell smoke until it reorganized its capital markets division in late 2001. A sharp young portfolio manager, Martin Halblaub, looked through reports provided by the Corvus trustee and noticed the portfolio substitutions. He began hounding Barclays for more information and asked Fitch whether it was still confident about its investment-grade ratings. Having happily pocketed its fee from Barclays, Fitch was slow to react. But by late 2002, the ratings agency couldn't ignore how blatantly Barclays had made a mockery of its diversity model. Once Fitch reevaluated the web of cross-holdings in Corvus and its siblings, it repeatedly downgraded the supposedly safest triple-*A* tranches to double-*B* or worse. Until the subprime crisis six years later, it remained the worst CDO performance on record.

Realizing that LB Kiel's $150 million investment was now all but worthless, Halblaub phoned Balducci and asked what had happened to Barclays' promise to look after his client. When Balducci prevaricated, Halblaub responded, "You're a complete asshole. I want to get rid of this whole investment and I'm going to sue you." The German bank filed a lawsuit in London's High Court in 2004, accusing Barclays of misselling, misevaluation, and misrepresentation, allegations that Barclays denied.[20]

This was not the only client complaining about the meltdown in performance, but Barclays persuaded its other CDO investors to quietly accept lowball settlements. HSH Nordbank (formed from the merger of LB Kiel and Hamburgische Landesbank) fought harder than the others. It used embarrassing press coverage and the threat of putting Bob Diamond on the witness stand to get Barclays to pay a substantial settlement, according to people familiar with the negotiations.[21] BPI was slower to act, but in February 2010 the little Italian bank faced Barclays in a London courtroom and, after a day of testimony, received an undisclosed settlement.

There were clear lessons for both sides. Credit derivatives were not for the naive investor. LB Kiel and BPI had stupidly outsourced diversification to an investment bank and a ratings agency, and paid the price. Lusting for profits, Bob Diamond had tried to rapidly grow a business that Barclays was unprepared for, and tainted the bank's reputation as a result. But these lessons were not apparent for some time, and the thinking in 2001 was that a grown-up approach to credit derivatives was now possible. J.P. Morgan and Deutsche Bank were about to push the delusion of financial innovation up another notch.

CHAPTER FOUR

The Broken Heart Syndrome

CDOs got a big push from J.P. Morgan and Deutsche Bank, which
brought their high-powered sales, trading, and quant teams into
the game. But to make real money, traders needed to do an even better
job of hiding the risk these investments carried. That required a Black-
Scholes of credit, *a new mathematical model that seemed to make the*
risk in credit derivatives disappear. Ratings agencies struggled to keep
up with the new innovations, while dealers raked in billions while
quietly paying off the most vocal of their disgruntled clients. A blip in
the market in 2005 suggested that all was not well with this picture.

Clash of the Cash Titans

There was a simple reason why the credit derivatives breakthrough
took place in Europe. The U.S. bond market was huge, liquid, and
sophisticated. Since the early 1990s, it was taken for granted that financial innovation came from America: the bond kings of Wall Street had
shown the world how to slice and dice pools of mortgages, credit card
debt, municipal bonds, and auto loans. It was in America where the
convertible bond and the CDO were invented. By this time, the bond
traders of Wall Street knew that their sinecures depended on their
ability to buy and sell everything they created. Sure, some aspects of
bond investing that people didn't particularly like, such as interest rate
risk, may have been hedged with derivatives. However, the fundamental reason to own bonds not issued by the government—getting paid
for taking credit risk—did not need to be messed around with by using

credit derivatives. If you liked the credit risk, you could buy the bond. If you didn't like the credit risk, you could sell it.

The situation was different in Europe. While governments were enthusiastic borrowers in the bond markets, all but the largest companies tended to prefer taking out loans with banks. And European banks were similarly defined by their lending, which was guided—and restricted—by geographical or relationship expertise. But underneath this tranquil surface, many people were desperate to buy or sell credit risk without appearing to do so. Like Sleeping Beauty, Europe was ripe to be awakened by a kiss from London dealers bearing a helpful tool: the credit default swap (CDS).

At Barclays, Bob Diamond's ambitious credit derivatives plans foundered because his bank could not consistently sell Oka Usi's complex deals or even price what he had created. J.P. Morgan, on the other hand, had the magic ingredients for making credit derivatives pay off. J.P. Morgan's European derivatives business was run by a former salesman, Bill Winters. He had moved quickly after the LTCM crisis to build up a network of highly motivated, brainy derivatives marketers who not only could shift J.P. Morgan's products across Europe, but could design them too. As Winters saw it, his experts were like artists in their derivatives creativity: "In music, you may reach a point where all the notes have been written and arranged in every way possible so that you cannot compose any new songs, but of course you always do write new songs, even if it's the same notes in the same pattern, but with a different accent. The same phenomenon is happening every day in the exotics and hybrids business."[1]

Andrea Vella was typical of the new breed of derivative supersalesman or "structurer" at J.P. Morgan. An Italian-born former aerospace engineer, Vella had dropped out of a PhD program at Caltech when a summer job at J.P. Morgan in London got him hooked on derivatives. Dominated by continental Europeans, the bank's financial institutions derivatives marketing (FIDM) team that hired Vella was the epicenter of the shift in power from trading to sales. As a former member of the team recalls, "We would listen to the client and shape something around what the client was looking for, and then hedge with the different traders around the different floors of the bank. Often the traders wouldn't know the full extent of the transaction."

While still an associate—the most junior rank at J.P. Morgan—Vella had impressed his bosses by selling a Bologna-based insurance company interest rate derivatives so complex, they were the financial equivalent of a Gordian knot. He was rewarded with a bigger account: Poste Vita, a Rome-based insurance subsidiary of the Italian post office, which sold long-term structured products to retail investors. Poste Vita was a leader in this booming Italian market, moving billions of euros every year. Such products typically work by combining a money-back guarantee with some exciting upside. To deliver this, a low-risk bond (perhaps a highly rated corporate bond) is packaged with derivatives linked to equities but also possibly interest rates or currencies. Naturally, London-based dealers flocked to Rome to sell derivatives to Poste Vita.

The problem with providing this exciting derivatives-based upside was that it was highly competitive, and Poste Vita knew how to play derivatives salespeople off one another to get the best price. So Vella focused on the boring, safe part: the bond that provided the money-back guarantee. What Poste Vita wanted for its customers was something financially perfect and as immutable as cash itself. In a meeting with the company's executives in March 2001, Vella realized that J.P. Morgan had a secret weapon in the form of credit derivatives.

Since their invention in the mid-1990s, credit default swaps were by now sufficiently well known among clients that J.P. Morgan was boasting about them in its industry award pitches. Consider how AXA Investment Managers, one of Europe's biggest mutual fund groups, sold default swap protection to J.P. Morgan on two European companies: French broadcaster TF1 and German clothing firm Adidas.[2] What was interesting about that? As traditional European companies that borrowed directly from banks, TF1 and Adidas didn't issue bonds. Here was financial innovation in action: the AXA bond fund had used credit default swaps to synthesize a bond the market couldn't provide. Bayerische Landesbank (BLB), a bank in Munich, bought default swap protection from J.P. Morgan to hedge its loan exposure to Swedish telecom company Ericsson and the sovereign debt of Argentina. That was interesting because BLB didn't have to sell its underlying investments in these credits. Even more interesting was that a woman who worked for the loan portfolio group at UBS was using J.P. Morgan's default swap desk to quietly offload the risk of loans UBS had made to its big investment banking clients, such as Nordic mobile phone operator Telenor. These clients all praised J.P. Morgan for allowing them to enter the trade when they wanted to, and exit it again, in whatever size they wanted, however volatile the market was. It was the best kind of advertising, and J.P. Morgan was telling the rest of Europe that its default swap market was open for business. Sleeping Beauty had arisen.

There was, however, a great deal about this new market that J.P. Morgan wasn't disclosing. Although they tracked the performance of bonds or loans, default swaps were unregulated over-the-counter derivatives and were not subject to the safeguards of traditional securities markets. In these traditional markets, not only do accounting rules require that companies report their debt to shareholders, but one can often find out who the biggest lenders are. There even exist databases, such as the Trade Reporting and Compliance Engine (TRACE), operated by the U.S. Financial Industry Regulatory Authority (FINRA), that publicly record the price and quantity every time a bond of a significant issuer changes hands.

What happens when default swaps get thrown into the mix? It might become public information that UBS had lent money to Telenor. But if UBS had hedged its exposure with J.P. Morgan, the real lender—in terms of getting paid for taking credit risk—was now J.P. Morgan . . . or perhaps an undisclosed third party that had taken the other side of the trade. With confidential default swaps, important information about borrower-lender relationships was now being obscured. Equally significant was how default swaps allowed parties without any existing exposure to a borrower to benefit from its bankruptcy. It was analogous to having a stranger take out an insurance policy on your life without your knowledge.

Around the corner from London's Liverpool Street railway station, Winters had a formidable competitor in Deutsche Bank. Under a former Salomon Brothers trader, Ron Tanemura, the firm had mastered the same kind of default swaps that J.P. Morgan clients raved about. In December 2000, Tanemura quit and the German bank turned to two ambitious Indian-born bankers, head of global markets Anshu Jain and his new head of credit derivatives, Rajeev Misra. The bank had some built-in advantages in Europe: it dominated trading in euro currency-denominated bonds and derivatives, and it possessed a sales infrastructure on the continent that was even better than what J.P. Morgan had. The two Indians hatched a plan to eat J.P. Morgan's lunch and snatch the precious industry awards that Bill Winters coveted.

Although subtle and arcane tools in their own right, credit default swaps that referred to single companies or countries were not enough to meet the goals of Jain and Misra and would not provide what Vella had in mind for Poste Vita. But now J.P. Morgan and Deutsche were about to plunder large swaths of Europe by following the script written by Robert Merton, and set spinning like a dervish his so-called spiral of innovation. Using the newly liquid market in "vanilla" or "flow" CDSs as a hedging platform, more complicated and more profitable derivatives would be traded, and the fledgling CDO market would be vastly expanded. Making the next turn of Merton's spiral work required a mathematical model equivalent to the Black-Scholes formula.

How Do You Amend the Broken Heart Syndrome?

In the late '90s, the Black-Scholes option-pricing framework appeared to be a triumph for the market approach, at least until LTCM crashed and burned in 1998. But even after the collapse of that behemoth hedge fund, the idea of pricing a financial contract according to the cost of replicating and hedging it out of simpler parts had a tremendous intuitive appeal. It was the financial analogue of pricing a car according to the cost of manufacturing it, filling it with fuel, and insuring it to drive on the road.

Better still, there was a built-in consistency check in the form of arbitrage. There is no reason why the price of a Toyota Prius must replicate the cost of everything that went into it. But as John Meriwether at Salomon and others demonstrated, derivatives allowed you to extract profit from the discrepancies between financial products and the raw materials used to construct them. As long as you didn't leverage up your bets the way LTCM had, this was a very low-risk exercise and tended to push prices toward their theoretical value. That boosted everyone's confidence in the market approach. Wouldn't it be great, the dealers thought, if the same trick could be done for CDOs? With default swaps increasingly liquid, couldn't you manufacture products by bundling together this raw material, with a dynamic replication recipe whose cost could be enforced by arbitrage? With such a replication recipe in place, any actuarial murkiness lurking in credit portfolios would disappear, and pieces of CDOs would trade every day just like options on the S&P 500 or the VIX index. Like the VIX, CDO prices would no longer be tied to a formula but would serve as valuable market intelligence for investors.

J.P. Morgan's secret weapon was that it already had such a CDO recipe in place—a trading formula it had invented to price its groundbreaking BISTRO deal in 1998. That was meant to shift credit risk off J.P. Morgan's balance sheet, but Bill Winters and his derivatives marketers wanted to adapt it so that they could create new deals for clients, and Anshu Jain and Rajeev Misra were following close behind. The recipe was called the *Gaussian copula,* and just as the "implied volatility" of the Black-Scholes formula provided a shorthand for the market's perception of risk, this model became common currency among dealers who began calling themselves *correlation traders.* Moody's and the other ratings agencies had already come up with a crude way of estimating how bundles of bonds or loans might default together, by modeling them as dice or coins according to the binomial expansion technique (BET). The power of the market was that it created a price for these uncertain events, so that the cost of default swap protection, say, on Ford Motor Company, gave a "market implied" default probability for Ford stock. The challenge for traders was to provide a bridge between derivatives linked to defaults on their own—single-name CDSs—and CDO tranches that depended on several defaults occurring within the same portfolio. Having triumphed with option pricing, did finance theory have anything to say about this connection?

Back in 1974, Robert Merton had applied the Black-Scholes framework to the struggle between lenders and shareholders to control and profit from a company's assets. As Merton pointed out, the company's equity and its debt both looked a lot like one of the option contracts he had recently written about.[3] Equity was a *call option* on the company's assets: either it was the amount by which the assets exceeded the liabilities, or it was zero. Debt was a *put option*: either you received the face value of the liabilities as repayment, or you seized the assets. By running the Black-Scholes formula backward, Merton showed that there was a way of using equity prices to infer what the debt of the company was worth. By pricing the debt of the company in this way, you also obtained an estimate for its default probability. In other words, you had a measure of how close the company was to going bust.

There was, of course, an arbitrage recipe involving trading stocks and bonds that enforced the pricing, but the real impact was conceptual: here was a mechanism that linked equity prices to default probabilities. By the 1980s, the consulting firm KMV began selling default predictions to bond investors—in competition against credit ratings agencies—by using a version of Merton's model. Their selling point was their superior information: equity markets, under the beady eyes of analysts and short sellers, might provide an early warning system of corporate bond defaults via the reverse-engineered Black-Scholes formula. KMV's resident quant, Oldrich Vasicek, made the intellectual leap in 1987—he realized that by modeling the assets of a company, Merton had opened a portal between two worlds: the opaque actuarial world of credit, where long-term investments either paid a modest return or occasionally lost a fortune; and the market world of equities, where daily prices suggested that stock returns were approximately modeled by the famous Gaussian distribution curve, commonly called a bell curve. The mathematical formula, dating back to Abraham de Moivre, showed that most price swings clustered around the average, while large gains or losses were rare.

Getting into equities provided huge advantages for the credit analyst. Replacing a bundle of loans or bonds with a bundle of stocks gave you the handy tool offered by Nobel Prize–winning economist Harry Markowitz: instead of relying on decades of historical default data, you could fine-tune diversification using the day-by-day information in market prices. Equally helpful was the idea of another Nobel economics laureate, William Sharpe, and others: that there was a "systematic" part of an equity portfolio whose risk could not be diversified away. In other words, owning two stocks is always better than owning one, and three is better still, but once your portfolio gets large enough the benefits diminish, while the risk of a market downturn impacting the entire portfolio stays the same. It was easy to identify the systematic risk with an index of stock prices (which is just an average), an insight that spurred the development of products such as equity index funds in the 1970s.

Vasicek seized upon all these ideas and applied them to credit. Exploiting Merton's "window" to work in the Gaussian world of the stock market, he identified a parameter, called *correlation,* that measured how closely individual stocks tracked the index.[4] Transformed back into the credit world, his model transmitted a downward swing in the index (perhaps the stock market, although he didn't spell this out) into a wave of corporate defaults sweeping across a portfolio.

Because it relied on many simplifying assumptions and was not backed up by empirical evidence, Vasicek's model was more of a provocative theoretical talking point than a practical, proven tool. And aside from leaning on Merton's model, it didn't provide an arbitrage recipe to enforce market pricing. But the invention of value at risk (VAR) in the 1990s provided a huge boost for the idea in practical terms. VAR, remember, was a method for sifting through trading book data to identify the worst that could happen in "normal" conditions— say, on nineteen out of twenty or ninety-nine out of one hundred trading days. At first sight, no one could expect VAR to apply to the opposite extreme: the opaque world of loans, which by definition were not traded, and stayed on a bank's books until they either were paid back or had defaulted. Yet the pressure for lending banks to please shareholders led inexorably to the idea of trading credit risk, and thus the credit default swap. Naturally, banks like J.P. Morgan wanted to shine a light into their own loan portfolios, in order to understand how to use the new hedging instruments. Vasicek's idea of a hidden Gaussian driver of loan defaults was like an unseen VAR model. Using Merton's window, translating debt into equity, the model brought the power of daily market information to uncover the level of risk lurking within a credit portfolio where nothing happened for years at a time.

The banking world of the late 1990s, where senior managers such as Peter Hancock or Marc Shapiro were casting around for ways to control credit risk and boost the return on capital, was ripe for an insight like this. Vasicek's model provided the intellectual foundation for a wave of credit risk models developed by banks and consulting firms, and was bought into wholesale by banking regulators. J.P. Morgan's version was called Creditmetrics, and it was in 1999 that a member of that modeling team, the Chinese-born actuary David X. Li, tried to give traders what they desperately wanted: a link between the market price of defaults on their own and the price of CDOs where defaults occurred together.[5]

Li was an actuary—he had never traded anything—but he did know plenty about trawling through mortality statistics to work out how life insurance products, such as annuities, should be priced. Particularly challenging were *joint-life annuities,* in which a married couple paid up front for an income for life, which lasted as long as either person was alive.

This may sound like a bad bet for the insurer, but it is actually quite safe to offer joint-life annuities because of *broken heart syndrome.* It is statistically proven, actuaries say, that once one member of a couple dies, the other typically dies fairly soon afterward (a famous example being the death of singer June Carter shortly after her husband, Johnny Cash, died). Actuaries had even developed a branch of statistics in the 1970s specifically to quantify this syndrome, known as *copulas.*

Using the analogy that the death of an insurance policyholder was like a bond defaulting (triggering a contractual payment from one party to another), Li applied the copula framework to the problem of lots of bonds defaulting together. And it turned out that the copula with the easiest mathematics, the *Gaussian copula,* was equivalent to the Vasicek model that connected multiple defaults via a single correlation parameter. As input, Li used the market prices of bonds or credit default swap spreads. As output, his analogue of the price of a joint-life annuity was the market price of a portfolio credit derivative, such as a piece of a CDO. But what was going on in the middle? Like Moody's BET, the Gaussian copula appeared to be just another actuarial rule of thumb, only in this case, Li was using it to connect one set of market prices to another. The difference was that while the Moody's BET was an inflexible rule book administered by a ratings agency, the mysterious correlation parameter in the Gaussian copula put the trader in control. Like the implied volatility that emerged from the Black-Scholes formula as the market's fear gauge, here was the tantalizing prospect of a new risk shorthand in CDO prices that supposedly broke open the complexity of the CDO. The Gaussian copula quickly became the lingua franca of credit derivatives traders, who dubbed it the *Black-Scholes of credit*.

A few quants were troubled by that comparison. They pointed out that somewhere along the circuitous route between Merton and Li, the replication-and-arbitrage recipe that enforced the market mechanism was dropped. The life-or-death question for a trading desk—Am I hedged against market moves?—was left unanswered. But it was easy to dismiss such quibbles when there were billions to be made.

Mr. Clip and the Repon Man

When Erik Stattin, the chief executive of Poste Vita, explained to Andrea Vella early in 2001 how he wanted a slightly better-performing but highly rated bond to provide money-back guarantees to his customers, the conversation was similar to that between Barclays and LB Kiel a year earlier. "We want a higher spread but we're rating constrained," the conversation began. "We want to diversify." Like his counterparts at Barclays, Vella saw a CDO as the solution that could provide slightly higher returns than a similarly rated corporate bond— in other words, it was slightly cheaper. And it would provide Stattin with diversification—the actuarial, not-putting-all-your-eggs-in-one-basket kind that reduced consumers' exposure to a single corporate bond.[6]

But there was a difference. The old-fashioned banks, such as Barclays, had exploited the yawning gap between the investment-grade returns to investors as determined by Moody's BET and the spreads earned by the trading desk from portfolios of speculative-grade debt. But they had to patiently earn their outsize CDO profit margins annually as a "carry trade" and would often have to hold back reserves out of caution in case their traders screwed up. On the other hand, if the Gaussian copula was indeed the new Black-Scholes, then J.P. Morgan could roll up all of these future annual profits into a single "present value" expressing the difference between a derivative and its hedge. To the salespeople, it appeared that staggering amounts of money were locked up inside the deal—money that, if the models could be believed, ought to be reflected in bonus payments. Sure, bringing together one hundred or so bonds in a CDO was a lot more compli- cated than Black-Scholes, which only involved a single asset, but the new breed of correlation traders were a lot geekier—and more pli- ant—than the previous generation of swaggering, larger-than-life traders exemplified by Oka Usi.

These new CDOs were not traditional securitizations, where assets such as mortgages or aircraft leases were transferred into a protected special-purpose company. Like BISTRO, the CDOs contained invest- ment-grade corporate debt and used credit default swaps as a building block, but were different in the sense that they weren't created to hedge loans on J.P. Morgan's balance sheet. The whole process was now run within a trading desk as a derivatives hedging problem. In an unregulated market, the only limit on the number of default swaps that you could write was investor demand for the CDOs you created. And the increased confidence that the model brought to the market boosted volume, making their profit much greater.

During 2001, the first of these new products hit the market. One was called a *credit-linked protected note* (CLIP). As a J.P. Morgan sales- man proudly explained to me, the bank had found a way of selling the very riskiest slice of a CDO—the equity tank of cash at the bottom that gets drained before anything else—to risk-averse German insur- ance companies. The bank achieved this remarkable feat by embed- ding the CDO piece into the coupon of a very safe bond issued by German mortgage banks, rather like a wafer-thin slice of poisonous Japanese *fugu* fish inserted into a roll of rice. This may have been my first encounter with a so-called single-tranche synthetic CDO, but behind the scenes, Vella was working on a much bigger deal.

Deutsche Bank's head of credit derivatives, Rajeev Misra, wasn't going to let J.P. Morgan hog the spotlight—and the profits. In April 2001, he poached one of J.P. Morgan's correlation trading technicians, Mark Stainton, effectively buying his competitor's technology. Although he had once traded interest rate swaps at Merrill Lynch, peo- ple who worked with him say that Misra's insights came from his sales background at Deutsche, which taught him about burying complexity in predigested, "TV dinner" formats.

Misra dismissed the CLIP product, claiming that J.P. Morgan was simply copying a Deutsche product called a *repackaged option note*

(REPON). Misra also argued that whatever Winters's team at J.P. Morgan was doing, Deutsche was doing it better, especially in the new arena of synthetic CDOs. Deutsche had not only invented its own variant of CLIP and claimed to be selling tens of billions of dollars worth of the products.[7] It also had bested J.P. Morgan at constructing synthetic CDOs in partnership with third-party fund managers, such as AXA. The idea was that the bank would earn money from arranging the product and trading the default swaps that went into it, while the fund manager earned a fee by picking the investments. Most important, the fund manager's independence would encourage investors to buy the structured product from the bank. Deutsche not only poached J.P. Morgan's client, proudly announcing its own CDO with AXA in 2002, but persuaded Asian clients such as Singapore's United Overseas Bank (UOB) to do similar deals. However, Deutsche's great advantage, its broad global sales network, exposed it to the same risks faced by Barclays: that the complex new products would be bought by the wrong people.

The Congregazione dei Figli dell'Immacolata Concezione was a Catholic lay order founded in nineteenth-century Italy. Run by priests, the Congregazione specialized in charitable works, running hospitals and children's homes in poor parts of Italy and other countries. Funded entirely by donations and bequests, the order's endowment had grown so large by 2001 that it began looking for places to invest. According to a source familiar with its operations, Father Lucchetti, head of the order's Italian branch, had been speaking to a fellow monk who had been a Goldman Sachs banker before taking his holy orders. The monk said, "Perhaps it is time for the Congregazione to consider moving out of conservative bank deposits and invest in the sophisticated new Wall Street products that offer both safety and higher returns." So in September 2001, Lucchetti took a short walk from his Rome headquarters to the office of a broker in Piazza Navona, a popular tourist spot with Baroque fountains. The Deutsche Bank saleswoman who shook hands with the priest was Sanaz Zaimi. After Lucchetti told her what he was looking for, she proposed a structured product that contained not only one of Deutsche's new single-tranche synthetic CDOs, but also an investment in a portfolio of hedge funds. The pitch document seemed to check all the usual boxes: diversification, independent management, and a built-in cushion of safety. After signing the inevitable waiver forms, Lucchetti agreed to invest €12 million of the Congregazione's money.

While the precise details of the Congregazione's deal with Deutsche Bank remain under wraps, documents relating to a similar transaction with a regional Italian bank in Umbria show just how toxic the CDOs were that Deutsche sold. The e-mail trail from Zaimi and the Rome-based brokers to the regional bank began in March 2001, and involved REPON, Deutsche's thinly sliced derivative-based synthetic CDO that exposed investors to a portfolio of corporate credits. It was the year the dot-com bubble burst, and analysts were warning that telecom companies were heavily exposed. But the magic of diversification was supposed to protect CDO investors. "Mezzanine tranches are robust to heavy sectoral losses," assured Deutsche's marketing material. "Even if Telecom, Auto and Retail sectors suffer 19 times historical losses, the BBB+ tranche will not suffer a loss." According to a Deutsche presale memorandum provided by Zaimi, "Maximum concentration in telecommunications as well as electronics will be capped at 8.5%." Comforted by this marketing material, in September 2001 the Italian bank paid $20 million for a deal called REPON-16. Completed at the end of October, this deal contained exposure to energy company Enron, which was only a month away from bankruptcy. Within eighteen months, five names included in the CDO had defaulted—Enron and four telecom companies, as a result of an exposure to that sector of nearly 11 percent (Deutsche insists that the client was aware of its last-minute tweaks). Given the timing of the deal, an observer might be forgiven for wondering whether Zaimi's Italian client was unwittingly performing a useful hedging role for the Deutsche Bank trading desk, having bought a type of CDO that in 2010 the SEC would characterize as "designed to fail."[8]

About a year after buying a similar deal, Father Lucchetti was alarmed when the Congregazione received a routine price report from Deutsche Bank indicating that his recently purchased structured product had plummeted in value. By this time, the priest had spoken to the regional Italian bank, which had made a similar discovery. Lucchetti was even more alarmed to hear that this bank had tried to visit the same broker on Piazza Navona, finding that its office had been stripped bare of its furniture and indoor plants, with no trace that it had ever existed. Meanwhile, the Swiss investment firm that was supposed to be managing the portfolio of hedge funds had gone out of business too. Father Lucchetti was streetwise enough to know he could not recover his order's investment by the power of prayer alone. He hired a lawyer who immediately wrote to Deutsche Bank demanding more information.

No explanation was forthcoming, and eight years later, the bankers who created the deal point fingers at one another when asked to justify how such a product was ever sold. People close to Sanaz Zaimi, now a top saleswoman at Bank of America, claim that she was far too junior to understand the complex products she was selling, and deferred to Deutsche's CDO structuring experts in her conversations with clients. Associates of one such expert, Paul Czekalowski, who was named in the trail of REPON-16 e-mails with the regional Italian bank, respond that such clients spoke no English while Czekalowski spoke no Italian—making them entirely dependent on Zaimi's fluent Italian to understand what they were buying. Friends of Rajeev Misra, now a powerful trader at UBS, say that these clients were far too small, and the bankers far too junior to him in the chain of command, for the deals ever to have appeared on his radar screen. Deutsche Bank's own public relations machine argues that it would be "illogical" to describe REPON-16 and its cousins as being "designed to fail," and that it was not Deutsche's job to advise clients what to buy. The bank does concede that it subsequently "further improved" its transaction approval process as the "market matured."

Deutsche Bank has confirmed what happened next: Father Lucchetti learned that the German giant was willing to buy its way out of an embarrassing situation. Deutsche quickly refunded the Congregazione its €12 million on condition that the priest pledged to keep quiet. Zaimi's regional Italian bank client also got its money back. Fortunately for Misra's bottom line, most of the bank's CDO clients didn't look at their price reports that carefully or were too embarrassed to complain if they did and noticed a loss. Unlike Barclays, which unwisely allowed itself to be dragged into the courts and the pages of the press when confronted by LB Kiel and BPI, Deutsche Bank mostly kept its problems out of sight.

Deutsche's Treat

Spain, like Italy, was fertile territory for derivatives, because it had an archipelago of provincial financial institutions ruled by a hate-to-lose mind-set. Deutsche Bank salesman Antonio Linares excelled in this market, crisscrossing the country, meeting the management of *cajas* (savings banks) in small towns. And he persuaded many of them to buy Misra's CDO products. Although Deutsche denies Linares's involvement, the lure of the financial iPhone caught the attention of Justo Palma, a fund manager for a mutual fund company called BZ Gestion in the city of Saragossa, northeast of Madrid, in 2001.[9] Palma invited several banks to propose a structured product for one of BZ Gestion's money market funds, and Deutsche Bank won the tender, selling a REPON-style product containing a single slice of a synthetic CDO.

Unfortunately, a money market fund is not the same as an insurance company, which holds its assets at book value. Palma's purchase was marked to market once a month, and as the provider of the product, Deutsche was obliged to provide its valuation. This quickly exposed a significant difference between the price Palma had paid and what the CDO was worth, even without any defaults in the portfolio. By 2002, BZ Gestion noticed that its low-risk fund was heavily underwater, and worse still, it was a kind of fund that Spanish regulators had banned from investing in credit derivatives. The company fired Palma, complained to Deutsche Bank, and promptly got a refund.

Meanwhile, other Spanish customers of Deutsche Bank were complaining to me about Deutsche's sales practices with CDOs. I called Misra and left a message, telling him that my magazine was running a story about BZ Gestion; Misra was traveling, but he immediately called me back from Tokyo at what would have been for him the small hours of the morning. "It's only a tiny little trade," he protested, implying that a few minor missteps were inevitable when creating a global credit derivatives powerhouse.

And in a sense he was right. His business was making so much money that he could afford a few missteps in selling inappropriate or toxic products to financial minnows, missteps that people close to Misra say he was unaware of at the time. It was relatively easy for

Deutsche to buy back problem trades from clients, which would often be repackaged into new deals. The bank's growing trading volumes and profits spoke for themselves: a month after I spoke to Misra, he boasted that his credit derivatives revenues had exceeded the $1 billion mark and duly collected his plastic trade magazine award for "credit derivatives house of the year."

It was a testament to the skill of derivatives salespeople, who were able to convince clients that these products had real value, that made such things possible. There was an enormous difference between what the customer paid for the product (in the form of a lack of risk premium) and the internal manufacturing cost calculated by the bank's traders. Indeed, as a Deutsche market risk manager innocently stated in an interview in 2004, his team encouraged the growth of the firm's single-tranche synthetic CDO business because the clients' ignorance of value gave Deutsche Bank a cushion against losses.[10] "Deutsche Bank salespeople may have performed a valuable risk management service [for Deutsche Bank]," I wrote, paraphrasing the risk manager's remarks. The bank was irritated to see such a statement in print because it gave the impression that well-intended governance procedures had made fleecing clients a company policy. But the real key to success here was simple: the client must never find out what the market price was for the product they'd been sold.

A Sucker for CDOs

September 10, 2001, was a traumatic day for J.P. Morgan's Andrea Vella. For months, he and his team of structuring experts in London had designed an investment product for Poste Vita's retail customers. It was a half-billion-euro monster containing derivatives linked to inflation and equity markets, and underpinned with a giant triple-A-rated slice of synthetic CDO to provide the money-back guarantee. Now the J.P. Morgan team was in Rome, listening to Erik Stattin tell them he had decided to do his first CDO-backed deal not with Vella, but with his rival, the derivatives sales genius at Credit Suisse, Guglielmo Sartori di Borgoricco. The next day, the 9/11 attacks on the United States convinced Vella that his idea was dead for good.

But he was wrong. At the meeting in Rome, Stattin had promised Vella that Poste Vita's second deal would be with J.P. Morgan, and over the next few months he was as good as his word. By February 2002, Vella was ready to close his first CDO deal for Poste Vita. There had been meetings with Italian regulators who gave the nod of approval. The CDO J.P. Morgan built for it would be called Mayu—"The name of a girl I know," Vella later said. Mayu was a Dutch-domiciled corporate android controlled by J.P. Morgan that took on the credit risk of one hundred investment-grade companies for ten years by selling default swap protection to the U.S. bank's trading desk. If Mayu had been constructed like a traditional securitization, it would have needed to issue $8.5 billion's worth of bonds to investors, in order to balance out the $8.5 billion of credit default swap exposure it had taken on from J.P. Morgan (equivalent to buying $8.5 billion in debt). However, Mayu was one of the new generation of single-tranche synthetic CDOs. Given Vella's specifications, the J.P. Morgan trading desk programmed the android to issue just a single tranche or layer of debt, amounting to €426 million, while hedging out the remaining $8 billion in the default swap market.

Meanwhile, Poste Vita had set up its own android, called Programma Dinamico, in the tax-friendly jurisdiction of Dublin, which invested in the Mayu CDO, along with the other derivatives. It then mailed out glossy brochures, featuring smiling Italians cavorting on beaches and yachts, that emphasized the dual marketing message of financial upside and underlying safety. The small print at the end of the brochures mentioned that the CDO carried Fitch's and Moody's triple-A ratings. Tens of thousands of middle-aged Italians invested €426 million with Poste Vita. What happened to their money? Only 93.5 percent was allocated to the Dublin-based android, Programma Dinamico. The remaining €27 million was pocketed by Poste Vita in the form of a fee.

When they analyzed the deal in 2004, some investment bank quants used Gaussian copula–type models to calculate the fair value of the Mayu CDO. They estimated that the manufacturing cost for the J.P. Morgan trading desk was about €28 million less than the bank received for Mayu on the day the transaction closed, in February 2002. To observers, it appeared that the €28 million (equivalent to $30 million at the time) was an example of the profit for J.P. Morgan that the new wave of derivative expert salespeople were able to point to at bonus time. The number shows what a good salesman Vella was: he had made Poste Vita and its thousands of Italian customers feel so safe in this deal that they were willing to leave €28 million on the table.[11]

People who know Vella downplay the idea that Mayu turned him into a multimillionaire star banker overnight. Whatever the truth, it wasn't just Vella who had created that warm, fuzzy feeling of security among his CDO buyers. One reason was that under Italian tax rules, there was no incentive for customers to look at the price of the CDO before the product matured (because if they bailed out early, they would lose any tax benefits). The structurers had apparently solved the problem of ensuring that CDO customers did not discover the market price. But it is hard to imagine that Poste Vita would have handed over the money had it not been for Fitch, which gave Mayu a triple-A rating, and for Moody's, which gave the same rating to Vella's next Poste Vita CDO deal.

Barbarians Among the Gatekeepers

As the gatekeepers of the bond market, the ratings agencies had an oligopoly backed by regulators that required investors such as insurance companies or money funds to buy investment-grade paper. This license to print money attracted shrewd investors, starting with McGraw-Hill, which bought Standard & Poor's in 1966; followed by France's Fimalac, which bought Fitch in 1997; and Warren Buffett, who acquired a 16 percent stake in Moody's in 2001. Meanwhile, the ratings analysts saw a new, lucrative revenue stream for these new shareholders: collaborating with banks to rate securitizations.

Rating securitizations was much more profitable than rating corporate bonds. It's not known exactly what Fitch was paid for rating Mayu in February 2002, but a Standard & Poor's CDO ratings invoice from 2003, disclosed as part of a court filing, gives an indication.[12] According to the invoice, S&P charged seven basis points for rating a CDO—for a $400 million deal, that would be $320,000, plus an additional "surveillance fee," which for a ten-year product would have been $350,000. That adds up to $670,000—about five times the fee for an equivalent corporate bond issue.

Spurred by these huge fees, the ratings agencies raced to transform themselves in order to keep pace with the business revolution being run by the credit derivatives dealers. It was a big cultural shift for them. At first, Moody's was defensive about the new developments, and in particular it seemed to be irked by KMV, writing papers that attacked the use of the Black-Scholes formula to estimate default probability, and tried to pick holes in KMV's performance statistics. The attacks suddenly stopped when Moody's bought KMV in April 2002 for $200 million. The venerable ratings agency had finally embraced the new commercial realities.

Meanwhile, S&P started showcasing its skill at measuring market-based correlation. By 2003, Moody's had jumped on the bandwagon and was talking about how to incorporate equity correlation into CDO ratings models.

In 2003, I watched Fitch's head of CDOs, Ken Gill, swanning before a sea of champagne-swilling bankers. That year, his firm's structured finance division brought in 60 percent of Fitch's €403 million annual revenues. At Moody's, structured products brought in more money in 2003 than all of what Fitch made in a year. And the engine of these revenues was in Paris, where Paul Mazataud was in charge of rating European CDOs. Educated in the French *Grandes Écoles* tradition to love mathematical rules, Mazataud was in the envious position of making his own rules—which happened to be rules that kept the CDO bankers happy and the money flowing in.

When I first spoke to Mazataud in 2004, he boasted about his ability to make wine from water. "We have many *AAA* tranches on the synthetic CDO market," he told me. "Maybe 50 percent are *AAA* rated." Far from defending the gates of an exclusive club of triple-A bond issuers, Mazataud was gleefully running a triple-A printing press.

To be fair to Fitch, Moody's, and S&P, most of the analysts building CDO ratings models were acting with integrity. They sincerely believed in their models, and they thought that incorporating Gaussian copula ideas or KMV's link to equity prices would make them better. Some of them agonized about the statistical weaknesses of triple-A ratings, which depended on near immunity from rare events that had never been witnessed in the nascent CDO market. Yet all this sincerity was being subverted by the pressure to be more profitable. Fitch, Moody's, and S&P all gave the banks access to their CDO rating software to help them fine-tune the machine they were operating. The bankers understood the Gaussian copula far better than the rating analysts did, and could simply reverse-engineer the rating software to maximize their profits on every deal. And triple-*A* ratings were the linchpin of the process, perpetuating the belief in rock-solid safety that made it possible for J.P. Morgan to make so much money from Poste Vita's investors.

What made it harder for J.P. Morgan to clip those Italian sheep was the disclosure in 2004 that—since the moment it was launched—Mayu had suffered a string of problems that epitomized the flaws in the system. According to Fitch, a few months after the CDO had been issued, one of the one hundred credits it contained defaulted when WorldCom filed for bankruptcy in July 2002.[13] J.P. Morgan happened to be a big lender and bond arranger to WorldCom (in March 2005, the bank would agree to pay a $2 billion fine to WorldCom investors). Buying protection from the Mayu android on $80 million of World-Com debt prior to its default might have conveniently hedged some of the bank's exposure. To be fair to J.P. Morgan and Vella, there is no evidence that Mayu was intentionally laced with debt that the bank knew was about to default. According to people close to the deal, J.P. Morgan selected a "universe" of eligible credits for Mayu, using the criterion that their default swaps were liquid. But *liquid* meant heavily traded, which in WorldCom's case was because unbeknownst to Vella, traders at J.P. Morgan and other banks were avidly buying default swaps to hedge their loan positions—an example of what economists call *adverse selection*.

However, that default significantly eroded the cushion protecting Mayu's investors from a loss on their triple-*A*-rated CDO—an unthinkable occurrence. (The Deutsche Bank REPON-16 product, with its five defaults, had been lower rated.) That's why, behind the scenes, Vella organized a restructuring of Mayu in 2003, buying up defaulted or downgraded credits from the portfolio and replacing them with highly rated ones, including seven pieces of CDO on J.P. Morgan's trading book. But all that fevered activity was not enough to retain the triple-*A* credit rating. This placed Fitch in a quandary, because as part of their scheme to ensure that investors never discovered the real CDO price, the banks had sworn Fitch and Moody's (which had rated the other J.P.

Morgan CDO) to secrecy . . . although that "secret" was comically revealed by Poste Vita's marketing material, which proudly told prospective customers about Fitch's and Moody's triple-A ratings. In Fitch's case, this information was now clearly false. Meanwhile, Poste Vita's Web site, which published prices for all its investment products, suggested that Mayu's market value had declined by 40 percent, along with other CDO-backed investments (the price bounced back a few years later).

In the summer of 2004, as I researched that story, I found the explanations of the ratings agencies alternately amusing and disturbing. There was the unflappable response of Fitch's Ken Gill, who listened carefully to what I told him and expressed regret at what had happened to Mayu. Then Fitch immediately put out a press release announcing the downgrade of the CDO (by 2010 it had fallen to a triple-B rating, one level above junk).

Over at Moody's, Paul Mazataud's flustered reaction to my phone call was more telling. Although no downgrade had been necessary for the J.P. Morgan CDO his agency had rated, Mazataud was far more sensitive to the charge of being in the pockets of the banks that paid him to rate CDOs. But he dug himself a deeper hole by trying to refer to Moody's triple-A rating of those CDOs as being "off the record," although thousands of Italians had a brochure touting it.

These two senior ratings officials, who were supposed to be the watchdogs of the credit markets, had clearly lost sight of their mission. Default swaps might have been defensible to a limited degree as financial innovations, and the original concept of CDOs, to free up bank lending, also had some justification. However, the boom in synthetic securitization driven by ratings was a bad thing for many investors. There was no real economic value being created in this process, aside from the salaries and bonuses of the bankers and the ratings agency analysts.

All the profits and press accolades made it difficult for a naysayer to be heard. One senior banker who had doubts about the symbiosis between banks and ratings agencies trafficking in synthetic CDOs was the head of sales at a big U.S. securities firm and later became its CFO. "It began as a useful risk diversification portfolio management tool, and then, as always, the derivatives guys worked out a smart way to make money on it. So what you have is the greed of dealers, and the negligence of the ratings agencies, who both understood that their basic business model couldn't be paid for by their conventional product, idiosyncratic fundamental credit risk."

But these profits drove the default swap market, and there was no holding it back. In 2004 the volume of asset-backed bond issuance (which includes CDOs) first outstripped the corporate bond market.[14] And it was in 2004 that the total notional size of the default swap market exceeded $4.5 trillion, with a gross market value of $131 billion. By 2007, it would grow to a staggering $51 trillion, of which roughly half were "multiname" contracts or synthetic CDOs valued at $330 billion.[15]

Selling the Unsellable

The early generation of CDO buyers had one thing in common: the dealers expected them to hold on to their investments and not worry about market value. But in order for new Gaussian copula models to yield the pot of gold that they promised, CDOs had to trade in the market. One of these early investors provided an impetus for this trading when a disastrous experience forced it to take action. Abbey National was once the United Kingdom's biggest building society, or thrift. However, after demutualizing in the 1980s, the new shareholder-driven bank was bitten by the same credit diversification bug that had bitten the Germans and the Italians. Its 2000 annual report said as much. The headline declared that the bank was "building shareholder value," and it allocated a quarter of its $150 billion balance sheet to the first generation of CDOs and other exotic securitizations then being sold by Wall Street firms.

By the summer of 2002, the folly of this strategy became apparent, as the post-dot-com downturn swept across Abbey's bond portfolio, resulting in the first of what would be $2 billion write-downs. Abbey fired its chief executive and, following a poacher-turned-gamekeeper principle for hiring, brought in two ex–investment bankers as CEO and CFO to clean up the mess. Neither was an expert in credit derivatives, but for that they hired Richard Williams, a seasoned credit derivative trader who had been in the CDS game since its inception in the mid-1990s and had participated in the arcane industry panels that standardized the legal form of the new contracts. It was a smart choice, since Williams was an insider who understood how cliques of derivatives dealers could keep investors in the dark.

When Williams first peered into Abbey's $10 billion CDO portfolio in 2002, he saw what a sucker his employer had been. The investment banks that put the early CDOs together, such as Oka Usi's group at Barclays, focused on one thing: closing the sale and extracting the arbitrage profit between what they earned on the assets backing the CDO and what it paid out. They had never planned to buy them back. "In 2002, you could buy the new issue, but there was no ability to trade them," Williams recalled. "But we had a significant portfolio that had to be disposed of." In plain language, Abbey was the sucker that now had to turn the tables on those who had duped it. It wasn't going to be easy. As a former trader, Williams was shocked to discover that the regular CDO valuations that dealers were obliged to provide to their clients were little better than fiction. Williams learned the truth when he asked dealers to name a price at which they would buy their CDOs back. "The prices given as bids didn't reflect that monthly marking process," he says. "There'd be a significant discount." Those valuations had already led Abbey to take billions in write-downs and sack its CEO. Accepting the prices dealers were actually prepared to pay for the CDOs would lose the bank billions more.

Williams went back to basics. For the early Wall Street securitizations of the 1980s, dealers had worked out their own prices for CDOs by assuming that owning one was similar to owning a portfolio of the underlying bonds or loans. By using ratings agency arguments based on diversification and subordination to persuade traditional banks or insurance companies to accept much lower returns on the portfolio, the dealers got to skim off the difference and make huge profits. Think about what happens if the investor sells the CDO back to its manufacturer—the dealer is no longer covered against the risk of the underlying bonds and has to start selling them. But doing that means giving up the fabulous profits locked in by the difference between the market approach and the actuarial approach.

And it gets worse. Suppose that the underlying market for bonds or loans has gone haywire, as it did for telecom, energy, and aircraft debt in late 2001 and early 2002. If the dealer constructed a CDO using such bonds before those markets tanked, it now had to sell the bonds (or unwind the default swaps that replicate owning the bonds) at a hefty loss. But Williams was determined to find a way to sell the unsellable. Maybe the traditional pricing method, burdened with what he described as "its very deterministic, static mathematics," was overreacting to market swings. "We took the Gaussian copula–type mathematics and strapped it onto the CDO portfolio, just to see what kind of numbers came out. We got some significantly better values than were being quoted." In other words, the mysterious correlation parameter could be bent to do Williams's bidding.

Knowing the tricks of the dealers who had pulled the wool over Abbey's eyes, Williams used the Gaussian copula to undermine their consensus and get a better price. "We set about 'educating' the market in what we perceived the value of the CDOs to be. But the banks replied, 'That's all very nice, but our bid is still here.' So we then set about creating some more competitive tensions in the marketplace, showing a deal to another investment bank, and talked them through the value, saying, 'We'd like you to put a bid on this.' It was fun. At that point we started selling. Eventually, we reached the end of our portfolio, which was a big relief."

The Great Car Crash

The estimated $30 million of up-front profit that J.P. Morgan stood to make on the Mayu CDO was, of course, not instantly there for the taking. It was a paper profit or present value (PV) that, according to a Gaussian copula–type model, expressed the difference between what the client paid on the basis of a triple-A rating and the ten-year cost of replicating the CDO from the one hundred default swaps that served as its raw material. As the synthetic CDO market grew, salespeople and traders at J.P. Morgan, Deutsche, and elsewhere wrestled with the problem of turning these PVs into actual revenues and, hence, their bonuses.

A few years earlier, these massive paper margins had given everyone comfort: there was plenty of profit to go around and to repurchase problem deals. But as the credit derivatives business grew, the costs grew as well. A former senior J.P. Morgan trader recalls, "They are incredibly infrastructure-heavy businesses—the run-rate expense of just having operational support and IT runs to the hundreds of millions per year. And in credit derivatives, for every single corporate name you have a CDS, so the complexity explodes exponentially." And with 50 percent of revenues typically earmarked for bonuses, any bank that couldn't get at these profits quickly risked having its top people jump to another, better-paying gig.

The challenge was in convincing bank auditors that Gaussian copula mathematics represented the true market cost of manufacturing a piece of CDO. The main obstacle there: the U.S. Financial Accounting Standards Board, based in Norwalk, Connecticut, had issued a ruling obscurely titled "Emerging Issues Task Force (EITF) 02-03" in 2003, which sensibly required that profits from derivatives that didn't trade in the market couldn't be recognized until the deals reached maturity. A deal like Mayu presented a significant problem for J.P. Morgan, according to one of the bankers involved. "You do a tailor-made portfolio for which the correlation is unobservable, and you are sitting on an enormous risk that no one can put a price on."

For the derivatives salespeople and traders who had already bought imaginary Porsches and Notting Hill houses with correlation booty wrapped up in a model-based PV number, EITF 02-03 was maddening. They didn't want to be told that the synthetic CDO profit they were convinced was rightfully theirs would stay locked away for a decade or more. And this delayed gratification also grated on the nerves of the senior management of investment banks that had poured money into the expensive infrastructure needed to trade the new products. How would they explain to analysts that their growth projections needed to be revised downward, because accountants had locked away those revenues and virtually thrown away the key?

Well, where there's a $100 million or two to be made, there's a way. Fortunately, for the stymied bankers, the Abbey CDO liquidation pointed a way forward. One of the buyers of secondhand Abbey CDOs in 2003 was ex–J.P. Morgan trader Jonathan Laredo, whose company, Solent Capital, typified the wave of hedge fund start-ups that from 2003 on raised investor funds to squeeze value from the fast-developing credit derivatives markets.

Unlike investors such as BZ Gestion or Poste Vita, these hedge funds were not buying on the basis of triple-A ratings, nor were they interested in holding on to CDOs long-term. Using borrowed money from banks, and run by ex-bankers, the hedge funds had to be able to sell everything at a moment's notice, and hence they were the truest believers in daily mark-to-market valuation. If the Gaussian copula truly determined the banks' buying and selling appetite, the hedge funds were happy to use it as well. However, the ability to sell at a moment's notice required abundant market liquidity. By 2004, default swaps linked to well-known companies were already liquid, but pieces of CDOs that had been constructed specifically for clients weren't.

To give the hedge funds enough confidence to trade in those pieces, the banks would have to standardize the concept of what a synthetic CDO portfolio was, by creating an index of the one hundred or so most liquid credit default swaps. This prompted the launch of corporate credit indexes such as the iTraxx and CDX, primarily for the hedge funds to trade, and that in turn led to the creation of tranches on these indexes.[16] For the big banks that pioneered the London synthetic CDO market, J.P. Morgan and Deutsche Bank, the prospect of earning income from hedge funds trading structured credit on a weekly basis was exciting. They no longer had to spend so much time chasing sleepy, ignorant, hate-to-lose investors in the backwaters of continental Europe, while paying off those who subsequently complained. But even more exciting was how the new indexes could be shown to the accountants as evidence that a traded market existed, which would allow arbitrage profit to be released into the bonus pools.

The derivatives marketing chief who oversaw J.P. Morgan's FIDM team, a Frenchman named Bertrand des Pallieres, was particularly keen to publicize what these indexes could do. "It will reduce the bid-offer price, and it also will probably reduce the production cost," he told me in 2003. "That's why it's a useful thing—you end up releasing the risk. It might be a mechanism for getting hedge funds much more involved."

Another group of bottom-feeders was interested too: the so-called interdealer brokers, such as Icap or GFI, that specialized in anonymously matching up derivatives dealers for a fee. By adding the new standardized CDO tranches to their broker screens on terminals such as those provided by Reuters or Bloomberg, these brokers made themselves handy reference points for pricing. According to a credit derivative trader at Barclays, "The brokers contribute to this because now the dealers have a way of checking, 'Am I too tight, or am I too wide on this?' So, it drives another mechanism that basically everyone agrees on the price."

The emergence of a few hedge funds and brokers that traded pieces of standardized synthetic CDOs with banks did not really make the market safer or even more transparent. Looking for the most bucks for their bang, the hedge funds wanted to trade the high-risk, high-return equity tank at the very bottom of the Cayman android hierarchy of investors, or the mezzanine slice just above it. But these were the most leveraged pieces of the CDO, with a stake of a few million dollars or so giving access to an underlying portfolio of bonds of a billion or more. And the hedge funds were using borrowed money to buy or go short these investments, increasing the leverage.

More worrying, most of the synthetic deals like Mayu that had been sold to investors were not standardized. How relevant was the price of an index tranche that a hedge fund was buying? Could you really assume that the mysterious correlation had been observed after all? Increasingly, dealers had to accept what they called *basis risk*—in other words, an assumption that apples can be hedged with oranges. The correlation traders and quants struggled to keep up with the complexity. The pages of industry journals resounded with debates with titles like "looking for the perfect copula": was it safe to use mathematical short-cuts such as "Panjer recursion," or did you need to string together dozens of computers in what were called *reusable valuation grids*?

Nowhere was the problem more acute than at J.P. Morgan, which dominated the credit derivative market and had the biggest positions. Deals like Mayu and dozens of others like it, adding up to trillions of dollars, were fed into a computer by the traders, an ex–J.P. Morgan banker recalls. "Every night the model would recalculate the positions, taking nine hours to run the numbers. Every morning the traders would come in and find their positions according to where spreads had gone." This was no longer the world of John Meriwether or Oka Usi. It was like something out of the movie *2001: A Space Odyssey*.

And then the real world played a practical joke on this not-so-little cottage industry. The two giants of the U.S. car sector, General Motors

(GM) and Ford, had long been saddled by ruinous pension fund and health-care obligations, and in May 2005, the ratings agencies abruptly downgraded GM and Ford to junk levels.

The huge outstanding debt of the auto giants made them popular targets for default swap bets, which ensured that they became prominent components of the new credit derivative indexes. The jump in the cost of GM and Ford protection rippled through the bottom layers of CDOs that contained them, which was enough to temporarily paralyze that market. In the ensuing brouhaha, the focus was mainly on the hedge funds rumored to have suffered losses, but the main pain was felt at dealing desks, notably at J.P. Morgan.

In one week, as the computers absorbed the new information, the bank's correlation desk lost $400 million. The geeky traders, who had effectively become the servants of their models, broke the bad news to the marketing geniuses who had crafted the transactions. According to one member of Vella's team, "The head of the trading desk met me and said, 'Dude, thanks to that transaction you put on our books, this is what we're suffering today: the risk can't be hedged.'"

According to a former senior trader there, "Things were really falling apart in 2005. They basically blew up from mark-to-market moves." The bank did a massive purge of its European derivatives operation, and in his letter to shareholders at the end of the year, J.P. Morgan Chase's new CEO, Jamie Dimon, scolded his derivatives bankers for "unacceptable levels of volatility." As a result of the fiasco, the bank was in no position to exploit the next wave of CDO innovation, however much it wanted to, and in 2007 would have a lucky escape as a result.

These losses proved what many quants had long known: the Gaussian copula model (and even its refinements) was a scam. As a Deutsche Bank quant said in a footnote to a 2002 paper published in an industry journal, "In the copula framework, spread risk is basically a model risk."[17] In other words, by not properly linking CDO prices with the underlying default swap spreads, the model itself became a risk to any trader who used it.

Once the GM/Ford excitement died down, however, the banks and hedge funds resumed trading the new credit derivatives indexes. In a sense, there was no going back: the banks already had trillions in default swaps on their trading books (measured by the notional or face value of the underlying bonds). As long as the indexes traded, it was possible to use elision to claim that virtually their entire book was "marked to market." Which meant that accountants would allow profits to be reported, and hence keep the innovation and bonus merry-go-round whirling.

The catastrophic car-debt collision of 2005 showed how sensitive credit derivatives pricing was to a change in mood of just a few market participants. It also underscored a lesson Poste Vita and other CDO investors had learned the hard way: the more that illusory safety was built into credit ratings, the more market volatility would result. The great arbitrage that powered all this activity was unethical and—more important—unsustainable.

CHAPTER FIVE

Regulatory Capture

Back in the 1980s, Fed chairman Paul Volcker decided banks needed a "speed limit" to curb their risky lending practices, but the large, sophisticated banks created collateralized loan obligations (CLOs) to evade the new rules. Volcker's successor, Alan Greenspan, argued that regulators should not impede the investment innovations, and in 1998, new rules loosened the restraints on the big banks. It was soon obvious, however, that regulators didn't have the skills or power to prevent banks from abusing the system. Given a last chance to tighten the rules in 2005, they blew it.

The Speed Trap

Looking back from today, years after the 2007–2008 crisis brought the banking system to a halt, a question often asked is, How did the regulators allow things to get so out of hand? How could they have been so blind? To answer those questions, we must travel back to the late 1980s.

Bank regulators are supposed to judge the strength of their charges and intervene when it is found wanting, but, ideally, do so without second-guessing what should be free market activity: risk-averse judgments by bankers about the uncertainty of their borrowers. To use a driving analogy for a regulator's job, this is akin to ensuring that drivers have licenses and their cars have passed mechanical inspections. But during the 1980s in the United States, it looked as if these "credit police" were too weak to prevent banks from getting in trouble in emerging markets and commercial lending in real estate. That's when the chairman of the Federal Reserve, Paul Volcker, began toying with the idea of setting a "speed limit" for banks.

The *speed* of a bank is its capital ratio, or leverage. The more loans a bank has made for each dollar of shareholder capital, the easier it is for an economic downturn to eat up the bank's solvency, and the more lethal the impact a crash is going to have on the confidence of depositors. The combination of Volcker's inflation-fighting interest rate hikes in the early '80s and poor commercial real estate lending decisions had produced the equivalent of a multicar pileup: over a thousand bank failures from 1981 to 1989, and a savings and loan crisis that would require hundreds of billions of taxpayer dollars to fix.[1] It was obvious to the Fed chairman that the banks had been driving too fast.

But what should the speed limit be? Bank regulators typically expressed such a limit (a leverage figure) as a minimum rather than a maximum—the lowest permissible equity capital buffer, expressed as a percentage of a bank's assets. During the 1980s, U.S. bank regulators had believed 5 percent—20 times leverage—was enough. It wasn't: not only did banks lend recklessly, but they found ways to make loans that didn't show up in their accounts, which allowed them to game the leverage ratio. So Volcker picked a bigger number: 8 percent. Expressed as leverage, that speed limit would restrict the amount banks could lend to private companies (including the off–balance sheet loans) to no more than 12.5 times their equity capital.

Volcker knew that enforcing his speed limit in the United States alone was insufficient. If Switzerland, for example, permitted 4 percent capital (or 25 times leverage), then Swiss banks would have an advantage in vying to make loans to U.S. companies. To build support for a single international speed limit for banks, Volcker approached the Basel Committee for Banking Supervision, a talking shop for central bankers based in the Swiss city of Basel. There, Volcker's officials learned about how European bank regulators had developed a theory of tailored speed limits, or *risk-based capital*. According to these regulators, corporate or emerging market loans were the baseline, the analogue of a winding country road that could be treacherous, and hence the 8 percent rule could apply. But a lot of the lending done by banks in Europe was to categories of borrowers that were much safer than that. So any international rule would have to tailor the capital speed limit to the types of roads it expected banks to "drive" down.

Europeans thought the 8 percent rule too draconian for residential mortgages, so Volcker's team accepted 4 percent there. Loans to banks in other advanced countries were seen as even safer, because Basel members thought they could trust each other to regulate banks properly.[2] As with raising the speed limit on a well-constructed highway, the committee agreed that banks could drive faster here, requiring 2 percent of capital—50 times leverage. Banks lending to the governments of developed countries were driving down a German autobahn, where unlimited speed was allowed—0 percent capital.

In order to persuade the foreign central bankers to agree to a global rule, the Fed officials agreed to use the Europeans' phrase, risk-based capital, in their discussions, although some feared that it was too prescriptive. By 1988, Volcker's campaign had yielded results: the Basel Committee agreed to adopt the 8 percent rule as part of a global regulatory rule book called the Basel Accord. Following the *risk-based* rhetoric, the speed limits on different types of "roads" for the banks—mortgages, corporate loans, bank lending, governments—were established through what became known as *risk weightings*. Although Basel I, as the new set of rules became known, was not legally binding, all the member governments of the committee pledged to implement it.

Volcker's 8 percent speed limit was turned into law in the United States via an act of Congress called the Federal Deposit Insurance Corporation (FDIC) Improvement Act of 1991. (The two U.S. mortgage agencies Fannie Mae and Freddie Mac successfully lobbied to have themselves categorized as high-speed-limit banks, even though they weren't subject to bank regulation.) Bona fide banks that fell below the 8 percent capital limit were pronounced *undercapitalized*, and if they didn't fix the problem, they were liable to be seized by the government. For good measure, the FDIC kept in place its old 20-times leverage rule that ignored the European idea of tailored speed limits.

But Volcker was no longer around to celebrate his achievement. The previous year, President Ronald Reagan had declined to renew his appointment as Fed chairman. He had been replaced by Alan Greenspan, whose libertarian philosophy was more in line with Reagan's zeal for deregulation. Greenspan did not interfere with the signing of Basel I—after all, it would help U.S. banks that wanted to expand into foreign lending markets; but he steadily pulled back from his predecessor's coplike approach to banks and instead made it clear that he believed in (and fostered) Wall Street innovation. If the 8 percent rule was an obstacle to Wall Street ambition, then Greenspan, like Ayn Rand cheering on the rugged entrepreneurs battling government interference in her novel *Atlas Shrugged,* was not going to stand in their way. As Greenspan put it in a February 1998 speech, "Many of these products, which would have been perceived as too risky for banks in earlier periods, are now judged to be safe owing to today's more sophisticated risk measurement and containment systems. Both banking and regulation are continuously evolving disciplines, with the latter, of course, continuously adjusting to the former."[3]

Speed Is Good

In September 1998, in an auditorium at London's Barbican Centre (better known for performances by the Royal Shakespeare Company and the London Symphony Orchestra), central bankers and regulators from around the world met to discuss modifying the Basel rules.[4] In the decade since Volcker's speed limits had become a global standard, much had changed in banking. Encouraged in part by the improved, level playing field, large banks had gotten bigger and increased their international exposure. As these banks became more confident in commercial lending, they chafed at Volcker's 8 percent rule.

The problem, as they saw it, was simple. The formula was a blunt instrument. It might make sense for those thousands of little regional banks whose governance couldn't be trusted to keep them out of trouble, but it was an unnecessary hindrance for the new, sophisticated breed of financial giant.[5] It was obvious to these giants that their loans to high-quality corporate borrowers, such as Walmart or IBM, did not need a full 8 percent of shareholders' money to be kept in reserve. And when it came to lower-quality loans, the giants knew they were smart enough to apply the brakes before any threat to depositors materialized. Most important, while the regional minnows of banking could only fulminate about obstacles they felt were stupid, the giants had the muscle to drive around them.

With their armies of lawyers and tax experts, and their global presence, the big banks were inventing new techniques to engage in *regulatory capital arbitrage*. They were shifting billions of dollars' worth of loans off their balance sheets into Cayman Islands androids that issued collateralized loan obligations (CLOs). That reduced the capital buffer of shareholders' money that they held against the possibility of loans' defaulting. With a smaller capital buffer required, banks could not only increase returns for shareholders but also make new loans. By the end of 1997, virtually every large bank had put together some kind of CLO deal—National Westminster Bank, Chase Manhattan, NationsBank, ABN AMRO, and Swiss Bank Corporation had all done it. Combining this idea with credit derivatives, as J.P. Morgan did that year with its BISTRO deal, was the obvious next step.

As they monitored all this innovation, Federal Reserve officials were in a bind. They had come up with the *risk-based* language in the 1988 rules, and the concept of risk weightings for different loan categories. But now the banks were saying, "If you want to regulate something that is *really* risk based, here it is." The Federal Reserve realized it was about to be left behind by innovations such as loan securitization and credit derivatives. At the Barbican conference that September, speakers from the Fed delivered well-intentioned warnings aimed at their fellow Basel Committee members, urging them to loosen the regulations they, themselves, had pushed for. "Overwhelmed . . . by the unstinting pace of innovation," the outdated Basel I capital rules could mask a deterioration in a bank's true financial condition, warned the Fed's in-house rule-making expert David Jones.[6] Another Fed official, John Mingo, cautioned that any attempt to ban a particular product, like default swaps or CLOs, would simply prompt banks to innovate a way around the restriction. Instead, regulators needed to update their rules to get in step with what the banks were doing with or without their permission.

The Accord Is Dead—Long Live the Accord

As they exploited new financial tools, like default swaps, to slalom around the Basel rules, the large banks, including J.P. Morgan and Credit Suisse, were politically savvy enough to offer regulators an intellectual justification for changing the rules. If their activities with special-purpose vehicles (SPVs) and credit derivatives happened to increase the speed limit at which they "drove," that increase in "speed" could be justified by their new technology. These banks argued that all their sophisticated technology made it possible for them to see economic reality in a way that eluded the Fed's out-of-date regulators. And the way they saw this "reality" was through mathematical models of credit portfolios.

The message was that, like value at risk (VAR), here was a radar system based on market information that regulators ought to pay attention to and ought to use. Banks argued that they needed to be allowed to use their own judgments of borrower creditworthiness in their capital calculations (in other words, let the bank's own credit police determine the speed limit for a specific lending business). When lending to a portfolio of such borrowers, banks should enjoy the diversification benefit of reduced overall capital requirements (or a higher speed limit for the entire bank, in other words) that the models predicted.

With Greenspan's cheerleading—and lending ideological support—the big banks soon won Fed approval for this change. But their real prize lay in turning derivatives and securitization into a factory production line: helping smaller banks exploit the technology to free up their balance sheets, and repackaging their loans into triple-A-rated CDOs that could be sold to hate-to-lose investors. The dealers knew, however, that European regulators were unlikely to be impressed by this proposal if U.S. banks and their consultants were in the midst of an intellectual skirmish over the relative merits of their respective models. So they tried to build consensus in 1998. As technical editor of an industry journal, I was directly involved. I published a technical paper by two Oliver Wyman consultants proving that all the loan portfolio models were mathematically the same when reduced to their simplest form.[7]

At the Barbican conference that September, I discovered that the bankers, consultants, and industry lobbyists angling for new capital rules had some heavyweight support. A soft-spoken, bespectacled Federal Reserve Board economist called Michael Gordy had produced a lengthy paper that made the same conclusions as the article I was about to publish.[8] He was one of the few regulator quants treated as an equal by investment bank quants, and his work would be hugely influential. The Oliver Wyman article and Gordy's paper made it hard for conservative regulators to claim that no coherent intellectual framework existed for reforming the old rules. "The development of credit risk modeling will be the catalyst for a major rethinking of theory and practice," William McDonough, the president of the New York Fed, told the conference approvingly.[9] He had just been elected chairman of the Basel Committee and used the opportunity to announce that the old 1988 accord would be replaced with a CDO-friendly version, which would come to be known as Basel II.

Britain's newly created Financial Services Authority (FSA), which made no secret of its mission to help London better compete with the United States as a global financial hub, approved. Supervisory tools should be based on the banks' methods, the FSA's managing director of financial supervision, Michael Foot, told the conference. Furthermore, said the FSA's chairman, Howard Davies, banks that built their own credit risk models should be rewarded by regulators.

The only prophecy of doom came from one of the few women regulators present, Patricia Jackson. Her team of researchers at the Bank of England warned that banks were far from being able to prove that their models were reliable. But the bank was about to lose its powers to regulate private sector financial institutions to the industry-friendly FSA. The head of Germany's federal financial supervisory authority, Jochen Sanio, was also troubled by the sudden embrace of advanced credit modeling and grumbled that "the issues may not be resolved."[10] However, the conference attendees shrugged off these quibbles.

The real drama that day was taking place offstage. Gossip during the conference's coffee breaks was about the collapse of the hedge fund Long-Term Capital Management (LTCM), based in Greenwich, Connecticut. The investment bankers in the audience were aware that trading portfolios were unbelievably volatile, and derivative markets were grinding to a halt as LTCM's problems cascaded through the financial world. This news put McDonough in an uncomfortable position, since he was urging foreign regulators to embrace the risk models used by the big banks, while his deputy, Peter Fisher, was at that moment sitting in a New York Fed boardroom trying to persuade the CEOs of some of those same firms to help bail out LTCM.[11]

Basel II, handed down in September, was hailed by most of the industry, but it fostered a dangerous illusion: that mathematical modeling and rule making could replace human judgment in banking. This would become painfully apparent with Basel's biggest loophole: the treatment of trading positions.

The Wet, Sloppy Kiss of Death

In the United States, where a multilayered government expressed the wishes of its founders for checks and balances, a multilayered system of financial regulation had grown organically. Each bank regulatory agency had its own creation myth—a bank crisis that was the reason for its existence. The oldest was the Office of the Comptroller of the Currency (OCC), created as an arm of the Treasury Department in the wild monetary years of the 1850s, followed by the archipelago of Federal Reserve Banks set up after a crisis in 1907. The stock market abuses and bank failures of the Great Depression spawned, respectively, the Securities and Exchange Commission (SEC) and the FDIC. The youngest was the Office of Thrift Supervision (OTS), founded in 1989 to shepherd "thrifts" or mortgage banks after the trauma of the savings and loan crisis.

At the top of the pecking order in the United States was (and is) the Federal Reserve. The Fed was not created to inspect banks; it was a *central bank*, and its employees proudly referred to themselves as bankers. From the chairman on down, it was staffed largely by economists rather than bureaucrats. Its cafeterias buzzed with high-minded debates about measuring inflation and controlling interest rates. But the Fed needed more than brilliant economists. Ever since the Great Depression, it had needed bank examiners, because each of the regional branches was a lender of last resort to the banks in its vicinity, charged with maintaining confidence and providing liquidity. Mac Alfriend was one such examiner; during a long career at the Federal Reserve Bank of Richmond in Virginia, he had built up a team of supervisors who would regularly commute down to Charlotte, North Carolina, to inspect two big institutions: Bank of America (BofA) and Wachovia. Within these banks, the full panoply of U.S. bank regulators could be seen at work: Alfriend's team of six Fed employees, along with fifty staffers from the OCC, in the bowels of Bank of America's headquarters, together with a lonely observer from the FDIC.[12]

Despite all the grand speech making and mathematical modeling being done by the Fed in Washington and New York, much of the regulatory work in the bowels of BofA's Charlotte headquarters between 1999 and 2002 was of the old-fashioned, pre–Volcker era sort. Yet there was one area in which the Richmond Fed was at the cutting edge. The market risk amendment to Basel I had been incorporated into U.S. banking regulations in 1998, which meant that Alfriend's team was required to check BofA's VAR models. These examiners took this task seriously, understanding that applying a quasi-scientific statistical testing framework in a moneymaking environment required the utmost skepticism. Applying such scrutiny on behalf of the Fed, and the taxpayers who stood behind it, Alfriend and his team were not afraid to challenge banks on their practices.

In addition to checking the back-office controls, data sources, and model assumptions BofA used to do VAR tests, his team also ensured they got a daily feed of the bank's end-of-day trading profit and loss (P&L). If the bank took a trading hit, Alfriend's team knew about it at the same time BofA chairman Ken Lewis did. More important, they knew how close the bank was to reaching its VAR limit and had the power to pick up the phone and ask why.

Early on, VAR seemed like a magic bullet for regulators looking to keep trading-heavy banks safe. When Alfriend's team first started looking at Bank of America's trading books in 1999, they contained only simple derivatives—mostly interest rate swaps and foreign exchange contracts—along with Treasury bills, corporate bonds, and equities. There were lots of data points in these heavily traded markets that could be fed into the VAR testing machine. By running all those numbers, Alfriend could reasonably feel that he was fulfilling his mission of keeping the system running safely. Yet as was shown by the collapse of LTCM, the use of VAR to calculate capital creates a dangerous incentive. When it implemented the Basel I amendment, the Fed required banks to hold trading book capital of at least three times their VAR number, with the line drawn at the one-in-a-hundred worst-case level.[13] As part of a capital requirement that banks could calculate for themselves based on their own models, VAR stopped being a testing mechanism for the skeptics. Instead, it became a tool for the legalized manipulation of shareholders, regulators—and, eventually, the taxpayers.

When one reads Bank of America's annual reports from between 1999 and 2003, a period in which the chairman's baton was passed from Hugh McColl to Ken Lewis, the focus on keeping shareholders happy is obvious. Even when revenues stagnate and earnings dip downward and up again, the cash dividends keep increasing, and the number of shares outstanding declines, the result of a buyback program. Nonfinancial companies are free to have as big or small an equity base as the market (and their creditors) will allow. But shareholder-owned banks are constrained by regulators, who want them to have a minimum cushion of shareholder capital at risk to protect depositors.[14] This is their speed limit. The more rigorously that speed limit is enforced by regulators, the more boring and "utility-like" banking becomes. Return on equity is modest because earnings are divided among a very large equity capital base.

But BofA, in line with its global banking peers, was promising more, delivering a return on equity above the 15 percent mark. If Lewis were to have any chance of hitting those numbers, he could not afford to have regulatory constraints forcing him to hit the brakes. As one senior Fed bank supervisor told me, "Capital matters a lot to banks, and in particular to the treasury function. Because they have to make those numbers, and they have to make them every quarter, they will do a lot of things to reduce the regulatory capital minimum." As we saw earlier, the 8 percent rule of 1988 had prompted the innovation of regulatory capital arbitrage using securitization technology. Measures such as shareholder value added (SVA), which Bank of America adopted in 2001, emphasized low-capital fee-generating businesses such as investment banking, versus capital-intensive businesses like balance sheet lending.

Basel's market risk amendment provided a new loophole because it allowed credit risk to be held on the trading book. The original version of VAR that had impressed Peter Fisher back in 1994 didn't involve credit risk at all: it was about things whose prices changed hour by hour, such as government bond yields, foreign exchange rates, and listed equity prices. In those days, credit risk was firmly on the actuarial side of the fence, buried deep in bank balance sheets and long-term corporate bond investors' portfolios. But then innovators like Peter Hancock found a way to trade credit risk using default swaps. As Greenspan said, regulators had to follow in the bankers' footsteps, and so the Basel Committee was lobbied in 1998 to tweak its VAR rule to keep up with banks migrating to the market approach. Perhaps mindful of the confusion that the term *credit risk* would cause, given that it officially reserved the term for the risk of default in the actuarial world, the Basel group chose the expression *specific risk* for the price risk of credit in a trading portfolio.

This amendment-within-an-amendment was what Federal Reserve Board officials would later describe as the "kiss of death," because specific risk laid the commercial banking sector wide open to the kind of greed-fueled delusion that crushed LTCM. Here's how it worked: if you could generate more earnings from increasing trading positions, while keeping VAR low, then the regulatory capital requirement would not keep up with the increased activity. That meant that share buybacks could continue and dividend payouts could keep going up. And the best way to keep VAR low was to invest in assets that didn't actually trade.

During its visits to BofA in Charlotte, Alfriend's team began to notice odd things. BofA was expanding into distressed debt, buying up the loans of troubled companies with the intention of turning the investments around and selling out at a profit; a traditional bank would hold such loans on its balance sheet. But BofA didn't want to hold expensive shareholder capital against loans anymore (and reduce its SVA figure) because it had a trading book to play with.[15] What was the VAR of the distressed debt BofA invested in? The bank had come up with a model and asked Alfriend's team to approve it. According to the new Basel rules, Bank of America needed to estimate the worst that could happen to its distressed debt 99 percent of the time. So it took a year's worth of daily price data, during which the loans barely budged. Even to a one-in-a-hundred day worst-case level, the VAR was negligible.

According to the Basel market risk amendment, which was now part of U.S. banking regulations, BofA could in principle hold four times this VAR as trading risk capital, a tiny fraction of the 8 percent of loan value in risk capital it would have held as a lending bank. The only caveat was that regulators had to approve the VAR model, and Alfriend's team rejected it. The Richmond Fed staffers argued that a year's worth of loan price data didn't reflect what was likely to happen to the debt in a full recession. The BofA officials responded by channeling the Chicago school of market-efficient economics, insisting that market prices reflected all possible information about the loans, including their potential for default. Alfriend's team held their ground, doubting that BofA had any intention of trading the loans it was holding.

The Fed examiners also spotted an analogous case where VAR was inconveniently big for Bank of America. The bank was making proprietary investments in exchange-traded funds (ETFs), a popular way of gaining exposure to equities using derivatives. Of course, no one ought to be able to fool a VAR model into thinking that an outright equity position (or its derivative) had a low VAR, given the historical volatility of equities. Indeed, that was the whole point of VAR, and why Peter Fisher had liked it so much in the first place. So what did BofA do? It attempted to put its ETFs in its loan portfolio, by using an accounting rule to classify them as "available-for-sale" securities. In this case, 8 percent was a smaller capital charge than would have been required using a VAR model.

A Trillion-Dollar Pizza

While the Richmond Fed was trying to quash these shenanigans in Charlotte, much bigger plans were afoot. The BofA gambit with distressed debt was troubling because credit risk—the kind of uncertainty that bank balance sheets were intended for—was finding its way into the trading book. Accounting rules made things worse because they gave management leeway to classify assets in ways that gamed the rules. The Basel amendment encouraged the gaming because of the way it handled credit risk in bank trading portfolios. Nowhere would this be more apparent than for CDOs, where the banks ran through the Basel loophole with a freight train. Recall that the difference between what an investor pays for a triple-A-rated product and the wholesale cost of replicating the deal from selling a bundle of default swaps in the market gets wrapped up into a single present value (PV). The more debt you can trade versus the slice of CDO sold to investors—or the bigger the leverage, in other words—and the PV goes up. Bankers hope that the client's deal and its hedge constructed from default swaps track each other over the lifetime of the deal, in order to justify calling the PV "revenue" and paying themselves (on average) about half of this revenue in the form of bonus money. The shareholders of the bank hope the bankers are right, so that they can pay themselves the other half of the PV in the form of "earnings." If the deal goes bad for the client, then neither the bankers nor its shareholders care (so long as the client is not able to sue the bank). That is how love-to-win traders win.

The shadowing of a synthetic CDO by its default swap mirror image over time is crucial.

If that fails (as happened to J.P. Morgan in the correlation "car crash" of 2005), then the PV may disappear, and even go negative, so that the bank is losing more on its hedge than it made from the customer. The more complicated the deal, the more uncertainty about this question, implying that the PV is not revenue at all. Even if the deal is allowed to take place, the PV should be held aside in reserve—possibly for years— until the question is resolved. Unfortunately, cash incentives had a way of settling the issue. Until the 2007–2008 crisis, the bonuses earned by derivatives bankers were considered separate from the risk models used to justify PV calculations. In fact, though, they are one and the same, because the deal and the risk model that "releases" PV are driven by bonus incentives. All this raises a huge dilemma for regulators. With great caution and integrity, a bank might do the right thing. But what if the bankers and shareholders get blinded by the incentives and throw caution and integrity to the wolves?

The first line of defense that Basel market rules required was a team of independent risk managers within the banks, with enough clout to stand up to profit-hungry CEOs—precisely the opposite of the sort of people the Richmond Fed encountered at BofA. If that barrier is breached, what is the next line of defense? For a deposit-insured commercial bank, it is the regulator who can force it to hold a risk capital reserve. Prudent regulation and trading profits are a zero-sum game: if the regulator demands more capital, there is less PV to be shared out between bankers and shareholders.

At the level of individual deals, the Basel VAR-based capital rules became an incentive for banks to "prove" that replication worked in order to reduce VAR and hence reduce the "tax" that cut into their immediate profits. The Gaussian copula–type models used by traders said that the likelihood of losing money on the leveraged bundle of debt sitting behind a triple-A CDO was much smaller than one in a hundred. Bonus-motivated bankers argued that because 99 percent of VAR was therefore zero, the majority of this leveraged position—the so-called super-senior tranches—required no regulatory capital. To get away with this, commercial banks first had to "persuade" the regulators charged with defending depositors and national banking systems from disaster. Alfriend's team of Richmond Fed examiners consistently rejected such arguments from BofA. As a former member of the team recalled, "Bank of America probably still hates us to this day because they spent two years trying to get some CDO models through approval, and they just never would do a good enough job of analysis. And we kept going back to the point, Is this model going to work through a crisis?"

One reason the Basel Committee brought together regulators from many countries was that if an international bank didn't like the answer it got from the Fed in Richmond, it could simply set up shop in London or Zurich and get an easier ride. That's why Volcker put so much effort into lobbying for a global 8 percent rule, and why his successors at the Fed came to London in 1998 arguing that it should be updated everywhere at once, in Basel II. Yet the exact problem Basel II was designed to solve was manifesting itself on the trading book. It started out in Switzerland, at the very moment the specific risk amendment-inside-an-amendment was approved by Basel in 1998. If you worry about BofA's risk managers' being more interested in justifying Ken Lewis's numbers than in reining him in, have some sympathy for the former Swiss banking supervisor, the EBK.

In Switzerland, banking dominates the national economy, and the country's two megabanks—Credit Suisse and UBS—dominate Swiss banking. In 2000, the balance sheet of UBS was double the Swiss gross domestic product. Somehow, the EBK regulators, who were reputedly paid on the same salary scale as a Swiss traffic cop, were supposed to rein in these megabanks.[16] Unsurprisingly, they chose discretion as the better part of valor, quietly giving blanket approval to specific risk models at Credit Suisse and UBS. At UBS, that regulatory decision gave carte blanche for huge CDO positions that would eventually prove devastating. A bemused official from the Federal Reserve later said, "One can see how much leverage there was in those trading books, particularly at the Swiss banks. But it was compelling, you know? You can hold 8 percent capital in your banking book, or you can hold next to nothing in your trading book."

One might have expected better from Britain's FSA, which was created in 1998 by then-chancellor Gordon Brown and took responsibility for bank supervision from the Bank of England. Given London's global reputation as a financial center, hopes were high for the newborn regulator, yet when it came to approving bonus-generating VAR models, the FSA proved to be one of the worst victims of regulatory capture. Perhaps the most important reason for this failure was that the FSA was conflicted from the very moment of its birth, having been instructed by Brown's legislation to "have regard" for London's competitiveness as a financial center. Compounding the problem was that the FSA lacked intellectual firepower, in stark contrast to Patricia Jackson's old team at the Bank of England, whose research challenged the banks' rosy assumptions. William Perraudin, an academic who served on this team, described the contrast: "One of the issues with the FSA is that they have been perennial consumers of other people's material. Everything's based on secondary sources, so they don't do calculations and try to understand something. They just read what somebody else has done."[17]

The FSA wasn't uniformly spineless. Woe betide any bank the FSA caught evading its compliance procedures. In such cases, regulators were not afraid to show their teeth, as they did with the London branch of Credit Suisse in 2002, forcing that bank's management to fire a slew of uncooperative staff. However, so long as a bank could jump through the FSA's compliance hoops, it did not question the underlying business models. Although not as generous as Switzerland's EBK, the FSA began handing out specific risk model approvals in 2000 that permitted J.P. Morgan and Deutsche Bank to vastly expand their credit derivatives businesses on a sliver of capital. This attracted the attention of the traditional U.S. investment banks— Goldman, Morgan Stanley, Lehman, Merrill, and Bear Stearns.

For New York firms that had found it difficult to trade derivatives under SEC rules that had not been updated since the 1970s, the new opportunities in Europe were hard to resist, so they set up London-based companies, such as Goldman Sachs International (GSI) and Lehman Brothers International Europe (LBIE), that would be legally distinct from the U.S. parent company and would be their preferred locations for derivatives deals. The FSA boasted that "international firms that have established their operations here welcome the flexibility of the U.K. regulatory regime."[18]

The SEC was troubled to see its flock migrating to London. Its investment bank supervisors were focused on regulating what were called *broker dealers*—the parts of the investment banks that traded stocks and bonds on behalf of U.S. customers. Legally speaking, derivatives weren't even on the SEC's radar screen. These broker dealers may have complained that the regulator's strict capital rules did not recognize any risk-reducing characteristics of derivatives hedging, but those rules were becoming irrelevant. In 2000, the U.S. Congress passed a law specifically excluding the fast-growing over-the-counter derivatives markets from SEC oversight.[19] The SEC supervisor with responsibility for the issue, Michael Macchiaroli, joked to me in 2001, "Swaps are like a pizza business as far as the law is concerned."[20]

The bane of Macchiaroli's life was what he called "unregulated affiliates" of SEC-regulated firms that exploited the loophole, including the new London-based entities. Because the different parts of firms like Goldman or Lehman (regulated and unregulated) were bound together by a web of mutual guarantees, he feared that a derivatives-laden affiliate might bring down the part that the SEC was officially responsible for.

The Fed had the legal power as a lender of last resort to enforce capital requirements to cover derivatives positions that exposed commercial banks to credit risk. By contrast, the SEC had no such power. "Until ten to twelve years ago, everything on a broker dealer's balance sheet was collateralized—cash on the barrel," Macchiaroli told me with a note of foreboding in his voice. "And then they got into derivatives."

A veteran lawyer who had worked at the SEC since the 1970s, Macchiaroli held a weak hand of cards. But Goldman Sachs took a strategic view of regulation and decided to invest some time teaching what it felt was its backward regulator about derivatives and VAR. Adapting an SEC initiative called *broker dealer lite,* Goldman reached a voluntary arrangement with the SEC, agreeing to trade some derivatives out of New York in return for a lenient VAR-based capital rule that matched what the FSA was offering in London. And the handful of SEC supervisors charged with monitoring this hitherto unsupervised activity would not need to get their hands dirty with complicated formulas—they only had to rubber-stamp the models Goldman came up with. Bob Litzenberger, who was then head of firmwide risk at Goldman, explained, "For the SEC, BD lite was an opportunity to learn about our business. They came in for the audit with a huge number of individuals. They found the resources and time spent somewhat exhausting, so they said that for subsequent audits—now that they had the model—they could take a much easier route. They would just certify the model and do a few tests without having to do a full audit. It was beneficial for both of us. It built a lot of trust."[21]

In writing its new capital rules, the SEC borrowed some of the Basel market risk language but leaned heavily on advice from Goldman regarding technical details. By 2004, the voluntary arrangement was formalized further. Other investment banks like Bear Stearns or Lehman Brothers had shown little inclination to follow in Goldman's wake. Macchiaroli disliked what he called Basel's "square roots and charts," but he recommended that the SEC sign up to the standard in exchange for the right to inspect all the investment bank books at holding company level. To make up for the lack of a Fed standing behind these firms, Macchiaroli insisted on his charges holding additional cash and excess capital. Unfortunately, the under-resourced team of holding company supervisors still lacked the legal powers to stand up to the investment banks in the way that the Fed could do with Bank of America. Over the following years, Merrill, Lehman, and Bear Stearns aggressively exploited the SEC's rules to fill their trading books with credit risk.

Dogs Chasing Their Tails

Assailed by arbitrage from all sides, the erosion of Basel I began to resemble a time-lapse movie of an elephant being consumed by maggots and other scavengers. I saw another side of this at the end of 2001, when I interviewed a UBS credit portfolio risk manager. Her job was to hedge loans that UBS made to clients in order to win investment banking business, and she did so by buying default swap protection from J.P. Morgan.

The old actuarial versus market approach dilemma came up in our conversation. With the prevailing buy-and-hold, portfolio-based approach to lending, safety in numbers kept the interest payments earned on loans low. In other words, the money that UBS had coming in was typically lower than the market-based premium that the bank would have to pay out for J.P. Morgan default swap protection. This is what bankers call a *negative basis trade*. Sure, the portfolio manager could offset some of this cost against the additional investment banking fee income that UBS would earn from its corporate borrowers. But there was another advantage, she explained. Suppose UBS had lent money to a client such as Nordic communications company Telenor. Under the Basel I rules, that loan would require 8 percent in capital to be set aside by UBS, to cover the risk of Telenor's defaulting. But with a default swap in place, UBS had replaced that risk with exposure to J.P. Morgan. Now, UBS would be covered against a default by Telenor . . . unless J.P. Morgan went bust.

However, exposure to J.P. Morgan was favored by Basel because it was a bank, requiring only 2 percent capital to be set aside. In other words, by hedging a loan with a default swap, the UBS portfolio manager had slashed the capital requirement by 75 percent.

Given the intent of Volcker and the architects of the Basel I Accord, it was all terribly ironic. Back in 1988, the Basel Committee surveyed the world and set the speed limit for bank-to-bank lending four times higher than plain old corporate lending. What did the banks do? They found a way of transforming corporate lending into bank lending (using default swaps) and got to drive at a much higher speed limit. And of course banks that sold default swap protection (taking on the corporate risk) didn't have to set aside 8 percent, because these were derivatives that were capitalized according to a VAR model.

That means the credit risks within banks did not go down or even stay flat under Basel I. They just migrated into price risk (so-called specific risk) and bank counterparty risk on trading books. And as bank balance sheets got bigger, evading the Basel rules became more and more important in order to keep shareholders and bank employees happy. With the regulators trying to catch up with what the banks were doing, and the banks anticipating what the regulators were doing, the financial system was starting to resemble a dog chasing its tail.

And there were more loopholes. As shown by Ken Lewis at BofA, the need to keep shareholders happy is a powerful incentive to reduce the numerator (the amount of bank equity). In addition to all the innovations that shrank the denominator, there was a way banks could have their cake and invest it too: make the numerator look big to regulators, while shrinking the equity base to pump up the return on equity. An invention called *hybrid capital* did the trick. As its name suggests, this was a very convenient halfway house between debt and equity. Hybrid capital was like debt in the sense that it was tax deductible and didn't have the voting rights or dividend payments that shareholders enjoyed. And it was like equity in that regulators (and ratings agencies) could be convinced it was *loss absorbent,* meaning that repayment could be deferred if the bank needed the cash. In much the same way as what an amendment-within-an-amendment had done for the trading book, an obscure Basel Committee agreement known as the "Sydney press release" from October 1998 undermined the integrity of bank equity. Although U.S. regulators retained a speed limit based on genuine equity, European banks began heavily exploiting this loophole.

The impact was profound, and eventually catastrophic. Starting in the mid-1990s, the BIS gathered derivatives data from all its central bank members, who obtained it from the banks they regulated. In 1998, just after the Basel trading book amendment was adopted, the world's banks had derivatives exposures (by gross market value) of $2.5 trillion. Ten years later, in June 2008, the figure was $20.3 trillion. Yet the equity market capitalization of the world's banks, a measure of the shareholder capital supporting these positions, only doubled during this time.[22]

Fed Up with the Fed

The Federal Reserve may have been at the top of the U.S. regulatory pecking order, but within the Fed itself, the New York branch was top dog when it came to regulating banks. This was hardly surprising given the dual importance of Wall Street as the engine room of the bond markets and as the base for the largest multinational U.S. banks. It was only natural that industry risk-management innovations like VAR were first identified by staff in the New York Fed's markets division, such as Peter Fisher, who transmitted the ideas to the rest of the regulatory community.

Ever since the regulatory blessing of VAR in the mid-1990s, the New York–based multinational banks had been growing rapidly. By 2003, when William McDonough retired as New York Fed president and was replaced by Timothy Geithner, an ambitious former Treasury and International Monetary Fund bureaucrat, bank supervision was equally important to markets.

If any U.S. commercial bank needed to be challenged, it was Citigroup. In 1999, when then-chief executive Sandy Weill had needed an act of Congress in order to fuse the SEC-regulated Salomon Brothers with Fed- and OCC-regulated blue-chip lender Citibank, he had taken care to reassure his new shareholders and supervisors about the importance of governance. A veteran ex-AIG and Chemical Bank executive, Petros Sabatacakis, was appointed chief risk officer of the new conglomerate and ordered to rein in the freewheeling Salomon traders. Sabatacakis was so tough in applying position limits that on the trading floor he was known as "Dr. No."

Then came Enron and the dot-com bust. Sabatacakis may have ensured that the bank (unlike Chase Manhattan) avoided significant losses in the shakeout, but Citigroup's conflicted role in bond underwriting, derivatives, and investment research left it open to the charge of having facilitated massive fraud at Enron and WorldCom. That led to the New York Fed and the OCC censuring the bank in July 2003, as part of a settlement in which it didn't have to admit wrongdoing.[23] Weill was forced to quit as chief executive (while remaining chairman).[24]

The incoming CEO, former general counsel Chuck Prince, may have seemed like a steady pair of hands on the wheel, but it was Prince who undermined the risk governance mechanism that Weill had put in place. Prince allowed Tom Maheras, the head of fixed income, to appoint his own risk managers. Feeling that his independence had been compromised, Sabatacakis quit in 2004 and was replaced by a

Maheras crony, David Bushnell, whose first move was to abolish Sabatacakis's trading book position limits.[25]

Hidden from public view, this weakening of internal risk governance made it ever more essential that Citi, the largest bank in the United States, was supervised properly. It was essential that the bank's day-to-day supervisors were not intimidated by the conglomerate and Weill, its charismatic chairman. A former senior New York Fed staffer recalls that the OCC seemed particularly cozy with Citigroup: "I remember being in a meeting in Citigroup, and Sandy Weill stopped by. He gave a big hug and a kiss to this lady examiner from the OCC . . . That didn't give me the feeling of tough supervision."[26]

The names of two of the New York Fed's key bank supervisors—head of bank supervision William Rutledge and head of risk management Brian Peters—appeared on the "written agreement" censuring Citigroup over Enron. Another key figure was Sarah Dahlgren, who from around 2003 onwards was the New York Fed's chief relationship manager dealing with the conglomerate. Rutledge was widely respected but was also a graying career bureaucrat (he retired at the end of 2010) who defended the status quo of balkanized U.S. bank regulation because he believed it was conducive to financial innovation. In conversations, he was careful and precise about defining what was *not* his responsibility.

Today, the New York Fed is shy about allowing Rutledge's key lieutenants, Peters and Dahlgren, to comment about their experiences (Dahlgren succeeded Rutledge after his retirement). Some idea of the challenges that these three and their staff faced during this time can be discerned from public documents and from the recollections of those who examined their work from the outside.

The Federal Reserve System has a governance mechanism intended to reinforce regulatory best practice. The Federal Reserve Board in Washington, D.C., provides centralized resources and sets standards for bank examiners based at the thirteen regional Federal Reserve Banks. In order to apply this governance, the Board has the authority to obtain information about the banks that were supervised within each region.

Setting the Fed's centralized standards for market and liquidity risk supervision was the responsibility of a small D.C.-based team of former regional reserve bank examiners. Federal Reserve Board staff say that amid the smooth and politically attuned bureaucrats who thrive in large government bodies, the market and liquidity risk team stood out. The team had a reputation for talking about issues in a direct fashion and letting the best idea win, regardless of who supported it. They wanted to apply the same style—and integrity—to managing trading book risk across the Federal Reserve System.

Around 2003, the market and liquidity risk team began trying to collect the trading P&L and VAR data feeds that some of them had seen at regional Fed offices such as Richmond. "We thought that we would pull things together, look for trends, get ahead of systemic risks, and see where crowded trades are," a member of the team recalls. The most important data would come out of New York: the daily P&L and VAR data for the biggest trading banks, J.P. Morgan and Citigroup.

It was a time when Fed staff recall being beset with distractions: the post–September 11 focus on money-laundering controls, or the vast exercise of preparing for Basel II. For Brian Peters, there was the additional burden of enforcing the post-Enron agreement with Citigroup. For whatever reason, Peters appeared too busy to talk to the market and liquidity risk team members when they approached him asking for daily trading data feeds from the giant New York banks. They returned to Washington, D.C., empty-handed.

Although the sources close to the New York Fed insist that the Board had the right to access whatever information it wanted, the market and liquidity risk team remembers things differently. To them, it was as if the New York Fed was on a different planet from its siblings. "It wasn't that they wouldn't provide information because we hadn't asked for it," a member of the team says. "They wouldn't provide information because they weren't forced to."

Partial access eventually came from a committee on Large Financial Institutions (LFIs) set up in March 2005 in response to complaints from Fed governors that the Board was not getting enough information about regional Fed banking supervision. As a result, the market and liquidity risk team learned that the New York Fed did not receive electronic daily P&L, VAR, or other relevant trading book information from Citigroup. Instead it received three-month-old reports photocopied from originals provided to the OCC. Was the New York Fed flying blind?

Even from the untimely trading reports that the New York Fed did receive, the staffers at the Federal Reserve Board became concerned that the New York Fed seemed to lack the expertise—and, just as crucially, the skepticism—to even ask the large banks the right questions. The team obtained information indicating that one major New York Fed–supervised bank had lost between $60 and $80 million trading in the nascent market for carbon emission credits. Up to the moment of the loss, the VAR loss estimate for this trading book had been approximately $1 million, on the basis that the bank's long position in emission credits had been rising steadily by small increments for the previous year.

Although it was not a substantial or dangerous loss for the bank, this was the type of model methodology weakness that could be indicative of broader problems. Such a weakness could have been picked up by a fulsome trading book or regulatory capital inspection; however, such inspections did not appear to have been undertaken by the New York Fed, despite recommendations from the market and liquidity risk team. Questioned about the need for such inspections, New York Fed bank supervisors complained to their Washington, D.C., counterparts about a lack of resources. One person on the market and liquidity risk team vividly remembers a New York Fed bank examiner shrugging off the emission trading losses, arguing, "Don't worry about that. We just have to respond to these things when they happen. We can't get ahead of these problems. We don't have enough people, and the bankers have a lot of smart people."

In May 2005, some of the concerns being voiced internally by Federal Reserve Board staff found their way into a confidential operations review of the New York Fed that has since been made public by the Financial Crisis Inquiry Commission. Entitled "Draft Close-Out Report, Large Complex Banking Supervision," the document highlighted Sarah Dahlgren's direct management responsibility for the New York Fed examiners at Citigroup.[27] The document then warned that "staffing at the relationship teams is under stress . . . as it pertains to the relationship teams' ability to conduct continuous supervisory activity. This is of particular concern when evaluating the Citi team."

Meanwhile, the market and liquidity risk team and others in the Federal Reserve Board supervision division had grown concerned that as large banks built up their trading businesses and accounting rules gravitated to fair value measurement, bank balance sheets were increasingly subject to short-term market moves that could lead to rapid falls in regulatory capital. A memo produced by the team pointed out the issues and risks involved in increased use of fair value and warned that a sudden freeze in certain markets might imperil bank solvency. But when the market and liquidity risk team tried to interest Dahlgren in their findings, she retorted, "I think our banks know how to manage to fair value," ending the discussion.

In 2006, the market and liquidity risk team attended a Citigroup risk assessment presentation to a committee of Fed examiners. When asked for the rationale supporting the designated satisfactory rating for interest rate risk, the New York Fed team could not provide any information. At another Citi meeting the market and liquidity risk team attended, the New York Fed examiners had been asked to come up with a list of supervisory priorities for the bank. They identified approximately twenty items and patiently explained why each one was important. Near the end, Peters interrupted and told his staff to cut the number of priorities to five or six because twenty was "too many." The Washington, D.C., team was stunned—twenty was *too many* things to check regarding the largest and most complex bank in the United States?

In the five years that the market and liquidity risk team struggled to improve the New York Fed's supervision of Citigroup, the conglomerate added almost a trillion dollars to its balance sheet—visibly and "invisibly." While sources close to the New York Fed might dispute the words and actions that the market and liquidity risk team attributes to its staff, they are curiously silent about its failings as a supervisor— failings that ultimately would hit U.S. taxpayers.

One of the sad ironies is that even the twenty priorities for Citigroup that Peters cut to the bone did not include the biggest problem of all: the way Citi was building up a $43 billion super-senior CDO exposure on its trading book. Both the New York Fed and its watchdogs in Washington, D.C., failed to spot a fundamental breach of the thin blue line they created: recording the super-senior CDOs as trading exposure and interrogating the bank's VAR model. A senior Federal Reserve Board official who is still angry about that screwup says,

"They didn't put them in their VAR. And that is a complete violation of all the rules. I mean this is just basic. You do not need to be a quant to catch this. They were supposed to be mark to market. But the attitude seemed to be, 'Why bother? They don't change in value. They're *AAA*.' They didn't put them in the VAR. You can stress-test your heart out. If it's not in the VAR, you're not going to get anything on it."

Passing the Bucks

The proposed Basel II bank capital rules, which had taken six years to compile, were ready in early 2004. They would incorporate Michael Gordy's correlation model, hard-coding into bank capital requirements the same kind of actuarial diversification benefit that underpinned investment-grade corporate CDO ratings. And banks would be able to feed into the model their "internal ratings" for loans on their balance sheets, with the idea that this would reduce the pressure for regulatory arbitrage. Banks that weren't sophisticated enough to build these lending radar systems would be allowed to use old-fashioned credit ratings.

The interminable meetings about Basel II around the world took their toll. In its rush to finalize the new rules, the committee adopted a few shortcuts, overruling its technical experts. One such expert was William Perraudin, who, while working with the Bank of England, had been assigned the job of analyzing how banks should allocate capital to pieces of securitizations. A key premise of securitization, and CDOs in particular, was a water-into-wine trick: how a portfolio of risky assets could be transformed into an investment-grade bond using diversification and subordination. That was enough to convince ratings agencies, but should bank supervisors be equally gullible? In other words, if a ratings agency said that a piece of CDO was triple *A*, could banks hold minimal capital against it? Perraudin's research suggested that while the bundling and slicing of risks in securitization had a positive effect, regulators shouldn't ignore the nature of the underlying assets in favor of ratings. But when it came time for the Basel Committee to consider this subtlety, time pressure ensured that it was left by the wayside. As a supervisor involved in the discussions recalls, "When everybody was getting blown out in terms of the length of this process, the decision was made—it's already complicated enough." The upshot was that Basel II contained a deadly incentive for European banks to buy triple-*A*-rated CDOs.

But the worst loophole in Basel II had remained almost unchanged from Basel I: the capital requirement for bank trading books and, closely associated with it, the treatment of liquidity. In 2003, officials at the Federal Reserve Board in Washington, D.C., were sufficiently concerned about the growing size of bank trading books that they made a concerted effort to get the issue onto the agenda of Basel II. In typical Basel style, a special subcommittee was formed in January 2004. It would consider "less liquid instruments held in the trading book," along with counterparty credit risk, for which the banks were keen to retain the hedging advantages exploited under Basel I rules. Because the SEC had just signed up the U.S. investment banks to the Basel II rules, Michael Macchiaroli was appointed cochairman of the joint group, along with Oliver Page, the FSA's head of financial stability and retail firms and a former Bank of England supervisor.[27]

Far too little has been written about the role of lobbyists in the decade leading up to 2007. For bank-funded lobby groups like the International Swaps & Derivatives Association (ISDA), the Bond Market Association (BMA), or the Institute for International Finance (IIF), it was not enough for the U.S. Congress or Basel to exempt vast swaths of the system from proper regulatory oversight. Any attempt to tighten things up, even marginally, had to be given the "whack-a-mole" treatment. Engaging in coordinated campaigns against the regulators, the well-heeled lobbyists stonewalled anything not previously agreed to. "Treatment of less liquid assets in the trading book . . . is essentially new," the lobbyists complained to Basel in December 2004.[28] "The questions raise complex issues . . . the Associations favor a thorough examination that should not be rushed." This bit of sophistry neatly inverted what was the real problem—that illiquid (or not frequently traded) new products like synthetic CDOs catastrophically undermined the statistical basis of VAR, creating a clear and present threat to the banking system.

Those who worked with Page remember him as a sincere and honorable man, and in the context of the FSA's conflicted objectives at the time it is hardly surprising that he took on trust what the not-so-honorable lobbyists were saying. "I saw the banks genuinely involved," Page says. "They were aware that it's no good what the regulator tells you about your capital needs. I could see that they were now engaged in sorting out and fixing what needed to be done to achieve a sensible outcome." Advising Page and conferring with the lobbyists was FSA head of prudential policy Paul Sharma, whose experiences with the United Kingdom's troubled life insurance industry made him a fervent believer in the benefits of market valuation. No less sincerely than Page, Sharma approvingly pointed to bank CDO models as an example of his philosophy: "We just need to assure ourselves that there's a certain amount of integrity. You're talking to the person who was going to allow portfolio tranche derivatives into our VAR models, precisely because we thought that our banks had got to the stage where they could begin to credibly model these things."[29] Macchiaroli had agreed to co-chair the committee, hoping that VAR-based capital would get a serious review, but on arriving for the meetings in London he discovered to his chagrin that VAR was not even on the agenda. Sitting at the same table as Page and Macchiaroli, the Federal Reserve Board officials argued for increased trading book capital in Basel II and they were frustrated by the views they heard in London. "Half the group said, 'No, the banks know their models. They can do this better than we can, we shouldn't be dictating to them,'" recalls a member of the Fed team, who then fruitlessly tried pleading, "Look how little capital there is here. By any measure, you can't look at 800-to-1 leverage and say it's okay. I know it's not a true measure of risk. It just can't be true." Despite his personal reservations, Macchiaroli eventually decided to go along with the consensus, and so did the skeptics at the Fed.

Although Page insists that the compromise he agreed to at the end of the subcommittee debates was "tough on the banks," in reality it was anything but. The urgent need to increase trading book capital requirements in Basel II was kicked into the long grass. The subcommittee's final report in 2005 called for "further work" on the notorious kiss-of-death, setting a comfortably distant deadline of January 2010 for any improvements.[30] The measure that Page felt was his greatest legacy, a requirement for improved stress-testing, turned out to be a toothless, face-saving palliative, because as Page concedes, it was never properly followed through. (Page retired from the FSA in March 2006.) None of the regulators involved wants to take the blame for it, but in that committee room, in those meetings, the FSA, the Fed, and the SEC blew the last big chance for regulators to prevent a catastrophic financial disaster.

CHAPTER SIX

Burning Down the Housing Market

Thanks to government sponsorship (Fannie Mae and Freddie Mac) and the deregulation of lending, subprime securitization produced bonds that were ideal for repackaging into CDOs. Soon, there was so much demand for CDOs that sourcing subprime mortgages was a bottleneck slowing down profits. Dealers cleared the bottleneck by inventing CDS bets on subprime bonds that could be bundled into CDOs instead of mortgage bonds. For the dealers to balance out these bets, they needed insurance companies like AIG to buy default swaps on the safest pieces of their deals, and they needed hedge funds like Paulson & Co. to bet against subprime. As the U.S. housing bubble began to burst in late 2006, the dealers bet against their own deals while selling them to unwitting investors.

Pickup on North Street

In March 2002, a seemingly innocuous meeting took place in the offices of Landesbank Kiel (LB Kiel), in the German port city of Kiel. Sitting at the boardroom table were a pair of Americans, Wayne King and Ken Karl, whose business cards were emblazoned with the crossed-keys logo of UBS. Facing them were Franz Waas, an executive board member at LB Kiel, and his new head of portfolio management, Martin Halblaub. The two Germans were part of a sophisticated international new wave in finance that made regional German banking slightly less boring than it had been for hundreds of years—and slightly more profitable. For LB Kiel's owners, it offered a way to shake loose from state ownership and taxpayer guarantees.

The pitch document the Americans brought to Kiel was for North Street 4, and they explained how it would "leverage" UBS's "global asset management expertise."[1] In reality, it amounted to UBS's setting up a Cayman Islands special purpose vehicle—a financial robot—that would invest in some $3 billion of investment-grade bonds. By *asset management,* UBS meant that it would move bonds in and out of the android over time. LB Kiel would be exposed to the "second loss" layer of this portfolio, a slice of risk some $500 million thick, for fifteen years. The investment was like the filling of a gigantic sandwich, resting on an equity layer that was supposed to protect LB Kiel, while the German bank was supposed to protect UBS from losing money on the "super senior" layer above.

Like LB Kiel's similar deal with Barclays eighteen months earlier, there was a built-in flaw with such sandwich arrangements. "You've got an inherent conflict of interest," a senior UBS official would later concede. "Whose interests are you actually protecting? Are you looking after UBS's interests, or the second loss provider [LB Kiel]?" Listening to the pitch, Halblaub felt uneasy about the inherent conflicts, and he hesitated to sign up to the deal. "What's the matter—don't you trust us?" joked Karl. There was nothing to suggest that Karl and UBS weren't sincere about wanting to help their client, and so Waas intervened—to abort the deal now would cast doubt on how serious LB Kiel was about entering new markets. LB Kiel agreed to buy North Street 4.

Initially, Karl filled up North Street 4 with corporate debt issued by familiar companies like Disney, the Burlington Northern and Santa Fe railroad, cable television company Viacom, and supermarket chain Safeway, among others. By October, with the approval of LB Kiel, many of these corporate stalwarts had been replaced by mysterious names such as INHEL 2002-A, OOMLT 2002-3, and NCHET 2001-NC2. In just seven months, some 70 percent of the North Street 4 portfolio had been replaced by securitizations, of which a quarter were funding U.S. subprime and home equity lending, as well as credit card loans and commercial mortgages. NCHET 2001 was a subordinated tranche—or the next-to-bottom layer—of a securitization deal backed by subprime mortgages from New Century Financial Corporation. INHEL 2002-A was a *mezzanine certificate* backed by mortgages sourced by IndyMac, a Californian bank.

Via a daisy chain that ran through the Cayman Islands, the UBS New York trading desk, and special-purpose companies in California, the burghers of Schleswig-Holstein, the ultimate owners of LB Kiel, were indirectly lending millions of dollars to aspiring middle-class American consumers eager to buy homes, cars, and those big-screen TVs. That was what LB Kiel wanted, an ultra-safe, diversified package stamped "triple-*A*" by century-old ratings agencies. The tool that joined cautious Germans and buoyantly optimistic Americans was the ABS CDO, the financial innovation that played a crucial role in stoking the housing bubble.

The Home ATM Machine

It would require another book to recount the long and tortuous history of the shadowy mortgage securitization ecosystem that LB Kiel stumbled into via its North Street CDO deal. Had it not been for two decisive factors, American mortgage lending might have stayed largely on bank balance sheets, as it did in Europe. One factor was the 1980s savings and loan crisis, which discredited traditional bank lending in the United States and forced troubled banks to sell their mortgages to Wall Street. Even more important was the role of the U.S. government in guaranteeing mortgages that got securitized. Since the 1960s, three government-sponsored enterprises—Fannie Mae, Freddie Mac, and Ginnie Mae—had bought residential mortgages from banks. Beginning in the 1970s, they had securitized these mortgages but insured investors against homeowner default, creating bonds known as *agency debt*.

The three agencies protected themselves from having to pay out on this insurance by imposing restrictions on the mortgages they would buy—insisting, for example, that borrowers make minimum down payments and document their income. But if they did have to pay out, where would the money come from? As the home lending market took off in the 1980s and investors flooded in, the two privatized agencies,

Fannie and Freddie, increasingly exploited the assumption that the U.S. government was standing behind them.

That assumption became so widespread that by 2002, agency debt was being bought in massive quantities by China and Saudi Arabia as a substitute for Treasury bonds. In the shadow of this government-backed, trillion-dollar market, a private sector mortgage securitization market emerged, including subprime as well as what were considered prime mortgages: those ineligible for the Fannie or Freddie umbrella because the amounts borrowed were too large (so-called jumbo loans) or where a creditworthy borrower didn't have the right documentation (known as *Alt A*). The packages of subprime and other "nonconforming" loans were controlled by financial robots lurking inside a mailbox that borrowed money from investors according to a program laid down by a distant investment bank. In the U.S. mortgage and consumer finance industry, the androids did not hide under a Caribbean beach umbrella along with other tax exiles. They wore the Stars and Stripes and the proud badge of an SEC registration, protected by Reagan-era 1986 tax reforms that nurtured home equity lending.

On the SEC Web site, there are currently about ten thousand androids listed, and most are mortgage related. They cluster like sheep around the financial giants that spawned them: Morgan Stanley has two hundred fifty androids, while Lehman Brothers left over one thousand of these orphans, each of them mindlessly sucking up repayments from borrowers and sifting the cash through pumps and valves to investors.[2] How did these mortgage robots get to be so numerous? Fannie and Freddie played a role, according to FDIC chairman Sheila Bair. She recalls how a combination of weak governance of the two mortgage agencies and government encouragement of minority home ownership kick-started the subprime boom: "I remember very well when I was at Treasury in 2001 when a broader government effort to expand homeownership was launched. It was well intentioned and turned out to be a significant driver."

She says that Fannie and Freddie got around restrictions on mortgage eligibility by letting Wall Street package subprime loans and then invest in the end product—with U.S. government backing. "I was very worried at the time, because Fannie and Freddie would not directly guarantee these loans, but they would buy the private-label mortgage-backed securities (PLMBS) that funded these mortgages. So, they really provided the market to buy these. And they loved it because they were like a hedge fund, right?"[3]

Yet Fannie and Freddie were not enough on their own. It took robot investors—CDOs bought by institutions like LB Kiel—to inflate a bubble. In other words, CDO robots investing in subprime robots. One can track where some of the money invested by LB Kiel went. Take the NCHET 2001 deal, whose full name is New Century Home Equity Trust 2001. Of the $500 million Waas signed over to UBS in March 2002, Karl invested $13 million in a slice of NCHET. He probably bought it from Citigroup's Salomon trading desk, which in turn built the android with New Century's name on it, and filed a form with the SEC telling them that the android lived inside Salomon's Manhattan offices. The actual lending had been done the previous year, when New Century lent about $500 million to some thirty-five hundred homeowners whose credit scores didn't qualify them for prime loans. The majority were in four states—California, Florida, Texas, and Michigan—and most of these subprime borrowers were using hybrid adjustable-rate mortgages to do a "cash-out refi." In other words, they were using their homes as an ATM.

Everyone's ideal of a traditional mortgage has cautious lenders helping cautious borrowers who end up owning a home after thirty years. In this new world of mortgages, people have little to lose and a lot to gain. About half the New Century borrowers were "stated income" or "limited documentation," what would later be known as "liar loans," and most were borrowing about 80 to 90 percent of their home's value. Those mortgages were financially suicidal as long-term products, affordable for just two years, after which so-called payment shock would arrive, driving the borrowers' interest rate up to as much as 15 percent. Any sane borrower would want to escape from shackles like that, either by refinancing (assuming house prices kept rising)—or by defaulting and handing back the keys.[4]

New Century very quickly got these primed-to-explode loans off its books—after all, it was not a bank, but rather a "mortgage finance company." Brokers handled the individual loans, and New Century gave them a cut of all the fees embedded in the mortgages they sold. Appraisers hired by New Century checked the value of homes that served as collateral. Then, in April 2001, the completed bundle of loans was handed over to Salomon Brothers. By September, NCHET was dressed up for market with its own investor prospectus, ready to start borrowing money. A company called Ocwen was appointed as "servicer" and, in return for fees, would collect money from the thirty-five hundred borrowers (and chase the deadbeats), while U.S. Bancorp was named "trustee" to look after the internal cash plumbing system on behalf of investors. The final step was to bring in Standard & Poor's and Fitch to provide ratings for the slices of debt that NCHET sold in the market. There was plenty to preoccupy the ratings agencies: they would crunch the actuarial math to show that mortgages in California, Texas, and Florida might diversify each other, as well as demonstrate how good New Century was at appraising houses and how good Ocwen was at servicing subprime borrowers. Branded with a single-A stamp, the $13 million slice of NCHET was paraded on the market and ended up in UBS's North Street 4 deal.

The long chain of specialists—mortgage brokers, New Century, Salomon Brothers, Ocwen, U.S. Bancorp, UBS, Standard & Poor's, and Fitch—that helped transfer excess capital out of Schleswig-Holstein into the California economy was, advocates claimed, the market working at its best. The expertise of all those specialists ensured that people in California could buy houses they never could have afforded in the past.[5] It ensured that LB Kiel's processed dinner, although full of unfamiliar ingredients, was safe to eat.

That said, North Street 4 was not particularly nourishing for the Germans, because the risk-processing specialists had already taken much of the "nutrition" out of it. On the $500 million investment LB Kiel made, Karl and his traders would enjoy the profits of trading $3 billion worth of bonds for up to fifteen years. In return, UBS was required to pay LB Kiel just $6 million per year as a return on its investment. Put another way, LB Kiel was paying a hefty "rent" in return for its heavily processed exposure to the U.S. consumer.

A rent-seeking opportunity like that was not going to be enjoyed by UBS alone. Wall Street was already looking for ways to crank that money machine up to the limit.

Revenge of the Dorks

Greg Lippmann had grown up in New Jersey's strip-mall suburbia and joined the investment bank First Boston (now Credit Suisse) immediately after graduating from college in 1991. He didn't look like your father's banker. Swarthy and lanky, with a piece of gum permanently wedged in his cheek, Lippmann grew his sideburns almost down to his jawline and shaved the ends into knifepoints, which gave him a faintly menacing, rockabilly look. By the mid-2000s he was trading asset-backed securities (ABSs) for Deutsche Bank, doing well enough to afford a big Manhattan loft apartment with a vast kitchen that he rented out to Italian cooking classes.

But Wall Street, like the rest of life, most often resembles high school, and ABS traders such as Lippmann looked enviously at people like Rajeev Misra, who had made it big in CDOs linked to corporate debt. With an office full of plastic trophies and a retinue of personal trainers and public relations flunkies, the black-clad Misra was a Deutsche Bank rock star. The way Lippmann saw it, these credit derivatives superstars were like the American football players in high school, with their body armor and bevy of girlfriends. The lowly ABS traders were the dorks in the marching band.[6] Theirs was a small business that most people didn't pay much attention to.

A few blocks away from Lippman's office, at the bottom of the island of Manhattan, Dan Sparks would bristle at that analogy. In his eyes, the Goldman Sachs mortgage desk was the football team—after all, he had briefly been a college player, spending a season as a walk-on for Texas A&M in his freshman year. Sure, he may have gone to a non-Ivy League business school (Texas A&M) and had eschewed Lippmann's frenetic Manhattan lifestyle for deepest suburban Connecticut. But Sparks was not stuck trading secondhand mortgage bonds, as Lippmann was. Having been made a partner in 2002 because of his trading prowess, Sparks became head of Goldman's structured product business a year later, putting him in control of trading and repackaging mortgages.

UBS's success with subprime-linked CDOs such as North Street was a sign that cautious investors around the world would buy into this obscure asset class, so long as it could be packaged with a good credit rating and had a prestigious fund manager involved. The problem was that the very nature of the subprime mortgage market kept it small—and safe. First there was the challenge of finding the mortgages. If Sparks wanted to compete with market-leading firms like Lehman Brothers and Bear Stearns that specialized in packaging newly originated mortgages into securitized bonds, he would need his own supply of product. The big suppliers at that time—such as New Century and Long Beach—were already selling their product to other Wall Street firms, and Goldman's head of loan origination, Kevin Gasvoda, was frequently on a plane to California and Nevada, where many subprime lenders were based. His carrot was a proposal to finance their operations—Goldman would lend them cash they could advance subprime borrowers, and in return would receive the mortgages it needed.

Building this pipeline took time. Assembling the half-billion dollars' worth of subprime loans needed for a new mortgage bond meant waiting six months while brokers rounded up enough financially strapped consumers. And that required a lot of boots on the ground. Sparks wanted to keep some control over the process and didn't like the idea of outsourcing. That meant hiring hundreds of people to run an in-house mortgage-servicing business for Goldman, and basing them in South Carolina and Texas to avoid paying expensive Manhattan overheads.

Even creating a mortgage bond factory was not enough to deal with the next challenge—rounding up enough mortgage bonds to supply a second factory building CDOs. In 2003, Sparks began hearing from asset managers—from well-known firms, like BlackRock, Trust Company of the West (TCW), and PIMCO, to obscure outfits—who wanted Wall Street firms to arrange subprime CDOs for them to manage. Unlike the North Street 4 CDO, where UBS's role was heavily conflicted, these new CDOs would depend on the independence of the manager to keep investors out of trouble. Knowing that it was their credibility as much as the credit ratings that underpinned investor confidence in these ABS CDOs, the better-known asset managers exploited their gatekeeper status. Wall Street firms would have to come to them and pitch for the privilege of CDO underwriting. Sparks assigned a member of his team, Pete Ostrem, to manufacture these CDOs, but he was quickly stymied by the bottleneck in

Goldman's incomplete subprime pipeline. Ostrem grumbled to Sparks about the challenge of satisfying the fund managers. "They're like, 'Hey, Goldman, you take all the risk, or most of the risk. Are you going to be able to deliver the longs? Do you have enough product?'" Ostrem had to scour the market to buy pieces of mortgage bond in the market to satisfy the CDO managers and win deals, but this highlighted a more fundamental issue. As with CDOs, the packagers of American mortgages depended on a carefully constructed pecking order of risk to convince investors that the product was safe. But if, like Sparks, you wanted to repackage these finely graded parcels of debt, they came in inconveniently small pieces. While the debt of companies such as Ford or IBM had hundreds of billions in outstanding bonds that could be traded in a flash, making CDOs out of mortgage bonds was tough. Consider again NCHET, the resliced bundle of New Century subprime mortgages in the North Street 4 portfolio.

At first sight, with $500 million advanced by New Century to subprime borrowers across America, there should have been plenty of debt for CDO builders to play with. Recall, however, that the arbitrage engine that kept the CDO business running was powered by cheap raw materials in the market, where cheapness is measured by the premium earned over government bonds. The triple-A output of this engine was an upper limit; there was nothing to be gained by feeding in expensive ingredients, because that cut into profits. To make CDOs built out of mortgage bonds work for dealers, the mortgage bonds needed to pay about 2 percent more than Treasury bonds. Think of NCHET as a large office building, say, thirty stories high, with the riskiest "floor" in the basement and the safest at the top. To find something suitable for North Street 4, imagine Ken Karl getting into an elevator on the top floor and descending floor by floor until he gets paid 2 or 3 percent more than the government bond rate. He has a long ride, because most of the floors of NCHET are triple-A rated—these parts of mortgage bonds would be bought by American pension funds and insurance companies, as well as Freddie Mac. Only when he gets down near ground level, perhaps four or five floors up, does Karl find what he needs. Just like the floors of a building that connect the entrance levels with the main part of the property, these ABS tranches of interest are called *mezzanine*, with ratings that vary from triple-B to single-*A*. And they represent a very thin slice of the building overall. The "M-2" slice of debt that Karl picked out of NCHET amounted to only $13 million. That may sound like a lot of money, but it would have been backed by just a couple of hundred homes and was, in Wall Street terms, no more than a rounding error.

Compare that with the $80 million of WorldCom debt that J.P. Morgan placed in Poste Vita's Mayu CDO at the beginning of 2002. That was the kind of building block you needed to attract European investors. By contrast, North Street's tiny piece of NCHET was all there was at that rating and spread; such things were slow and tricky to trade. The only good news was that it was impossible to lose more than $13 million. If Sparks or Lippmann wanted to use the same piece of NCHET that Karl had secreted away in North Street 4 for another CDO, there was nothing to be done except wait until Karl decided to sell it. Although the margins you could earn in this thinly traded market might be high, volume would always be low, and for Wall Street traders, volume equals status. As Lippmann was acutely aware, credit derivatives gave the industry rock stars a twofold advantage. They could trade in whatever size was appropriate to the products they were creating for investors, and by hedging themselves, they could make risk apparently disappear, further increasing their trading volume and profit. And investors were eager to lap it up.

As Easy as ABCDS

In the summer of 2004, Daniel Sparks took a nonstop flight from New York to Dusseldorf in Germany, accompanied by Jonathan Egol, a junior Goldman analyst to whom Sparks had recently given a trading job. As Barclays and UBS had already demonstrated, any self-respecting credit derivative innovator needed a German investor in its back pocket. But Sparks and Egol, who could barely find Dusseldorf on the map, needed help in finding one. Bleary-eyed from their overnight flight, Sparks and Egol were met at the airport by two Goldman salespeople who had flown in from London, the center of Goldman's European empire run by Michael Sherwood. One of Goldman's original default swap visionaries, Sherwood was the man behind the firm's secret derivatives deal with Greece in 2001. Since that deal, his European power base within

Goldman had grown. It wasn't just the fact that London was eclipsing New York as a financial center, attracting some of the firm's best traders and corporate advisors. Sherwood had built a network of super-intelligent derivatives salespeople and marketers, poaching from J.P. Morgan and Deutsche Bank and fostering relationships with clients on the continent. Stepping off the red-eye, Sparks and Egol slotted seamlessly into this network as Sherwood's salesmen guided the sleep-deprived Americans into a chauffeured Mercedes that swept them to the shiny headquarters of a bank called IKB.

The tubby German man on the other side of IKB's boardroom table was Dirk Röthig, and he had been complaining for months to London-based salespeople about the obstacles he faced in buying CDOs linked to subprime and other forms of securitized debt. Like LB Kiel, he saw the robot-on-robot investments as a safe means of cashing in on the American consumer, and he had a secret, behind-the-scenes mechanism to invest far more than LB Kiel ever could. However, as more Europeans latched onto the trend in 2003, Röthig saw deals that had been promised to him by London banks being snatched away as prices soared. The problem was what in industry jargon was called the "ramp-up period"—it took six months or a year for a CDO arranger and asset managers such as PIMCO to purchase all the small pieces of subprime mortgage bonds that met the necessary criteria for the deal, a time-lag that allowed dealers to profiteer at IKB's expense. As he explained to Sparks, what Röthig was looking for was something that could be cobbled together fast and invisibly, like the synthetic CDOs that J.P. Morgan and Deutsche Bank had pioneered in Europe using corporate debt.

Egol had been working to satisfy Röthig's request for months, and as they had dinner with the Germans before catching the evening flight back to New York, Sparks gave his blessing to an innovation that would bring the excitement of credit default swaps into the subprime mortgage bond business. Recall that derivatives have the subversive property of being able to instantly and invisibly replicate things that traditional finance makes difficult. In great secrecy, Egol had done precisely that, devising new default swap contracts that were subtly different from the normal corporate kind. A collection of several hundred New Century mortgages scattered across California and Florida don't all default on

the same day, as Enron did in December 2001. First comes *delinquency,*
when homeowners fall behind on their interest payments, followed by
foreclosure, and finally the sale of *real estate owned* (REO) properties.
It happens in dribs and drabs; every time a warning letter goes out in
Florida or a sheriff changes the locks in California, the valves and pumps
inside the robo-corporation's cash plumbing system silently open and
close according to their programmed instructions.

Seasoned mortgage bond traders such as Lippmann were familiar
with these robot cash plumbing systems. Since the 1990s, mortgage
packagers had adopted a standard software package, called Intex, that
worked out the plumbing on a computer. The traders had not only
their own copies of Intex, but also Bloomberg terminals that did the
same calculations. These were used by traders to value secondhand
mortgage bonds like NCHET. With all this standardization in place, it
was straightforward to construct a derivatives replicant of a subprime
mortgage bond, overlaying virtual reality on top of what was already
robo-finance. Soon after the Dusseldorf meeting, in June 2004, Goldman sold IKB a tailor-made synthetic CDO called Abacus 2004-1. Like
J.P. Morgan's Mayu, the deal was *static*—it didn't have a manager such
as TCW involved—and it was constructed entirely from the new mortgage bond default swaps. The revenge of the dorks was under way.

Goldman may have got there first, but Deutsche and other dealers
were close behind, designing similar contracts. Toward the end of
2004, Lippmann realized that other dealers were doing what he was
doing, when his clients starting demanding subprime derivatives
resembling ones they had already traded with someone else. He saw
that niggling legal differences would increase risk and damage client
confidence in the new derivatives, so he contacted four other dealers
with a proposal: "If we all agree to the same contract, we can avoid
these legal risks and grow our businesses." Gathering for weekly
evening meetings over take-out food at Deutsche Bank's U.S. headquarters on Wall Street, Lippmann and his rivals thrashed out a standardized version of the new default swap contract that paid out gradually as the piecemeal subprime default process took place.

This Wall Street get-together would have important ramifications.
Until then, mortgage bonds typically sat inside insurance company or
pension fund balance sheets (and more recently CDOs) until maturity.

The consequences of gradual default were hidden from view. Each ABS owner had made an actuarial bet on repayment and house prices, and dealt with the outcome in private. In that sense, despite being securitized, the U.S. mortgage market had something in common with traditional banking in Europe. What Lippmann and the others did was turn subprime mortgage investment into a two-way horse race where the market could bet on the outcome. No longer would traders be "shackled to the cash market," as Lippmann liked to complain had been his sorry fate.

As with the earlier version of credit default swaps linked to corporate debt, the derivatives would allow him and other dealers to *go short*, or bet against mortgage bonds—bonds they owned, or bonds they didn't own. And the new contract ensured you got paid—or had to pay up—immediately, because the contract stipulated that counterparties had to settle up each time new homeowner defaults eroded a subprime bond beyond an initial threshold. Rather than waiting until the official maturity date of the bond, when, as Lippmann put it, "the entire cookie was eaten," he convinced his fellow dealers that "a payment is made each time a bite of the cookie is taken." That meant the price of these default swaps was acutely sensitive to shifts in the housing market, serving as a broadcasting system from one trading desk to the next.

As the discussions among dealers continued into 2005, Lippmann invited more of his competitors to participate. When arguments broke out, Lippmann patiently explained how standardization would be the key to volume. By June, the contract was agreed upon, and it was ready to trade.

Sparks was pleased to have the tools he needed to leapfrog his competitors and satisfy the demand for CDOs. But he and his more old-fashioned colleagues also felt troubled. "This is a long-only business—this might ruin it," complained one of them. Sparks agreed. "I think these derivatives are going to spread risk throughout the world."

The Smartest Guys in the Housing Market

Despite his reservations, Sparks was already applying the new innovations to add millions to Goldman's profits. Röthig was so pleased with his tailor-made synthetic CDO that he demanded more, and Sparks and Egol set up a production line to crank out the new products, which would be given the Abacus brand name. Egol was the mortgage equivalent of what people in the world of corporate default swaps call a correlation trader. Correlation trading is all about selling just a few slices of a CDO to investors and replicating the rest by doing proprietary trading in the underlying default swaps, with the help of a model such as the Gaussian copula. Sparks was skeptical about using models to extract money from illiquid new markets like subprime derivatives, and he kept a close watch on what Egol was doing.

Meanwhile, in the non-derivatives world, Goldman's subprime mortgage pipeline was starting to deliver the goods, and in recognition of his successes, Sparks was promoted to run mortgage bond origination as well as trading. Gasvoda had built relationships on the ground; during its 2004 financial year, Goldman issued over $30 billion in subprime mortgage bonds.[7] On paper at least, Sparks had another job, as chief executive of the Goldman Sachs Mortgage Company; run by Gasvoda and employing over two hundred people, this company bought the underlying loans from the originators across America and repackaged them into dozens of newborn mortgage robots with names like GSAMP Trust. Sparks was one of the people who signed the SEC registration documents. But that was just a sideline from his main job, running Goldman Sachs's U.S. mortgage business.

Meanwhile, Pete Ostrem was busy creating CDOs for Goldman asset manager clients. He was very different from Egol, the geeky derivatives wizard. While he would use some of the new subprime derivatives to manufacture CDOs, Ostrem preferred buying the underlying "cash" bonds whenever possible. It was what Sparks approvingly called an "originate, clean up, and move on" business. After taking its fee—which was about 1 percent of the proceeds and was often taken in the form of an equity stake at the lowest, riskiest layer of the CDO—Goldman could discreetly step out of the picture and prepare for its next deal.

There was one obstacle. Ostrem could keep the CDO managers happy with the help of subprime derivatives to "deliver the longs" that they demanded. But there was one part of the CDO that the managers weren't interested in, because the returns were too paltry to attract investors. The super-senior tranche, sitting above the triple-A piece that the manager did find investors for, was Goldman's challenge. It was a problem because Ostrem would have bought the $1 billion worth of subprime mortgages that went into the CDO and held them on Goldman's balance sheet using repo borrowing. But unless he could sell that topmost slice of the CDO, Goldman would still have to "fund" several hundred million dollars' worth of assets, something it was loath to do.

This was also the problem with the Abacus CDOs Egol was pumping out. The models that ratings agencies used might have said the risk of losing money was as close to zero as the laws of probability would allow, but Sparks, who was responsible for the risk of Goldman's mortgage portfolio, still wasn't convinced—he wanted to shed that risk.

Once again, help would come from London, the territory of Michael Sherwood. With his salesforce, Sherwood not only would hold the key to shifting Goldman's hard-to-shift product, such as the topmost layers of Sparks's CDOs, but also had figured out a way to act as middleman for the rest of Wall Street. The trick was pulled off with a careful reading of the Basel banking rules. European banks, unlike those in America, did not have absolute leverage ratios restricting the size of their balance sheets. The only thing holding them back was the risk weighting, or "speed limit," applied to different types of lending. However, if European banks could buy triple-A-rated assets and combine them with a default swap transacted with a bank as counterparty, their capital ratio could be as small as 1.6 percent. That amounted to a leverage ratio of more than 60 to 1, or even higher, if you took into account the softness of European rules on what qualified as capital.

Although super-senior pieces of ABS CDOs did not provide enough of a return for normal investors, for highly leveraged European banks the paltry returns could be sufficiently magnified to become an attractive proposition, even after paying a default swap premium to a counterparty. It was different from the way LB Kiel invested with UBS, where at least the Germans had a stated interest in getting exposure to the U.S. real estate market. Here, armed with a triple-A rating and the protection of a default swap, an investor had little incentive to investigate what they were buying. The larger European banks, such as Société Générale or UBS, were already buying triple-A-rated CDOs to cash in on this regulatory arbitrage and were asking dealers to sell them default swaps on their investments. The Goldman European sales force had a list of second-tier banking clients on the continent, firms like Germany's cooperative savings bank Deutsche Zentral-Genossenschaftsbank, Switzerland's Zürcher Kantonalbank, and Dutch agricultural lender Rabobank, and wanted to sell them an entire package of CDOs and default swaps. But where was the all-important default swap protection going to come from?

Sherwood was on good terms with Joseph Cassano, the chief executive of AIG Financial Products (AIGFP), who lived in London. Founded in the 1980s and backed by its parent's triple-A rating, AIGFP had developed a reputation for making huge, complex derivatives trades linked to interest rates, equities, or currencies that even Goldman wasn't big enough to handle. These were famously lucrative trades from which Cassano and his team kept 30 percent of the profits. The problem of hedging super-senior risk wasn't new, especially for those dealers who constructed CDOs out of riskier components. However, in Cassano, Goldman had a man who had been involved in the market from the beginning, right back to when J.P. Morgan pitched him its groundbreaking BISTRO deal in 1998, a man so confident in selling this unusual form of protection that he would sell Goldman as much super-senior subprime CDO hedges as it wanted—eventually totaling $23 billion.

It was a quintessential Goldman move. Sherwood was a specialist in what one might call "elephant hunting." The deal that he and Addy Loudiadis orchestrated in 2001 to help the Greek government conceal billions of debt using secret swap contracts was one example of his prowess. By channeling business through a single large counterparty, Goldman could steer clear of the credit and reputational risks that came with spreading business across a range of smaller clients, one of whom might default or complain about the transaction.

While Sherwood remained invisible in the background, Goldman salespeople swung into action, led by Andy Davilman, who was based in New York. Goldman would stand in the middle of two back-to-back default swap transactions: buying protection from AIGFP on one side and passing it on to the European banking client on the other. A former Salomon trader working for Goldman in New York, Ram Sundaram, would be the middleman. Sparks, meanwhile, was invited to

London, where he met Cassano's underlings and then attended meetings at AIGFP's U.S. headquarters in Wilton, Connecticut. For Sparks, here was a suitable "elephant" that could do two things: provide a default swap sweetener to persuade European banks to buy the super-senior pieces of Ostrem's deals, and provide a direct hedge to the Goldman trading desk on Egol's Abacus deals.

Sparks already knew American International Group, whose American General life insurance subsidiary was a heavy buyer of the mortgage bonds Goldman issued. But this elephant was on a different planet. AIGFP resembled the hedge fund Long-Term Capital Management (LTCM), another secretive financial firm run by a mixture of sophisticated derivatives geeks and aggressive risk takers. There was Gary Gorton, a brilliant finance professor from the Wharton School who had a consulting agreement to build AIGFP's models.

Unlike LTCM, this elephant was backed by the world's biggest, triple-A-rated insurance conglomerate. AIG's regulatory structure would serve as a lesson in how an assortment of unconnected, well-intentioned regulations could be exploited by highly motivated innovators. In 1999, AIG asked the Office of Thrift Supervision to be its holding company supervisor. The OTS was supposed to regulate small savings and loans institutions, but if the law permitted a sleepy regulator to take fees for supervising a giant conglomerate, why should it complain?

This proved very convenient in 2004, when the European Union agreed to recognize certain U.S. regulators as being equivalent to its own financial supervisors. AIG had set up a bank subsidiary in Paris, Banque AIG. The French bank supervisor, the Commission Bancaire, didn't look too closely at Banque AIG because EU law deferred to the OTS as being responsible.

Of course, Banque AIG was really just a front for AIGFP, which shared premises with the bank's office in London. The bank was a shell where Cassano booked his default swap trades. But because it was a European bank, it fell under the Basel umbrella and ensured the capital benefits from the super-senior default swap trades with the likes of Société Générale.

Cassano set some conditions with Goldman. Rather than relying on credit ratings, AIGFP would send Gorton and his other quants to crawl over Goldman's CDO factory, tweaking the machinery if necessary to ensure they were happy with the mortgages underlying each deal before writing protection. For Cassano, having Gorton was like having a one-man ratings agency in his back pocket, and he enjoyed showing him off to the analysts who tracked AIG's stock. So confident was Cassano in his moonlighting professor that, over time, AIGFP would end up selling protection on $500 billion of CDOs. The elephant was truly in the bag.

Goldman insisted on one condition. Triple-A-rated counterparties such as AIG traditionally refused to sully themselves with the two-way collateral agreements between lower-ranked mortals in the derivatives market. Many dealers accepted this status quo. But for all except a few triple-A sovereign clients, Goldman refused to do business without such agreements. Pricing credit at its market value was almost an article of faith at Goldman, and derivatives counterparties were no exception to the rule. Reassured by Gorton's actuarial analysis, Cassano and Andrew Forster, a former J.P. Morgan banker who ran AIGFP's credit trading desk in London, were relaxed about Goldman's request. At least in 2005, the super-senior layer of CDOs barely traded, staying hidden on the balance sheets of banks or insurance companies. What possible event could result in a price decline sufficient to trigger a collateral call? "They thought the market was so stable it didn't seem like a big give," one of the Goldman team recalls. Agreeing to Goldman's terms would prove a fatal mistake for AIGFP.

The opportunity to buy subprime CDO protection from AIGFP lasted for about eighteen months. At the end of 2005, Gorton's actuarial model told Cassano that it was time to stop selling protection on subprime CDOs, but by the time that last deal went through in the summer of 2006, AIGFP had written protection on seventy different deals, with a total subprime exposure of $80 billion.[8]

The Great American Vulture

The standardization of asset-backed credit default swap (ABCDS) contracts in the summer of 2005 was like turning on a fire hose. By the end of the year, something like $100 billion of the contracts had been traded. And most of the buyers of subprime mortgage bonds in this derivative form were themselves androids—new CDOs that had been programmed to fill themselves with pieces of subprime mortgages. By

2007, this automated CDO purchasing of replicated subprime would reach the one-trillion-dollar mark.

Back in 2002, when ABS traders were still the dorks in the school band, there were flesh-and-blood investors—banks, insurers, and hedge funds—who liked to analyze and buy the riskiest pieces of U.S. mortgage bonds, keeping the market safer for more cautious investors such as pension funds. Replacement of these formerly critical buyers with CDO androids buying on the basis of credit ratings meant that no one cared about the mortgages themselves any longer. No wonder lending standards collapsed and money was handed out to *NINJAs* (borrowers with No Income, No Job, No Assets). No wonder that a culture of "liar loans" prevailed in America.

The traders in the new derivatives had their work cut out just feeding the great CDO factories, overcoming the bottleneck of supply in the cash market. These CDOs would sell protection on subprime mortgages, and the ABS trading desks would use the newly designed contract to buy it from them. Having bought protection, the desk would be short subprime—in other words, they would make money if the subprime mortgage market collapsed. At this point, in early 2005, dealers in the secondary ABS market had no interest in being short. If they had a view, it was to be long like everyone else, in order to meet the growing CDO demand. At Goldman, where Sparks managed Egol and his Abacus deals next to Gasvoda and his pipeline of new mortgage bonds, Egol was kept on a tight rein and was ordered to keep his position flat, balancing out Sparks's exposure elsewhere. But at Deutsche Bank, where the units buying and repackaging mortgages operated as distinct fiefdoms, the silo structure gave Lippmann the freedom to think for himself about the short view of subprime. But who would want to bet against the American consumer? At the "ABS West" industry conference in Phoenix, Arizona, in February 2005, Lippmann participated in a panel discussion with an ex-Deutsche trader, Steve Kasoff, who now worked for a hedge fund, Elliott Associates. Kasoff had been considering buying subprime CDOs but needed a way to hedge what he planned to buy. Excited, Lippmann realized he had an investor to whom he could sell a short position.

According to people familiar with the deal, Elliott was interested in shorting $500 million of subprime in a single trade. The problem was getting to that kind of size. Lippmann had a brainwave. Armed with subprime default swaps, Lippmann would turn himself into Deutsche's equivalent of Jonathan Egol.[9] Shortly after the conference in Phoenix, Lippmann set up a pitch meeting at Elliott's New York offices. Kasoff listened as Lippmann proposed structuring a special Abacus-style CDO for the hedge fund's benefit. There was a fiefdom at Deutsche Bank, called "CDO primary," that operated (on a bigger scale) the same kind of traditional CDO factory that Ostrem ran at Goldman. Lippmann agreed to work in partnership with this group to create something similar to Abacus. After both sides agreed which bundle of bonds would go into the deal, Elliott bought subprime protection from Lippmann, who in turn bought it from investors in the new $500 million CDO. Called START (Static Residential) CDO 2005-A, it was completed in June 2005.

Meanwhile, the Deutsche sales force had been speaking to John Paulson, a wiry New Yorker who ran what was then an obscure family of hedge funds that specialized in distressed debt and mergers and acquisitions (known as *event arbitrage*). Although Wall Street dealers would later boast about having "put John in the trade," Paulson says that his long track record in sniffing out distressed debt opportunities had attuned him to the impending collapse. Over the years, he had transformed himself into a financial vulture, waiting for disaster. "When spreads tightened to all-time lows in early 2005," says Paulson, "we felt that you weren't being paid enough for risk, so we shifted from a long focus to a short focus. We believed we were entering a credit bubble, so we were intensely focused on trying to find the best short opportunities in credit. By examining various credit markets, we felt the subprime mortgage market, particularly the lower tranches of subprime mortgage securities, as well as CDOs, represented the most mispriced securities."[10]

Had Lippmann and a handful of other dealers not succeeded in decoupling mortgage credit risk from the underlying bonds, Paulson would be an obscure figure today. But Paulson was smart enough to see that the same unchecked innovation that allowed Wall Street's CDO machine to deliver processed investment food into deepest Germany and elsewhere was giving him the opportunity of a lifetime. Recall how subprime mortgage bonds can be imagined as a fifty-story building, where CDO builders had to take the elevator down to the mezzanine level to get the juice they needed. The foundations of the building were the U.S. housing market; if the pace of house price appreciation flagged even slightly, let alone stalled or dropped, the mezzanine floors of mortgage bonds would be underwater. For that risk, investors received about 2 or 3 percent per year more in interest than they would have received for investing in Treasury bonds issued by the U.S. government. The use of derivatives innovation to strip out that credit risk from the underlying subprime bond meant that Paulson could pay 2 or 3 percent of the value of a bond like NCHET each year, with the possibility of getting paid the bond's entire value if house prices went down.

Paulson also figured out that the stream of annual 2 or 3 percent payments for this bet didn't have to go on forever, something that was public knowledge for anyone who read SEC filings for the likes of NCHET. They knew that two or three years after signing their mortgage document, the borrowers would be hit with that payment shock, which would triple or quadruple their cost of borrowing. Continuing house price growth might give them one last chance to refinance, but once that escape route closed, they were doomed. That meant you could short a $10 million–thick slice of mortgage bond for a maximum outlay of about $1 million. If subprime performed as most people then expected, Paulson would lose all of this investment, but if it went bad, he'd pocket a $10 million profit. Of course, with a credit derivative, you were no longer constrained by the size of the original bond. Scaling up the bet and paying Lippmann an annual stake of $2 million, Paulson stood to make $100 million. Put $20 million on the table, and $1 billion was there for the taking.

Paulson had already done his first $100 million subprime trade in summer 2005 with Bear Stearns, but now he wanted to do more, and was now raising $1 billion to set up a credit fund specifically focused on shorting subprime. Deutsche's CDO primary group obliged by cooperating to build more Abacus-style START CDOs as they had done for Elliott Associates, booking the default swap components through Lippmann's desk. The urbane Deutsche Bank trader became a confidant to the tetchy hedge fund manager. Despised by other Wall Street mortgage dealers for his bearish views, Paulson had found a receptive insider to talk to, while for Lippmann, exposure to the great cynic proved infectious. As he and his quants crunched the numbers, Lippmann realized that the upside of the short mezzanine subprime trade outweighed the downside so much that he really couldn't lose. In November 2005 he persuaded Deutsche Bank to allow him to make his own proprietary bet against subprime. It wasn't difficult. As a market-maker, all Lippmann needed to do was to buy slightly more protection than he was selling, leaving his trading book lopsided on the short side. In the pre-2008 unregulated era of derivatives, separating client-facing business from proprietary trading was not something large banks made a big fuss about.

But why stop there? Lippmann began to bypass the Deutsche CDO primary group in order to grow his trading business, according to former employees of the bank. He started his own virtual CDO factory, assigning London-based subordinates to attach bundles of derivatives (or correlation trades) to bonds that Deutsche was able to issue very quickly on the Irish Stock Exchange, with names like Eirles, Ixion, Syrah, and Coriolanus. Other firms like Morgan Stanley, Bear Stearns, and Citigroup ran similar operations, but Deutsche was the biggest player.

Along with the derivatives he was selling to Wall Street's mainstream CDO factories, Lippmann's virtual CDO factory helped bring in a flood of additional subprime protection from around the world, with the help of Deutsche's global salesforce. It was more than could be matched up with Lippmann's own proprietary position and Paulson's and Elliott's short, prompting Lippmann to seek out new would-be Paulsons. By early 2006 he became adept at giving rapid-fire presentations to more orthodox hedge funds that specialized in emerging markets and high-yield corporate bonds. Their first response was that shorting subprime was too unfamiliar for their comfort-level. Thinking on his feet, Lippmann shot back that shorting subprime was indeed outlandish—so much so that it would provide a perfect hedge for their big high-yield and emerging market positions. By 2007, Lippmann would become one of the biggest synthetic CDO players on Wall Street, all as a result of the special derivative he had helped design.

Meanwhile, a new innovation was being prepared that would make it even easier for hedge fund managers and traders to bet against subprime. Having agreed on a standardized subprime default swap contract in the summer of 2005, Sparks, Lippmann, and the other dealers immediately saw a further opening—to create an index of the new default swaps. Trading single-name default swaps and constructing bespoke CDOs out of them might look very profitable for the dealers on paper, but auditors were touchy about letting them recognize profits unless there was a visible market price. Hedge funds and dealer desks trading subprime derivatives also demanded liquidity, because they always needed to be able to close out their positions at a moment's notice. It was natural for Goldman, the Wall Street firm most obsessed with market pricing and hedging its own risk, to take the lead. Sparks assigned a clever young ex-nuclear physicist, Rajiv Kamilla, who convinced Lippmann and the other bankers to jointly construct a subprime derivative index based on the slices of mortgage bond they were trading the most. The dealers agreed that the new index would be sliced into five layers that mimicked the structure of mortgage-backed bonds, and would be updated every six months to include the twenty most popular subprime names. Given the name ABX, the new index was launched in January 2006.[11] Because the ABX prices would be compiled and disclosed publicly every day, the broadcasting impact would be even greater.

Waiting for the Flood

In the summer of 2006, the booming U.S. subprime market was starting to show cracks. Ameriquest, a medium-size subprime lender, settled a predatory lending investigation by federal prosecutors and was forced to drastically scale down its operations. The Federal Reserve, which was charged with financial consumer protection, issued an edict tightening up standards, demanding that adjustable-rate mortgage (ARM) borrowers be told the full cost of their loans. Imperceptibly, the U.S. residential housing market reached a peak and started down. The Federal Reserve was also raising interest rates.

At Goldman Sachs, though, the subprime pipeline was flowing at higher and higher speeds. Gasvoda's team was processing billions in new mortgages every month. Goldman was sucking up home loans from all over America and spitting them out through its production line of GSAMP androids. The process was running at such a fevered pace and with such a high level of automation that Sparks and Gasvoda, like the rest of Wall Street, were desensitized to what was going on at ground level. They were complacent about due diligence reports that suggested loans were declining in quality, and failed to pass this information on to investors or ratings agencies.[12] They didn't see that originators such as Countrywide were encouraging borrowers to lie on their applications or were bullying real estate appraisers to inflate valuations of properties. By 2006, 40 percent of U.S. subprime mortgages had *silent seconds*—additional home equity loans that increased borrowing power to well above 90 percent loan-to-value (LTV); 50 percent, or $250 billion worth of subprime mortgages, were limited documentation, or liar loans, and so were Alt A mortgages, of which $450 billion were issued and turned into bonds that year. Taken together, subprime and Alt A were almost eclipsing Fannie and Freddie's annual prime mortgage lending, and the two government-sponsored giants were themselves piling into subprime bonds as investors.

Yet for all his stoking of Goldman's mortgage machine, Sparks was being told by his bosses that he had to do more. It wasn't enough for Goldman to be ranked ninth in the mortgage bond league tables. To get higher up, there was a simple solution that Goldman's competitors had pursued. Ever since Lehman Brothers had bought subprime lender BNC in 2000, Wall Street firms knew they could win instant market share by acquiring mortgage companies, thus guaranteeing an increase in loan volume. "Don't you know that First Franklin, Equifirst, and Saxon are up for sale?" Goldman's senior management would chide Sparks. "I can't understand why anyone would pay that much for them," he would reply when Merrill or Barclays or Morgan Stanley would triumphantly announce their latest acquisition.

Although he was catching a lot of heat, Sparks stood his ground. He preferred a hands-off relationship with the originators, one that could be ended quickly. Sparks was also getting banged from the other side, from his traders, who had followed Lippmann's lead in helping hedge funds taking short positions against subprime using default swaps, and wanted to do the same trade themselves.

Charged with managing the risk of the mortgage book, Sparks had to explain the downside for his eager traders. And the bogeyman he used was that cranky angel of death, John Paulson. In the summer of 2006, the question on everyone's lips was, What if Paulson is wrong? After all, the ABX index was staying stubbornly close to 100 percent, even for the lowest tranche, which was supposed to be the canary in the coal mine for a subprime meltdown. "There's this huge short out there named John Paulson," Sparks warned his traders. "He isn't really a mortgage guy, and nobody knows how much capital he has. If he gets margin called because the market goes against him, this market's going to go straight up, and you're never going to be able to cover your shorts. Never."

Looking back, Paulson insists his confidence never wavered. Like a vulture circling high over the suburbs of Phoenix, Arizona, and California's Inland Empire, Paulson knew exactly where the bodies would fall. He had their zip codes; he even had their street addresses. He knew that half their income was going to mortgage payments, and he knew the date when payment shock would hit them. He knew which mortgage bonds were juiciest to short, such as those issued by Lehman Brothers, which had the worst underwriting standards, while he avoided those done by Wells Fargo, because their standards were the highest.

The dealers who traded with Paulson in 2006 tell a different tale. They say he was worried about having to explain to his investors that he would need to pay additional default swap premium to renew his bet for another year. Paulson's complaints to Lippmann about the lack of performance of his trade became strident. "Look at the facts," he lectured Lippmann. "We should be making money. Why isn't this working?" Lippmann, beset by other hedge fund clients whom he complained were "crying like babies," reassured Paulson. "I had to hold his hand," he says.

Unfortunately for those on the other side of Lippmann's trades, most of them did not benefit from his hand-holding. No more so than the buyers of his virtual CDOs, the single-tranche bundles of derivatives that Lippmann's traders packaged up as Dublin-listed bonds. Deutsche's global sales force latched onto these products, and in a repetition of the first CDO boom of 2001, sold them to far-flung clients that had little understanding of what they were buying. Consider Bangkok's Bank Thai, which in October 2006 invested $50 million in a Lippmann creation called Coriolanus Series 39.[13] Lippmann's traders started out with tiny slices of Countrywide and other mortgage bonds and amplified each one up to eight times. Piling leverage upon leverage, Lippmann's traders stacked together seventy-five of these subprime swaps into a *notional portfolio* that was $1.4 billion thick and then carved out Coriolanus Series 39 as a thin slice from close to the bottom of this virtual financial skyscraper. Within just over a year, the product would lose 98 percent of its value.

Having seen similarly thin-sliced Deutsche corporate debt CDO products like REPON-16 blow up in clients' faces after the dot-com crash, the firm might have been expected to protect its clients from products that people close to Deutsche Bank now admit were "bad." But the problems at the beginning of the decade had barely registered with senior bankers at the firm, such as Rajeev Misra, and these executives lacked direct responsibility for the sales and compliance functions that had dealt with the earlier generation of soured deals.

The Long and the Short of It

The first smell of blood finally hit the subprime market in November 2006. Dan Sparks first detected it when Kevin Gasvoda phoned him that month with some strange news. The obscure subprime originators, who doled out money advanced by Wall Street dealers in return for home loans that fed the giant securitization pipelines, were starting to wobble.

The incidents recounted by Gasvoda stemmed from a standard protection mechanism Wall Street firms had for their mortgage loan pipelines, called *representations and warranties*. As part of their contractual agreement to purchase loans from origination companies, firms like Goldman could demand their money back if the loans were obviously defective. It was just like consumers' having the right to return a defective washing machine. Up to that point, Goldman and other dealers had only performed the minimum due diligence on the subprime loans they bought, so confident were they that they could immediately be sold. But now the frauds that had been building up in the subprime mortgage machine were finally coming to the surface. The originators and brokers had scraped the barrel: they were now lending to such hopeless prospects that mortgages would default within a month or two after closing. These *early payment defaults* obviously couldn't be securitized, which was why Gasvoda was trying to recover the money Goldman had advanced to the mortgage finance companies. "It's a breach of an agreement," said Sparks. "They have to buy them back."

As far as Goldman's bottom line was concerned, the issue was little more than an irritant. Most of the subprime loans in its warehouse seemed to be performing and could still be securitized and sold to investors. Indeed, the whole point of the warehouse was to insulate the assets inside it from the ups and downs of the market. It was through the innovation of the subprime derivative broadcasting system that the defaults caused Goldman trouble—but ultimately would save the firm. Returning to the analogy of a layered mortgage bond as a multi-story building in a flood, the Intex models based on house prices and foreclosure rates said that the lower floors were still perfectly safe. But if you took the market prices of default swaps and fed them backwards into Intex, those same lower floors were flooded. That fed into the triple-B-minus category of the ABX index that tracked this mezzanine layer of the building. And because Sparks's traders owned a $6 billion long position in this index, a modest decline in the ABX had an immediately noticeable impact at the firm.[14] At the start of December, Goldman's mortgage unit had ten days of consecutive trading losses. The losses weren't large, but they were distressing for a firm not accustomed to losing money.

Closing its 2006 financial year at the end of November, Goldman reported record annual profits, including $14.2 billion from fixed income trading, of which over $1 billion in gross revenue came from mortgages. But was that business now unraveling? Sparks knew how his bosses—president Gary Cohn, CFO David Viniar, and CEO Lloyd Blankfein—would react to the losses. He had just been given a long-awaited promotion to the firm's risk committee, which meant he would now be required to attend the Wednesday morning risk committee meetings that Viniar chaired, and Cohn and Blankfein often attended.

Sparks found himself in an unwelcome spotlight beside his peers. "This is really puzzling that you're having these issues," said Blankfein thoughtfully. "It doesn't make sense," added Cohn, more brusque and direct than Goldman's brainy CEO. "Every other market we operate in is booming." American house prices were flat-lining, not declining, according to Goldman's reckoning. The ten days of losses had not breached any VAR limit, and credit spreads were still at record lows. But the derivatives radar system that Sparks was using could not be ignored. "Look, we get it," Viniar said. "It's OK if you make less money but we have to reduce the risk." On December 14, 2006, the CFO assembled Sparks and the senior members of his team for a special meeting.

Goldman needed a lot of mortgages flowing through its pipeline to make the kind of money the mortgage department had been making. The firm reported securitizing around $5 or $6 billion of subprime and commercial real estate loans per month throughout 2006. And at the end of the year, there were over $10 billion of subprime loans sitting inside Goldman as the pipeline bifurcated into the mortgage bond and CDO production lines that Sparks ran. Their prices weren't budging, but the fact that these warehouses of cash securities were invisible to the derivatives radar was a troubling sign. Then Viniar focused on what the radar did pick up: Sparks's trading positions. "You're too big. Let's bring this closer to home," he told Sparks as the meeting ended. "Let's be flatter. Let's be aggressive distributing things."[15]

As Sparks communicated Viniar's orders to cut risk, latent tensions among the Goldman mortgage team began to emerge. There was Gasvoda and Ostrem, respectively creating mortgage bonds and CDOs for the firm, and they needed to be long in order to do it. Then there were the traders—David Lehman, Michael Swenson, and Josh Birnbaum—who together with Egol collectively functioned as Goldman's equivalent of Greg Lippmann. Out of the three, Birnbaum was intensely self-confident (even by Goldman standards). It was Birnbaum, say former colleagues, who had purchased the long position in the most threatened layer of the ABX index back in the spring, and who had made a lot of money for Goldman on the trade. Even before Viniar's directive Sparks had had to force the headstrong young trader to cut back. "He was the longest guy in the market," a senior Goldman trader recalls.

Now Birnbaum would have to go the other way and bet against subprime, in order to cancel out those long positions that Ostrem and Gasvoda had. But how would Goldman perform a 180 without revealing its cards? Because dealers could post ABX bid and offer prices on Reuters terminals and trade with one another using brokers, it was easy to figure out who was trading heavily and which way they were positioned. Birnbaum insisted that he could fool the market. "Given how much ABX we purchased through the broker market, the world would think we were long for the foreseeable future," he told Sparks.[16] While selling off his long ABX trade, Birnbaum proposed selling default swaps on individual mortgage bonds to the most uncritical buyers imaginable: the vast stampede of ABS CDO androids robotically snapping up every mortgage bond they could find. Birnbaum could quietly step in, buying protection or, in other words, shorting subprime bonds that Goldman didn't own.

But Pete Ostrem, who had put together over $10 billion of CDOs for Goldman in 2006 and was keen to beat his record in 2007, expressed alarm. He ran a factory almost recognizable to laypeople: it brought in mortgage bonds as raw materials and converted them to CDOs at a profit. These cash mortgage bonds (and Goldman owned $7 billion of them) hadn't gone down in price the way the derivatives had. This meant that the subprime CDOs that Ostrem built looked less attractive to customers than synthetic CDOs constructed purely from derivatives.[17] By selling these subprime derivatives to Goldman's CDO competitors, Birnbaum was undermining Ostrem's business.

Tension between Sparks's underlings was not new. Ostrem had also clashed repeatedly with Jonathan Egol, whose Abacus transactions, constructed out of subprime default swaps, also competed with what Ostrem was doing. The Abacus factory didn't have a warehouse—it simply faced the trading desk. Investors like IKB and AIGFP took the long side, selling protection to Egol, who took the short side, accumulating a position that by 2006 had reached $14 billion in size. Ostrem saw that as a threat, and Sparks had long struggled to defuse frictions between his acolytes. Now he had to keep the headstrong Birnbaum in line. The two rivals on the trading floor would have to work together, Sparks explained. Ostrem would retool his CDO factory to start doing Abacus-style deals, providing Birnbaum with an outlet—invisible to the Street—in terms of subprime default swaps that he needed to short.[18]

Wall Street Turns on Its Clients

The first quarter of Goldman's 2007 financial year, which ran from the end of November to the end of February, was pivotal for the mortgage team. In December and January, as the mezzanine floors of the ABX became more and more inundated, the traders were changing their views. It was getting harder and harder to sell long positions in the market. Birnbaum, Lehman, and Swenson began to suspect that Paulson was right and that they needed to get into the "big short" while there was still time.

Meanwhile, down at the level of subprime originators, the virus of early payment defaults that Gasvoda had first detected in late 2006 was spreading to the warehouse of mortgage loans that the originators had transferred to Goldman after advancing cash to home owners. Because of the problems Gasvoda was having, Sparks had started to write down the market value of the originators' mortgages, and that meant asking for additional margin to cover the difference. But when Sparks made his margin call, the originators couldn't pay. As Gasvoda recounted to Sparks, "We just sent our guys in to collect some files. And they kicked our employees out of their building with a security guard." Sparks and Gasvoda began to realize that the same thing was happening at all the Wall Street firms—they were demanding their money in buybacks or margin calls, and as a result the mortgage originators were dying like flies. Sparks was left with subprime mortgages he couldn't sell and loans that weren't being repaid.

As he attended the weekly risk meetings with the heads of nine other key Goldman risk-taking businesses, Sparks felt himself once again under attack as he explained how the mortgage pipeline had unexpectedly malfunctioned. Particularly attentive was Craig Broderick, the firm's head of credit risk management, who was equally perplexed that the client margin calls had suddenly turned ugly. "We're not taking big risk positions here," said Broderick. "We're just acting as an intermediary on a really safe basis earning relatively low returns."

Goldman considered itself to have world-class risk management, but here was something their risk managers had completely missed. How could a mortgage pipeline business that Broderick characterized as "pretty low-volatility, pretty highly liquid, pretty customer franchise-oriented" misbehave in this way? "We haven't been modelling this stuff well," Sparks told him. "Our risk metrics are really, really bad." Throughout 2007, Sparks's mortgage traders would repeatedly clash with Goldman risk managers over the signals being given by the firm's risk management systems.[19]

Fed by Birnbaum's growing short positions, Pete Ostrem's CDO business may have boomed during the first quarter of 2007, just like its competitors, but Sparks was focusing on the warehouse of unsold mortgage loans and bonds. He and the firm's financial controllers were now updating the value of Ostrem's and Gasvoda's warehouses using the information they were getting from the mortgage bond market, as well as derivatives including the ABX index. That was an innovation that terrified subprime originators like Fremont or New Century—when used to calculate margin calls by Wall Street firms, the new derivatives radar system was literally putting them out of business. Seeing everything holistically—"these are all just positions now," Sparks would tell his team—meant that Goldman saw the world in a new way, differently from its clients. It was also radically different from the way the rest of Wall Street did things. The giants of the subprime CDO market—Merrill Lynch, Citigroup, and UBS—had the biggest warehouses of all, but persisted in ignoring what the radar system was saying.

Does it matter if a Wall Street firm changes its industrial process from something recognizable—buying raw materials, warehousing them, and repackaging for distribution—to something based on derivatives, where it is taking a proprietary position against its clients? The end products look almost the same, but the motives of the manufacturer can be very different. With the warehouse model, the traditionalists like Merrill or Citi had to eat their own cooking, to the extent that demand might suddenly fall away, perhaps due to a product quality issue, leaving the wholesaler stuck with unsold inventory. However, with a derivative contract, the buyer and seller remain connected, and if the buyer loses, the seller has to win. When Goldman began taking short positions against the buyers of its Abacus CDOs in 2004, the conflict wasn't an issue. The size of Goldman's traditional mortgage warehouse, along with its long positions in derivatives, far exceeded the Abacus positions, so on a net basis, Goldman was indeed eating its own cooking.

In late 2006, this changed. Alerted by the signal of the ABX, Sparks's traders realized that short positions were not just bookkeeping, but a proprietary bet they needed to win. Over a nine-month period from November, Goldman allowed its warehouse of almost $8 billion in unpackaged subprime loans and $7 billion in mortgage bonds destined for CDOs to gradually run down to $3 billion, while Sparks's traders accumulated new short derivative positions that went as high as $12 billion. In fact, from February until December 2007, Sparks's traders were never less than $2 billion short subprime.[20] Although it was not until May 2007 that Sparks officially pulled the plug on Ostrem's warehouse-driven CDO factory—telling his team "I don't care, shut 'em all down" and handing the positions to Birnbaum—from December 2006 onwards, anyone buying a subprime CDO from Goldman was unwittingly betting against the firm's superior insight and market knowledge. While investors like IKB are described as "sophisticated," the truth is that they were anchored in the cash warehouse world, where Wall Street was as exposed as they were. In testimony to Congress, and in private interviews, Goldman officials insist that the firm did not conspire to bet against its clients. But by imperceptibly changing from a cash warehouse to short derivatives positions—which it knew was more than mere bookkeeping—Goldman made itself look evil and Machiavellian.

None of this was remotely illegal in what was an unregulated market—the small print of derivative contracts points out that a dealer owes no fiduciary duty to the investor and may be actively betting against them. And in defense of Goldman, it was now doing what Deutsche Bank had been doing since 2005—matching up hate-to-lose CDO investors on one side with Greg Lippmann's proprietary bets or bearish hedge fund managers on the other, such as John Paulson and Elliott Associates.

Lippmann's multiple roles as market-making middleman, virtual CDO manufacturer, and Paulson-style high-roller who stood to benefit from the meltdown of products that Deutsche and other banks created would be enough to make any observer of Wall Street queasy. And the way Deutsche's sales force peddled Lippmann's virtual CDOs to less-sophisticated institutions across the world shows financial innovation at its socially harmful worst. Yet it would be unfair to pin the blame on Lippmann. Well before the crisis broke, Lippmann was open about shorting subprime to the extent of annoying his colleagues who still believed in the U.S. housing market. They resented the premium he paid for protection, which cut into their bonus pool. Lippmann even offered subprime derivatives protection to LB Kiel (by then re-named HSH Nordbank) in 2006, but the Germans were unable to get board approval for the transaction, which would have saved them $3 billion. In contrast with Lippmann and his openness, Goldman's secret last minute 180-degree turn is all the more shocking.

Ironically, it was Goldman's belated attempts to follow in Deutsche's footsteps and match up subprime bulls and bears that eventually landed the firm with a $550 million SEC fine. At Goldman, a key figure was Fabrice Tourre, a young French derivatives marketing wizard who had been posted to New York from Europe to work with Jonathan Egol. With Viniar's orders to "get closer to home" ringing in his ears, Sparks had to find a mechanism to stop his growing short positions from getting too big. "Fab," as everyone called him, had a marketing pitch: he proposed "renting" the Abacus platform to hedge funds like Paulson & Co.

After overcoming opposition from Sparks's traders, who wanted to earmark the Abacus platform for their own short-selling, in March 2007 Tourre arranged a synthetic CDO called Abacus 2007 AC-1 for the purpose of allowing Paulson to short a billion dollars worth of subprime. The detail that landed Goldman and Tourre in the SEC's gunsights was a minor tweak to the static Abacus template: Tourre brought in a monoline insurance company called ACA to select the specific subprime bonds in the CDO while allowing Paulson extensive influence over the selection. ACA, which via its monoline entity took on $850 million of super-senior exposure, seemed unaware of Paulson's true role, and so was IKB, which bought $150 million of triple-A-rated Abacus notes. In his personal e-mails, Tourre couldn't help referring to the uselessness of all this innovation. "This product is a creation of pure intellectual masturbation," he confided to a friend, unwittingly writing the epitaph of an entire industry.[21] The irony is that had Goldman matched up Paulson and IKB directly in the style of Deutsche Bank, or allowed Birnbaum to take the other side of IKB's subprime bet via an Abacus CDO, the firm would probably have stayed out of trouble.

The full-scale meltdown of the financial system was now only a couple of months away. To understand why it took so long to happen, why Goldman and its rivals were able to keep selling subprime CDOs as long as they did, we need to ask the following question: why did investors like IKB not pay closer attention to what they were doing? The answer is that they thought they didn't need to.

CHAPTER SEVEN

The Eyes of Satan

Having flooded the market with seemingly safe investments larded with subprime money, the traders created zombie banks to buy them. Brick-and-mortar banks liked these zombies, because they evaded accounting rules and bank regulations, and increased profits. Hungry for higher fees, ratings agencies encouraged the growth of this new market and undermined governance. Wall Street saw the zombie structured investment vehicles (SIVs) as ideal "dumb money" customers for buying subprime CDOs and began setting them up specifically for this purpose. But at the first whiff of trouble in 2007, investors fled this market, causing the zombies to collapse almost overnight. Banks were forced to bail them out, which increased their subprime problems.

Mutual Fund Destruction Society

In 2005, two conservative investors in the Pacific Northwest were contemplating the manifold comforts of cash. At the Washington State treasurer's office in Olympia, deputy treasurer Doug Extine managed $8 billion of state funds in what was called the Local Government Investment Pool. Over in nearby King County, which contains the city of Seattle, investment officer Mike Smith managed cash reserves of $4 billion. Their mission was different from that of long-term investors such as insurance companies or pension funds. Whatever investments Extine and Smith chose, their employers needed the added assurance of liquidity—that the investments not only were safe, but could be converted to cash quickly.

Although their goals were nearly identical, the two men took divergent approaches to their investing. Extine handled his pool like a giant deposit account, looking for safety.[1] He parked money at dozens of federally insured banks and invested in government-backed IOUs such as Treasury bills and mortgage agency discount notes. Smith was slightly more adventurous. He bought lots of non-government-backed IOUs, known as commercial paper. It wasn't a big risk—these IOUs had been around since the 1970s and were issued by big companies such as Coca-Cola and General Electric. The IOUs matured every three months or so; how much could one lose in that period of time?

In fact, Extine knew exactly how much. A few years earlier, Washington State had bought commercial paper, a lot of it from California utility companies. In early 2001, the utilities suddenly defaulted, and the treasurer's office lost millions of dollars. Like Smith, Extine had once believed that the top commercial paper credit ratings were an assurance of safety. Like Smith, he didn't have time to investigate the creditworthiness of commercial paper issuers, so he learned his lesson and stuck to Treasury bills and CDs.

There were also some governance differences between the two investment funds. As part of a centralized state treasury, Extine was somewhat insulated from the pressures of local government. Smith, on the other hand, answered to his politically appointed boss. By investing in commercial paper, Smith could deliver an extra couple of million dollars in returns per year, which made a difference in Seattle, where schools, museums, and other services were always clamoring for additional funds.

Washington State is a long way from Wall Street, and the San Francisco representatives of the banks, such as Barclays and Morgan Stanley, who traveled up to Olympia and Seattle, were a far cry from the high-powered salespeople found there and in London. Extine would politely send them on their way, but Smith was intrigued by their pitches for commercial paper issued by unfamiliar finance companies with odd names like Rhineland, Tango, McKinley Funding, and Mainsail II.[2] The ratings agencies wrote approvingly about these IOUs, which were known as asset-backed commercial paper (ABCP). Little did he know that he was about to be a guinea pig for the latest tricks of love-to-win investment bankers and their ratings agency accomplices. Driven by short-term gains, they found in people like Smith the ultimate twist in a challenge that had spurred financial innovation for centuries.

The assurance of liquidity that Extine and Smith craved—the idea that their investments could be redeemed, dollar for dollar, whenever cash was needed—was nothing new. It was behind one of the oldest financial innovations of all, the invention of banking. How do banks get away with taking depositors' cash and lending it out to borrowers who won't pay the money back for years? Like the Cowardly Lion, the Scarecrow, and the Tin Man getting green spectacles from the Wizard of Oz, the depositors happily walk around thinking their cash is available whenever they want it. Woe betide any bank whose depositors take their green spectacles off. The need to keep the illusion intact (and to save the economy from bank runs) was the driver behind the invention of central banking and deposit insurance. But what happens if you dispense with banks, and central banks as well? What happens if an unregulated free market creates a parallel system that connects depositors with CDOs, subprime mortgage bonds, and a web of derivatives? The answer emerged in the summer of 2007, when people like Mike Smith discovered that the assurance of liquidity— the ultimate basis of banking confidence—had been subverted into the ultimate depository of concealed risk.

The origins of what became known as *shadow banking* go back to the early 1970s, when U.S. banks were predominantly small, safe, and so heavily regulated that they couldn't even set their own interest rates for customers. From the customers' perspective, this safe but clunky and expensive system was ripe for improvement. Big corporate borrowers wanted to reduce the cost of bank loans, and the newly invented commercial paper or IOU market was a great way of doing that. Money market mutual funds sprang up to give shortchanged bank depositors a better deal. Like Smith, these money market funds bought commercial paper because the extra returns gave them an edge over traditional bank deposits. Over time, the money funds started investing in short-term repo agreements as well, helping to prop up the growing balance sheets of investment banks like Goldman Sachs and Lehman Brothers.

Looking at this upstart market, the traditional lending banks could argue that if their depositors took those green spectacles off, Uncle Sam would be there to protect them in the form of the FDIC's guarantee, which stood at $100,000 per customer in 2007. Money market funds responded that they didn't need this protection because they weren't "borrowing short and lending long," as banks did—IOUs and repos were only short-term investments, not long-term loans. That distinction let them build up the confidence of their customers with a myth worthy of the Wizard of Oz: "We never break the buck." In other words, for every dollar you invest with us, you will get at least a dollar back. This was an astounding claim, in part because the contractual small print on mutual funds made it clear that the redemption value of funds depended on the price that its assets could be sold for in the market: there was no guarantee your cash would be returned. Yet mutual funds succeeded in fostering a perception that investors were guaranteed to not lose money. Taking full advantage of such (misplaced) customer confidence, money market funds grew to over $2 trillion by 2007.[3]

Banking in the Shadows

In the late 1980s, this alternative U.S. deposit-taking system—growing steadily and inexorably—came to the attention of a mismatched pair of bright young bankers at Citigroup. Nick Sossidis is a Greek-born bear of a man with a blunt and forceful manner. Stephen Partridge-Hicks is restrained and public school English, and has a photographic memory for dates and contracts. It was a time when large banks were starting to feel shareholder pressure to shrink their balance sheets and increase equity returns, and securitization technology was being devised to achieve this. Citibank had not yet become the behemoth financial conglomerate of Sandy Weill and Chuck Prince. Partridge-Hicks and Sossidis were proud of their employer, but they would find their loyalty to Citi challenged by some of their big clients.[4] The hate-to-lose Japanese banks and Swiss insurance companies were annoyed by all the products the Americans were trying to sell them, because everything had risks attached—high-rated bonds exposed the Japanese or Swiss to interest rate or currency risk, and junk bonds added credit risk. Was there any way to invest in just the highest-quality assets and have the risks stripped away?

The next generation of innovative bankers would have produced a CDO in answer to such a request, but as Partridge-Hicks and Sossidis listened to the complaints, it sounded as if the Japanese and Swiss wanted to buy shares in a *bank*. After all, for every dollar of shareholder money, banks could build up a tower of high-quality assets financed by customer deposits. After paying the depositors their interest, shareholders could reap the rewards. The problem was that the Japanese didn't like the direction in which banks such as Citi were going. Rather than a bank promising to pay shareholders 15 or 20 percent returns on their investment every year, the Swiss and Japanese wanted something safer and more boring. Just a couple of percentage points more than the risk-free rate was fine for them.

Sossidis and Partridge-Hicks had a brain wave. If they couldn't find a real bank for the Japanese and Swiss to invest in, they would create one. It would be safe and boring: it would restrict itself to investing in the very safest assets—the debt of highly rated banks, for example, and the topmost slices of the new kinds of securitizations that Citi was doing with its credit card portfolio. Sossidis and Partridge-Hicks knew that they could use the well-understood and straightforward derivatives linked to foreign exchange or interest rates to strip away risks the Japanese or Swiss didn't like. Although their creation wouldn't have a central bank in the wings ready to bail it out if things went wrong, Sossidis and Partridge-Hicks would argue that their new bank was so safe that it wouldn't need one.

But where would this new bank find its depositor base, which would provide the funding for the billions in ultrasafe assets in which it was going to invest? How was the new bank going to pay for all the branches and armies of bank tellers it would need to take in billions of dollars in deposits? And how was it going to get regulatory approval? Partridge-Hicks and Sossidis soon realized that a ready-made solution was the army of depositors that had already been assembled by U.S. money market funds, and other institutions looking for places to park their cash. If their new bank could sell IOUs to these funds, then it would have, in effect, outsourced its deposit taking to the likes of Schwab or Fidelity.

With this final spark of inspiration, Partridge-Hicks and Sossidis were ready, and in September 1988, the world's first shadow bank, Alpha, began operations. An up-and-coming Moody's analyst, Raymond McDaniel, worked with the Citibank duo to ensure that Alpha achieved the top "A-1+/P-1" commercial paper rating for its IOUs. Another shadow bank, Beta, followed a year later.

In the same way that money market funds were not officially deposit-taking banks, Alpha and Beta were not officially banks. In fact, they were early forms of the Cayman android, special-purpose vehicles (SPVs) managed from Citigroup's London offices by Sossidis and Partridge-Hicks. But unlike the tens of thousands of CDO androids that would swarm inside Cayman mailboxes, or the American mortgage androids already proliferating across the United States, these were different. The idea of a typical CDO or ABS is that the android borrows its money in a single swoop. The alchemy of subordination and correlation is harnessed toward this single moment of debt raising, whether it happens in a couple of big gulps or as a programmed series of tiny sips.

Instead of a one-off debt-raising debut, Sossidis's and Partridge-Hicks's new creations would need to raise money again and again, every time one of their IOUs expired. The money market funds would have to be able to inspect the androids in all weathers and from all quarters. Since the IOUs had to be investment grade in order for the funds to buy them, credit ratings agencies would also be regular visitors to the android pen. Fortunately, these two financial craftsmen had an infectious passion for their creations and watched over them carefully, patiently dealing with the ratings agencies, keeping their investors happy—and getting paid a handsome fee for their services.

However, keeping an eternal bloom on Alpha and Beta's cheeks could not be done by loving care alone. Citigroup provided the workshop for Sossidis and Partridge-Hicks, and as they got Alpha and Beta off the ground, having a hundred-year-old U.S. bank standing behind them helped the sales proposition. But what would happen, if for some reason Alpha and Beta's investments performed badly, and no one wanted to buy its IOUs? Could Citigroup be relied upon to inject the billions needed to pay off all the expired short-term borrowing? Partridge-Hicks and Sossidis put in place a crucial umbilical cord to their parent bank—called a backstop facility—but took care not to rely on Citi to provide all the money that might be needed. It turned out to be a wise move. In 1990, an emerging-market lending crisis had swept across the banking industry, and now having Citi's name on one's business card was anathema. Suddenly, the investors in Alpha and Beta feared that the umbilical cord might flow the other way, sucking the lifeblood out of the two androids. "Citibank? I don't want to see that—those guys are a disaster," the Japanese now told Partridge-Hicks. "I want the Alpha Beta guys." "But we *are* the Alpha Beta guys," he replied.

Meanwhile, accountants and regulators were starting to debate the ramifications of that umbilical cord between a bank and its offspring. It was easy to prove that the securitization androids behind the basic forms of CDO and ABS were distinct creatures, separate from their creators. But the idea of the android continuously borrowing money, with an umbilical cord there to provide an emergency cash supply, raised questions about whether it was really distinct or not. As they debated the finer points of these questions with Citi's senior management, Sossidis and Partridge-Hicks became more and more impatient. From talking with investors, they had reached the conclusion that the umbilical cord was a bad idea. If the android became diseased, it could infect the sponsoring bank, just as a diseased bank could kill its android offspring. In 1993, they decided to leave Citi and create their own perfect financial android, capable of surviving without any parent bank's support. It would be a "narrow bank," doing the boring stuff that flesh-and-blood banks like Citi were forgetting how to do. They called it Sigma and brought it to life two years later.

Dusseldorf's Dr. Frankenstein

With Sossidis and Partridge-Hicks out of the picture, Citi cloned a stable of androids. Other banks—such as Dresdner Bank, HSBC, and Standard Chartered—copied the idea, attracted by the prospect of getting paid for managing highly rated assets off their balance sheets. For all the muttering by the two inventors of the shadow bank concept, no one else thought that the umbilical cord—and its pledge to back up the android IOUs—was a bad thing. The benefits were too great. If regulators forced flesh-and-blood, brick-and-mortar banks to hold fixed amounts of capital against even their safest loans, then the androids could buy these loans instead. They could then hold the loans in an unregulated Cayman mailbox, freeing up their parent banks to do more profitable, albeit riskier, lending. And there were activities that banks had been doing for commercial customers from time immemorial but were no longer shareholder friendly: advancing cash to businesses against their orders from customers, or discounting receivables, for example. The androids could be programmed to do this instead. And since the money market funds (performing the time-honored role of deposit taking) were happy to buy the android IOUs, the shadow banking system could quietly grow.

Like the CDO and ABS businesses, the new financial androids produced a flock of specialist human attendants. Because of their need to borrow continuously, as lifelike operating companies, the job of supervising them was more intensive than it was for CDOs. It required constant monitoring and testing. A good number of these attendants were at ratings agencies and law firms, but they also learned their trade at banks that specialized in the more humdrum types of service, with job titles such as *trustee* or *CP placement agent*. Typical of this breed was Dirk Röthig, who had picked up inside knowledge of the high-maintenance androids during stints at accountant Deloitte and then at State Street Bank. Like so many financially minded continentals, he followed the job market to London and New York. But early in 2001, Röthig was surprised to hear that his education in an arcane corner of international banking made him a person of great value in his home country. He soon found himself sitting in a boardroom in Dusseldorf, listening to a bank chief executive on the make named Stefan Ortseifen.

This was around the time that LB Kiel was looking beyond its North Sea horizon and buying CDOs from Barclays and UBS. Ortseifen felt that his shareholder-owned bank, IKB Deutsche Industriebank, was a cut above the staid *Landesbanken,* with their cautious boards of local politicians and union officials. IKB was well regarded for its lending to midsize companies in Germany's industrial Ruhr heartland, but it had no spare cash with which to buy CDOs. Any excess money was plowed back into lending, so Ortseifen could not invest directly, as LB Kiel had done. But he argued that by doing what it had done perfectly well for seventy years—lending to domestic companies—IKB was gambling its shareholders' money on the vicissitudes of the German economy. As he explained to Röthig, "I want to be a risk manager, not a risk taker." In order to buy unfamiliar foreign assets that would diversify its risk, IKB would have to create an android. Ortseifen made Röthig, a journeyman in the android world, an astounding offer: under the supervision of IKB's two treasury managers, he would build and control his own shadow bank from scratch, with a team of dozens of android attendants.

Unlike the vehicles Sossidis and Partridge-Hicks had designed for Citibank, Ortseifen's android, called a *conduit,* would not need the picky Japanese investors who performed the role of equity investors in a shadow bank. Ortseifen didn't want anyone else involved—his highest priority was keeping the German tax authorities away from his new android. So Röthig got to work constructing a web of Channel Islands purchasing companies and Delaware charitable trusts that would be "advised" from Dusseldorf.[5] This spadework was necessary because his creation had to do the stuff that LB Kiel was now doing in baby steps, but on a much bigger scale: it would buy CDOs and ABSs in the billions and borrow to pay for them by selling commercial paper IOUs to American money market funds and treasury cash managers such as Mike Smith, out in the Pacific Northwest.

In March 2002, Röthig's new android, Rhineland, was ready to take its first breath. There would be an umbilical cord, allowing IKB to rake off profits from the difference in interest between what the android bought and what it owed. For a handsome fee, Fitch and Moody's rated the IOUs Rhineland would regularly spit out and repay a couple of months later. To replace the Japanese equity investors, the two ratings agencies came up with a model to calculate the "enhancement," or extra capital, that IKB needed to put aside in reserve.

There was a trade-off here. Other conduits that invested only in triple-*A* assets did not have to post an enhancement, but Rhineland was going for lower-rated investment-grade CDOs and ABSs to boost IKB's returns. Of course, like all the other umbilically supported androids, IKB had to promise that it would step in and repay the IOUs if the CDOs went south. But Fitch and Moody's didn't worry too much about IKB's ability to do that. Better still from Ortseifen's perspective, the Basel banking rules laid down that this "standby facility" required no shareholder capital to be set aside—in other words, the "speed limit" of such lending was infinite. And so, completely off the radar screens of any regulator, Rhineland was up and running.

I didn't hear about this scheme until late 2003. It was bonus season for the Wall Street firms, and in the bars and nightspots of London's West End, credit derivatives bankers couldn't help but brag about the client who was making them rich by buying so many of their CDOs. They *loved* Dirk Röthig. When I finally met this tubby German banker, it was late at night at a popular Mayfair club called Annabel's, and Röthig was drinking whiskey with some Merrill Lynch CDO salesmen. He struck me as a reluctant and awkward star—a stable groom who had been promoted to jockey and was now riding a giant thoroughbred.

Röthig chafed at the suggestion that some kind of mind-over-matter mastery was required to pick the right investments for a beast of Rhineland's size. Rather, it was a question of software and control systems used by his team of thirty-five. "We are using proprietary tools which we developed, as well as the common things like RiskMetrics, Intex, Wall Street Analytics. We use these special tools across asset classes to analyze them," he told me in measured, slightly accented English. "I would say that it has proven a worthwhile investment, because we have not faced a loss so far."

I had been writing about the Basel rules since 1998, and I could see that what industry analysts called an arbitrage conduit was merely the latest tweak in a series of ingenious innovations to get around regulatory agencies over the last decade or more. Conduits made sense for banks on both sides of the Atlantic: in America, with its leverage limits, conduits were a way around the rules. In Europe, the inflexible Basel I speed limits were the motivation. Trusting that the banks must be driven by rational economic self-interest, regulators could only follow in their wake.

Gradually it dawned on me that the self-interest was less rational and more selfish, driving individuals to extract "rent" from each step of the innovation process. Because Rhineland bought riskier pieces of CDOs or ABSs than other conduits, the banks that sold it the products earned higher fees.[6] And those were just the fees for originating the securities. Behind the scenes, the banks were making a lot more by trading the difference between the price Röthig paid for CDOs and their internal manufacturing cost, calculated by the bank's default swap trading desk. That was more like 5 percent of the value, depending on how much juice the traders could extract from the arbitrage between ratings-based and market-based pricing.

With Rhineland buying about $3 billion of CDOs every year, the top dozen credit derivatives dealers were making about $200 million annually from this one client. No wonder Röthig was so popular, and no wonder CDO salespeople were using their IKB revenues as a calling card with headhunters. In January 2004, I asked Röthig how it felt to be such a cash cow. He shrugged and said, "It's a win-win situation for both sides." Indeed it was. Despite overpaying banks hundreds of millions for CDOs, Rhineland could get away with paying a virtually risk-free rate of interest on the IOUs it was selling to money market mutual funds—over $50 million in annual revenues for IKB.

There was something disturbing about Röthig's insouciance, especially as dealers were assiduously flattering him, and telling me how clever he was at "pricing CDOs to the last basis point."[7] The ratings agencies, earning millions from rating both Rhineland's investments and its IOUs, were equally complimentary. Yet here was an android that had been programmed by Ortseifen to buy $3 billion of CDOs and other securitized bonds every year, whether they were a good thing or not. I began to suspect that while Röthig thought he was in charge of Rhineland, the real puppet masters were the originating banks and ratings agencies. They were happily stuffing it with their creations on one side and selling its IOUs on the other.

Yet the faster it ran, like a hamster on the wheel of innovation, the more confident IKB got about its skill as an investor. It became heavily involved in buying subprime bonds and CDOs containing subprime. A few months after I spoke to him, Röthig hosted a visit from Goldman's Dan Sparks and Jonathan Egol to discuss what would become the Abacus production line of subprime CDOs. In December 2005, Deutsche Bank's Greg Lippmann made a courtesy call on Röthig, finding him adamant that U.S. house prices would keep rising, and protect the CDOs his Rhineland android was voraciously buying. By 2006, Röthig had left IKB after a row with management, but by now Ortseifen was addicted to the cash coursing through IKB's veins via that umbilical cord. He could not imagine the possibility that this child might grow up to be a monster that would suck his bank dry.

Banking by Photocopy Machine

Stephen Partridge-Hicks and Nick Sossidis had followed their principles to the letter. As their investors had requested, they created a beautiful android called Sigma that was boring and virtuous. It would not buy subprime, even if triple-*A* rated. It would buy just the safest and simplest assets, and apply a limited amount of leverage (borrowing roughly twelve times its capital in the form of IOUs, about a third of the leverage of commercial banks like Citigroup), to extract a return of about 2 percent above the risk-free rate. To carry out the job of constructing and controlling Sigma, Sossidis and Partridge-Hicks set up a company in London's Mayfair district they called Gordian Knot, after an ancient rope puzzle Alexander the Great "solved" with one slash of his sword.

Alexander's celebrated act was a metaphor for how Sigma had untangled itself from the umbilical cords that bound other androids to large banks. Sossidis and Partridge-Hicks thought long and hard about the problem. They believed they had cracked it in 1995, when Sigma first drew breath, but changed their minds in 1998, when John Meriwether's LTCM had to be bailed out and dismantled by the banks that had lent it money. At first sight, an android like Sigma was completely different from LTCM. Instead of issuing IOUs to buy bonds with a maturity of several years, LTCM built up a huge web of derivatives and securities by borrowing directly from dealers via repo and collateral agreements. These positions were priced at market value every day, and if they went against LTCM, the fund had to transfer cash to the dealers. Once the market suspected that the fund was in trouble, the valuations rapidly worsened, it started hemorrhaging cash, and it went into a death spiral.

Partridge-Hicks and Sossidis realized with alarm that Sigma bore an unfortunate resemblance to LTCM. Suppose the appetite dried up for its IOUs. Without an umbilical cord from a parent bank, or a syndicate of lenders, Sigma was dependent on what was called *market value termination,* where it would sell its assets at market value to repay short-term IOUs as they matured. But LTCM had shown that if the market suspected a forced liquidation, it would drive down the price of assets that needed to be sold. That would mean even more had to be sold to repay the IOUs, driving down market prices even more. And what made things particularly dangerous for Sigma was that for some of the obscure bonds it was supposed to own, only a few million dollars' worth needed to be traded for a billion-sized portfolio to be revalued.

Although the appetite for Sigma's IOUs had not dried up in 1998, Sossidis and Partridge-Hicks decided that there was no time to be lost protecting their precious creation. Over the next five years, the two men pored over legal technicalities, coming up with ways to ensure that no investor or lender could ever force Sigma to unwillingly price its assets at market value. For example, the vehicle began issuing slightly longer-term IOUs called *medium-term notes* that didn't fall due as quickly as commercial paper did, as part of the new system called *cash flow continuation*. During this time, Gordian Knot, the management company, grew to employ eighty people, and Sigma continued buying assets until it was close to $40 billion in size. Although it was completely invisible to most people, Sigma's two creators fervently believed that they were doing a service to society, acting as a "banker to the banks," encouraging new, responsible lending by investing in securitizations.

Yet for all their skill in refashioning Sigma, it was still a Cayman android performing a banking role without a central bank. Aside from the ratings agencies that stamped its IOUs, Sigma's only regulation was indirect, via Gordian Knot's supervision by London's FSA. As for the money market funds that by now were heavily investing in its IOUs—Fidelity, the Reserve Primary Fund, Vanguard, and J.P. Morgan Asset Management—they had become completely dependent on credit ratings that their regulator, the SEC, required them to use. So Partridge-Hicks and Sossidis spent years explaining their new protections against an LTCM-type crisis to Standard & Poor's, Fitch, and Moody's, hoping to get the benefit of increased confidence from the ratings agencies. They hoped that by giving the ratings agencies exclusive inside access to Sigma's exquisite machinery—and paying them $1 million a year apiece in fees for rating Sigma's IOUs—they would support their android without interference.

But they didn't account for the commercial pressures in the ratings business. Having spent so much time learning about the workings of Sigma, the ratings agencies would not be satisfied with an investment return of just $1 million a year. Executives at the three agencies were given mandates to meet revenue growth targets by exploiting innovations like Sigma. The result, according to Sossidis and Partridge-Hicks, was that Gordian Knot's secrets fell into the hands of competitors. And that meant more android banks. Some were so-called conduits like Rhineland; by 2006 these had grown to almost $500 billion, measured by the IOUs they issued. But others were copies of Sigma or seemed to be closely related to it. With names like Parkland or Whistlejacket, most of these new androids had umbilical cords to parent banks, while failing to incorporate Sigma's new anti-LTCM crisis protective measures.

Most of the copycats seemed to emerge from Moody's, where Raymond McDaniel, the analyst who had originally rated Sossidis's and Partridge-Hicks's first creation at Citibank, ascended the ranks, becoming president in 2001 and CEO in 2004. Sossidis and Partridge-Hicks first noticed this when a team of analysts suddenly left Moody's in 1998 to set up a *structured investment vehicle* (SIV) for the Bank of Montreal. The analysts had been involved in the rating of Sigma and had been given inside knowledge of its workings. That was suspicious enough, but Sossidis and Partridge-Hicks felt things had gone too far when another pair of analysts who had intimate knowledge of the post-LTCM improvements at Sigma left Moody's in 2002 to create SIVs for Dresdner Bank and HSBC.

There is no evidence to suggest that Moody's was giving its staff free rein to take a client's intellectual property and use it to create their own start-ups—which would in turn become new, lucrative clients of Moody's. Moreover, Partridge-Hicks and Sossidis were handicapped by the fact that it is hard to patent financial innovation. What Moody's and its staff did was perfectly legal, and McDaniels and his senior executives in New York brushed aside Gordian Knot's complaints. Today, Moody's declines to comment on any aspect of its relationship with Gordian Knot.

Sossidis's and Partridge-Hicks's suspicions were further enflamed when they began to see ratings agency reports that lumped together their beloved android with the copies under the catch-all term structured investment vehicles. That proved, they thought, that the agencies were repackaging the insider knowledge picked up from rating Sigma as a new "product" to be sold to prospective android creators hoping to build top-rated IOU machines. In January 2004, Moody's published what it called its *capital model,* a seventy-eight-page formula-strewn SIV recipe book that even included computer code. Developing and testing such complex financial research and software would normally cost much more than the few million dollars per year that Moody's was then making from SIV ratings.

Sigma-clone androids began to multiply fast, accumulating total assets of around $450 billion by early 2007. Almost a trillion dollars of IOUs were being sold by SIVs and conduits to the money market mutual funds and other short-term investors. Here was the shadow banking system at its height. But there was one more twist to come. By 2004, the blueprints for how to create androids like Sigma or Rhineland were no longer secret. Would-be creators could practically buy their ratings models and legal advice off the shelf, and after a few months' legwork, they could direct their android to start buying CDOs or subprime bonds, and sell IOUs to fund the acquisitions. The big investment banks were cashing in at every step—from providing the more humdrum trustee or IOU-selling services to the androids, to exploiting their appetite for hate-to-lose investments. But the CDO creators, who had become investment bank superstars by concocting value out of nothing within a much cruder android package, wanted a piece of the action.

The androids were willing buyers of their products, but there was only so much schmoozing one could do with the robot masters like Röthig, who in any case insisted on spreading his business across as many as twenty dealers. And not all of the new generation of androids were buying CDOs or subprime mortgage bonds. So the CDO inventors began to think of ways to cut out the middleman and muscle their way into the IOU market directly.

Run from the Shadows

Ratings agencies might have worked out how to boost revenue by cross-pollinating ideas worked out in secret at places like Gordian Knot. Investment banks, on the other hand, worked in a high-paced frenzy of mutual envy, plagiarism, and adaptation. I saw this firsthand after my story about IKB was published in February 2004. In it, I named three banks rumored to have made the largest revenues selling CDOs to IKB and Rhineland the previous year: J.P. Morgan, Lehman Brothers, and BNP Paribas. The article also mentioned how accounting standards bodies were targeting androids like Rhineland, proposing that the presence of an umbilical cord meant that they should be on the bank's balance sheet. This idea, called *consolidation,* filled the banks with dread.

I got another insight into how financial innovation worked when I spoke to a London-based Morgan Stanley credit derivatives salesman. He pooh-poohed the idea that his competitors were doing that well out of Rhineland. "I would seriously challenge that anyone really has $50 million in their front pockets due to any trading clients associated with tranched risk or correlation," he said. I had an inkling why: Morgan Stanley's quants were notoriously skeptical about the Gaussian copula, and the bank's traders were less willing to book a profit up front when arbitraging the difference between ratings-based and market-based CDO pricing.[8] But there was also a note of envy in the salesman's voice—suppose his competitors really were making that much money?

It was the umbilical cord problem that Sossidis and Partridge-Hicks had thought so carefully about that gave Morgan Stanley a way into this business. The threat of consolidation (which came only in 2007) was perceived in 2004 as potentially reducing the supply of IOUs. It was Wall Street's job to find a way of making up any potential deficiency. As a result, the Sigma idea of stand-alone IOU-issuing androids was "a hot topic of conversation" at Morgan Stanley, this salesman told me. But who could fill the role of Gordian Knot, which had spent so many years lovingly designing and running Sigma?

At this point the salesman let something slip. "Cheyne is looking at this," he said, dropping the name of a London hedge fund, Cheyne Capital, big in CDOs. It was an outgrowth from the days when CDOs were launched as a means for fund managers like America's TCW or France's AXA to increase the size of their bond funds by exploiting a bit of Cayman Islands cash plumbing. Credit hedge funds like Cheyne had a far more incestuous relationship with the banks. Founded by ex–credit derivatives traders (Cheyne's founders were Morgan Stanley alumni) and offered generous lines of funding from their former colleagues, these funds obviously generated trading revenues for the dealing desks. But they also provided subtle but important additional services to the banks.

We have already explored one of these roles: the trading of new credit indexes like the iTraxx, CDX, or ABX that allowed dealers to book profits on much larger bespoke CDO positions with hate-to-lose investors. Equally important was the ability to step in as managers of CDO deals, earning a fee for *stock picking*, or ensuring that bad assets were weeded out of the CDO before they could do damage. The attraction for investors is that this is done independently of the arranging bank, to avoid conflicts of interest. LB Kiel (and its later incarnation, HSH Nordbank) had the misfortune of getting caught twice by such conflicts, first with its Corvus deal in the wake of Oka Usi's departure from Barclays in 2001, and second by UBS in 2007 with North Street 4. On paper, at least, a fund manager (or a hedge fund) was supposed to prevent conflicts like this in return for a management fee or possibly a stake in the CDO. By owning the equity layer at the bottom of a CDO, taking the first hit from defaults, they had "skin in the game"—an incentive to protect the layers above.

Most credit fund managers genuinely cared about protecting the interests of all their investors, rather than looking to extract short-term profit and accumulate fee-generating assets. However, the new wave of credit hedge funds faced a conflict because unlike traditional fund managers, such as AXA or BlackRock, that have their own sales forces, they depended on the banks to bring in CDO investors. By accepting CDO mandates, some funds vastly increased their assets under management, and hence revenues. While trading on their status as independent fiduciaries, some of them unwittingly ended up being tools of the banks, which stood to make the most money on any deal.

These kinds of issues were in the air when London-based Cheyne Capital joined forces with Morgan Stanley in 2004. Cheyne was well regarded and made a concerted effort to break into the SIV market by poaching staff from Gordian Knot and Citigroup. Having such a manager on board provided convenient cover for Morgan Stanley's mortgage department. The U.S. bank had an unabashed motive to originate and sell as many subprime mortgage bonds as possible, which it was pumping out in huge numbers. And with the help of the ratings agencies, it had the Sigma recipe book, which revealed the secrets of creating umbilical-free living and breathing Cayman androids. Morgan Stanley then did something innovative when it built an android called

Cheyne Finance. It would be based in Dublin, rather than the Cayman Islands, because the Irish government had decided to nurture an unregulated android-servicing center at the mouth of the River Liffey. For the sake of appearances, it resembled Sigma, in order to receive the approval from Moody's and S&P as a new member of the so-called SIV family. That would allow it to issue the triple-A-rated IOUs that money market funds and treasurers like Mike Smith were buying. A sales trip by Morgan Stanley bankers down to the Persian Gulf would bring in the equivalent of Sigma's long-term Japanese investors, in the form of Abu Dhabi Commercial Bank, which bought *capital notes* in the SIV. However, on the inside the android was effectively a giant subprime CDO arranged by Morgan Stanley that Cheyne agreed to "manage." Notwithstanding the hedge fund's sincere efforts to protect investors, the android would get stuffed with the all-American sub-prime mortgage androids, including notorious originators such as New Century, Countrywide, and IndyMac. Launched with a size of $4 billion in the summer of 2005, the Cheyne Finance SIV would grow to $10 billion by the summer of 2007.

While it was a clever ruse to hide a CDO inside a Sigma imitation in order to snare IOU investors like King County, Morgan Stanley was not the only bank to figure out how to get these hate-to-lose investors into the CDO market. Since parting ways with Sossidis and Partridge-Hicks in the early 1990s, Citigroup had built a big CDO business and in 2005 succeeded in selling commercial paper IOUs directly out of a CDO it arranged called McKinley Funding. One of the buyers was Mike Smith.

Meanwhile, Cheyne Finance quickly attracted imitators. Vince Balducci, who replaced Oka Usi as head of credit derivatives at Bar-clays, had hired a young Irish banker named Ed Cahill from J.P. Mor-gan. Late in 2005, just before Morgan Stanley won a credit derivatives award from an industry publication partly for its SIV ingenuity, Bar-clays salesmen began pitching a rival design of subprime-buying android to their clients. Called a "SIV-lite" by Cahill, it was even more stripped down than Morgan Stanley's invention and gave Barclays cru-cial powers to tweak the android's workings. The British bank brought in a Geneva-based hedge fund, Avendis, to run its first $1.6 billion SIV-lite, Golden Key, which launched just before Christmas in 2005. A Lon-don credit hedge fund called Solent (founded by ex–J.P. Morgan banker Jonathan Laredo) was hired to manage the second one, Mainsail, in 2006. Once again, the triple-A-rated IOUs from this android ended up in King County's portfolio.

What had started as a quest by Sossidis and Partridge-Hicks to construct a Platonic ideal of a bank had turned into something weird. The new generation of SIVs and SIV-lites were virtually indistinguishable from CDOs and served as funnels to pour subprime bonds into the portfolios of unwitting hate-to-lose investors. The twist was that investors were convinced that their money was not only safe but also liquid. The bankers who created the products—at Barclays, Morgan Stanley, and elsewhere—received their bonus payments soon after the deals closed and, by contrast with Gordian Knot, had no long-term interest in their creations. Meanwhile, the credit hedge funds, ratings agencies, and android trustees all took their management fees. The role of the ratings agencies was critical. Their willingness to morph existing models into new product areas facilitated what were basically bait-and-switch tactics by banks.

Remember how CDOs are rated: it depends on the idea that bundling together loans or other assets diversifies away risk and, together with a cushion of subordination, makes things ultrasafe. Behind the scenes, banks would bully the agencies into accepting parameters or inputs for the model that would keep the profits flowing. Consider, for example, *asset correlation,* a key parameter in calculating the loss probability in a credit portfolio, and hence the rating of CDOs. Moody's, S&P, and Fitch happily adopted the intellectual pretense that asset correlation—which the banks wanted to be as low as possible—could be applied to ratings-dependent androids as if it were some independent natural phenomenon that could be quantified, such as wind speeds over Greenland. Investors understood none of the commercial pressure behind the ratings arms race. They started out buying CDOs based on corporate bonds, which they *just about* thought they understood. They failed to appreciate how the dealers had picked the corporate CDO market clean of profits by 2003, and how by recycling androids into new CDOs, the dealers could renew the cycle. By placing slices of corporate CDO into €100 million "CDO-squared" for its client Cassa di Risparmio di San Marino (CRSM), Barclays booked €25 million of gross profit on a single day in July 2004.[9] When applied to bundles of subprime mortgage bonds fed into CDOs, the intellectual pretensions of the ratings agencies was stretched to breaking point. If one mortgage bond linked to adjustable-rate NINJA loans in California and Nevada defaulted, they all would, because they were all exposed to the same kinds of borrower. Hiding behind small-print caveats such as "data will tend to be sparse for newer or more exotic sectors within structured finance," Moody's and the others spread the illusion of safety across $500 billion of triple-A-rated securities.

By helping the CDO privateers of the City of London and Wall Street break into the IOU-issuing world of Gordian Knot and Sigma, S&P and Moody's gave the innovation cycle a last, fatal burst of energy. (Fitch failed to establish a foothold in the SIV universe.) It was here that the intellectual flimsiness of the two revenue-hunting ratings agencies became obvious. A CDO may be a dangerously overengineered android, but its flaws can be hidden from view as long as you don't have to sell it in the market. You can't really be sure whether the correlation model was right or wrong until you have waited for the CDO debt to be paid back.

The new generation of umbilical-free SIV androids were constructed around the idea that people like Mike Smith would keep buying their IOUs every three months. Banks and ratings agencies had "photocopied" some of the ideas used to build Sigma, but corners were cut in the process. The ability of Cheyne Finance or Mainsail to own billions in subprime bonds completely depended on the money market funds' being happy to bet again and again that android uncertainty was preferable to cash. If liquidity suddenly dried up, the subprime bonds owned by Cheyne Finance or Mainsail would have to be quickly sold in order to repay the IOUs. For Moody's and S&P, this was a very different proposition from understanding the long-term default behavior of bond portfolios, where at least they could draw upon their decades of rating experience. They were now effectively rating market confidence and the liquidity of assets.

A perfect example of how ratings agencies overreached in trying to turn market water into actuarial wine was a bizarre product that briefly flourished in late 2006 and early 2007. The Constant Proportion Debt Obligation (CPDO) was invented by ABN AMRO, a second-tier Dutch investment bank that eventually became part of Royal Bank of Scotland. The idea was that an android would be programmed to buy and sell derivatives on a credit index, such as the CDX or iTraxx, in such a way as to maintain a fixed coupon that was attractive to investors. If the spread of the index widened (in other words, prices of bonds went down), the robot would buy more derivatives to try and make up for the losses. If prices kept falling, the robot would eventually blow up and lose investors their money. Moody's European head of structured finance Paul Mazataud, the man who helped rate J.P. Morgan's Mayu CDO in 2002, agreed to sell triple-*A* ratings on CPDOs, on the premise that the market meltdown scenario was statistically unlikely. The product flew off the shelves, other banks copied it, and ABN AMRO received a trade magazine award for "Deal of the Year."[10]

It proved to be the worst mistake of Mazataud's career. When the quants at ABN Amro received copies of the Moody's software Mazataud's team was using to determine the triple-*A* ratings, they discovered that the code was riddled with errors, of a type so elementary that any junior programmer should have spotted it.[11] ABN (which was making millions from selling CPDOs to investors) kept quiet about its discovery, but a U.S. bank tipped Moody's off. By early 2007, Mazataud became aware of the errors, which if rectified would have required a hefty downgrade of the products. A ratings committee meeting was convened to discuss the issue, but rather than confess its errors and downgrade a billion dollars of CPDOs, Moody's chose to keep quiet and hope for the best.[12] After the meltdown in CPDOs finally took place, and the cover-up became public, Moody's fired Mazataud, who today works for the French railways.

We Create Our Own Customers

During the early months of 2007, the trickle of collapsing U.S. subprime originators turned into a steady rain pounding down on Wall Street's mortgage desks. The invention of subprime default swaps allowed this once obscure regional lending market to be amplified and transmitted around the globe. However, despite the increasing erosion of the ABX index, the apocalyptic triumph of the shorts was still in the future. The consequences of allowing such a huge, leveraged, and unregulated off-track betting game on U.S. housing to flourish were as yet unimagined.

In early 2007, only the subprime mortgage bonds (residential mortgage-backed securities, or RMBS) were starting to suffer the effects. Via the ABX, the price signal was clearly visible. But there the flow of information stopped. There was no indication in the second stage: the triple-A-rated CDOs that bought the mortgage bonds. Nor was the gathering deluge foretold in the third stage: those SIVs and conduits that invested in these CDOs and RMBS and issued the ultimate product, the asset-backed commercial paper or IOUs that looked like cash. Even though these were all creations of the market, the arbitrage engine that drove them was designed to conceal market signals. It took six months for the subprime decay to work its way down the chain.

One reason it took so long was that the risk-takers—the buyers of the bottommost equity layers of CDOs whose investments were a hostage protecting the hate-to-lose investors higher up—were not actually taking significant risks. The trend was typified by a hedge fund from Evanston, Illinois, called Magnetar Capital. Running the fund's CDO strategy was Dave Snyderman, a former fixed income trader at Citadel Investments in Chicago. In mid-2006, Snyderman raised $1 billion in capital for what he would call the Constellation fund. The fund would take stakes in the equity or very riskiest slice of $50 billion worth of subprime CDOs that were created under its influence. The strategy had an additional twist in that Magnetar would also go short in the mezzanine layer of CDOs—the next level above equity—using default swaps.[13] In the wake of the financial crisis, some observers accused Magnetar of ulterior motives. They suggested that Snyderman was part of a plot by dealers to fool hate-to-lose investors into buying more senior layers of CDOs by presenting him as a genuine long-only investor while hiding the fact he was simultaneously short. Snyderman insists that this simply wasn't true, pointing out that his long-short strategy was no secret.

According to Magnetar, the truth was far more prosaic. The firm did not have a view either way on subprime. As Snyderman would say, it was all in the tradition of "going short Pepsi and long Coke."[14] Having spent his career building long-short trades designed to arbitrage hidden value in securities like convertible bonds, Snyderman applied the same logic to pieces of subprime CDOs, building an each-way bet because he didn't know which way the dice would fall.

All the same, the Constellation CDOs left an uneasy taste in the mouth. Arguably, they would not have existed without Magnetar's involvement as equity investor. But the crucial governance mechanism of CDO equity as a "hostage" against losses to reassure other investors had been undermined by Magnetar's each-way bet. And it is unclear that the arrangers actually told investors what Magnetar was really up to. Would you want to live in an apartment block whose ground floor janitor stood to get rich if the building burnt down?

Recycling unsold CDOs into CDO-squared deals was another way of staving off the final reckoning. Imagine a sausage factory where the manager finds the produce past its use-by date and no longer fit for human consumption. By tossing that tainted meat back into his grinders, the manager avoids having to write it down at a loss. The same thing happened in the CDO market, suppressing price information from the imploding subprime securitization market. The recycling worked because CDOs usually buy assets at *par*, or 100 percent of face value. At UBS or Citigroup, for instance, CDO arrangers would "mark to investor," assuming that the presence of a triple-*A* credit rating would guarantee a price of 100 percent for the output of their production line.[15] And because secondary market trading in pieces of CDOs was much more sparse than trading in the underlying mortgage bonds, where a lively two-way market existed by early 2007, placing these pieces in other CDOs meant that investors were unlikely to figure out what was going on.

Something like this happened after Oka Usi's departure from Barclays, when his Roman-named CDOs were recycled into each other late in 2001. It took months of back-and-forth questioning before Martin Halblaub realized the truth. And of course, the ratings agencies made the process easy because they classified CDOs as another "industry sector"; the CDO-squared was a familiar (albeit not well-understood) product. The 2007 crop of CDO-squareds would be linked to about twenty or thirty other CDOs, which themselves contained hundreds of other CDOs along with thousands of subprime mortgage bonds. A Merrill Lynch CDO chief, Ken Margolis, was so proud of his CDOs' investing in one another that colleagues recall him giving a presentation at a corporate offsite event with a slide entitled "We create our own customers."

Attempts to depict their cash flow plumbing graphically, as nested concentric rings of CDOs, earned them the sobriquet "eyes of Satan" (see figure 1). One notorious 2007 Merrill Lynch deal contained *itself* as an asset. When the bank's computers tried to calculate the interest due on the first payment date, Merrill's systems crashed.

The banks also became more desperate to sell bits of CDOs to *anyone*. While Merrill bankers had not been clever enough to invent something like Cheyne Finance, they did have a huge network of brokers in the United States to call upon. By the spring of 2007, a number of unusual sales began to take place. The city of Springfield, Massachusetts, discovered that about $12 million of surplus cash it had entrusted to Merrill Lynch brokers had been surreptitiously invested in CDOs. In Dallas, Texas, a telecom company called MetroPCS found that Merrill brokers had diverted some $130 million of its cash into

FIGURE 1

The "eyes of Satan"

A depiction of a CDO-cubed deal created by Merrill Lynch in early 2007. The node at the center of the graph represents the CDO itself, whose investments in other CDOs are represented by the inner ring of nodes, which in turn invest in each other, and additional CDOs represented by the outermost ring of nodes. These CDOs also used default swaps to invest in hundreds of mortgage bonds, which have been left out of the diagram for reasons of simplicity. To fully document a transaction like this would require a prospectus hundreds of millions of pages long.

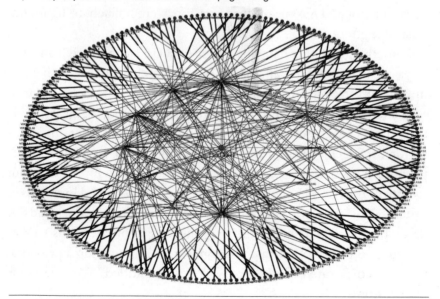

CDOs. Meanwhile, a pair of brokers at Credit Suisse managed to place some $1 billion of CDOs into their clients' portfolios with the simple ploy of replacing the letters *CDO* with *student loans*.[16] Ralph Cioffi, portfolio manager of a CDO-buying hedge fund sponsored by Bear Stearns, summed up Wall Street's desperate mood on the eve of Armageddon: "I think we need to go into outer space to find new buyers of CDOs."[17]

Not only were the big CDO-issuing banks desperate to stick their clients with the increasingly putrid inventory of their subprime warehouses, they were also in the business of fooling their own shareholders and regulators. Citigroup, for instance, reported during the first two quarters of 2007 that it had limited its subprime exposure to $13 billion—a big number, but not problematic for a huge diversified giant like Citigroup. In fact, Citigroup was concealing an additional exposure of $50 billion, via super-senior tranches of CDOs it had created. That detail that would eventually lead to a $75 million SEC fine.

The bank's regulators should have detected a deception of that size, and they had every incentive to look. As subprime finance companies began to topple like bowling pins in the first part of 2007, the Federal Reserve Board was sufficiently worried to request all the regional Federal Reserve banks to report on subprime problems in their region. For the New York Fed, an obvious object of concern was Citigroup, but their overly cozy relationship with senior management at the bank hobbled effective oversight and blocked the board in Washington, D.C., from learning what was really going on there.

There is disagreement about exactly how and when Fed chairman Ben Bernanke was briefed on Citigroup's subprime exposure. One former Federal Reserve Board official distinctly remembers an "entourage" arriving in D.C. from New York that spring to give a presentation to the Governors in the Federal Open Markets Committee (FOMC) meeting room, recalling how a female New York Fed bank examiner told Bernanke, "Citi doesn't have any additional subprime exposure."[18] However, the Board itself has no record of such a meeting taking place before September 2007, and New York Fed sources deny its existence. Whatever the facts behind the anecdote, Bernanke did claim in March that "subprime was contained" and in May that "we see no serious broader spill-over to banks." Had Bernanke known the truth he would have blanched.

Pop Goes the Bubble

The day the triple-*A* subprime CDO bubble began to pop was June 22, 2007, when Bear Stearns closed a leveraged hedge fund it managed and liquidated the fund's triple-*A* CDO assets. Two and a half weeks later, Moody's and S&P finally acknowledged that something was wrong with subprime, recognizing what the investment banks packaging the loans had known for months: that payment shock, fraudulent lending, and inability to refinance was driving the American homeowner off a cliff. A mass downgrade of mortgage bonds on July 10 was followed by warnings that subprime CDOs were next.

What alarmed investors and bankers was the acknowledgment, made explicitly by S&P, that the methodology used for rating subprime bonds was flawed. Within days, the highest, safest layers of the ABX index fell from par to the mid-90s, from where they would never recover.

On July 11, 2007, Andrew Forster, the head of AIGFP's credit trading desk in London, was talking on the phone to his American colleague, Alan Frost. They had just heard about the ratings agency announcements, and Forster was worried about the impact this would have on the $80 billion of CDOs AIG was exposed to. "We're going to have enormous downgrades," Forster said.[19] The downgrades would force people to sell, which would hammer prices. AIGFP earned over $50 million a year on the protection it had written on the CDOs, but it now faced the possibility of losing hundreds of times that amount. Frost dared to think the unthinkable: "Is there concern that that event could cause us to have to mark . . . ?" Forster cut him off: "We can't 'have' to mark it. Then we're fucked, basically."

The following day, Forster joined his boss, Joseph Cassano, to brief AIG senior management.[20] The company's CFO, Steve Bensinger, and chief credit officer, Kevin McGinn, listened as Cassano assured them that AIGFP's super-senior default swaps only had "modest" exposure to market pricing, and in any case, pricing had "remained largely stable." Forster kept his mouth shut, but he knew that the second stage of securitization had been breached. Even then, the $20 trillion shadow banking system was hiding behind the third stage, where the impact of the growing subprime crisis was still invisible.

On July 17, 2007, Nick Sossidis and Stephen Partridge-Hicks visited the offices of Standard & Poor's and Moody's in New York. The two founders of Gordian Knot had done well with their perfect android, Sigma, earning several million dollars per year apiece. Achieving this sort of income required persuading skittish investors to lend a lot of money to Sigma—some $57 billion in a combination of capital notes and commercial paper IOUs. Part of that was due to Sossidis's and Partridge-Hicks's skill at creating what they described as an old-fashioned bank outside the regulated banking system. But equally important were the triple-*A* ratings paid for by Sigma when it issued debt.

After LTCM's downfall in 1998, Sossidis and Partridge-Hicks had seen their enemy: it was the market approach to credit where a loss in confidence could freeze liquidity, pushing prices down and forcing borrowers to sell their assets. Gordian's two leaders had carefully retooled Sigma from within, attempting to protect their android from the specter of liquidity risk. By 2007 they were proud of their work and wanted the ratings agencies to give them additional credit for it. "Here's the results," Partridge-Hicks began the meetings with S&P and Moody's officials on July 17, speaking in his sincere, soft-spoken English manner. "The average life of our liabilities has doubled. We've mitigated contingent liquidity risk."

At Moody's, the Gordian duo were greeted by some of the firm's most senior staff, in deference to Raymond McDaniels's long history with them. There was Brian Clarkson, president, and Noel Kirnon, global head of structured finance. On speakerphone from London was the French accent of Paul Mazataud. At S&P, the panel of officials was headed by Joanne Rose and Richard Gugliada, the firm's senior structured finance ratings managers. In each meeting, the response was the same. Both Moody's and S&P officials nodded politely as Partridge-Hicks concluded his presentation. "Very impressive," they both said.

Now it was Nick Sossidis's turn to speak. The bearlike Greek was not self-effacing like his English partner. Detecting a slight hint of condescension, he took a more confrontational approach. "You don't look that impressed," he growled. He and Partridge-Hicks were frustrated with the ratings agencies. There were the old allegations of plagiarism, but they needed to keep the ratings agencies on board, so both partners bit their lips about that. But impossible to ignore was how Moody's and S&P had encouraged a boom in SIVs and SIV-lites that had piled into subprime mortgage bonds. The last straw for Sossidis was seeing Sigma lumped together as part of the "SIV sector" in Moody's and S&P reports. "You rated all these other competitors, you haven't applied the same high standards we have in running our business," he fumed. "They're increasingly commoditized, increasingly flaky, and there's a guaranteed problem coming here. Look at how much work we've done: we explained our improvements to you in 1999, we got it down in 2003. We think we've done a bang-up job improving the business and making it more resilient to a liquidity shock. You need to differentiate us more because there's a liquidity crisis coming and we're going to get tarred with the SIV brush if you don't help us reposition ourselves further away from the SIVs."

Partridge-Hicks could see that his partner's diatribe was falling on deaf ears. Moody's and S&P had too much at stake—if they downgraded Sigma's fly-by-night competitors, that would simply prove how foolish they had been to give their IOUs the highest ratings in the first place. Sossidis made one last plea: "Look, guys, we're trying to run a proper banking business here." The chill in the room was palpable, and the meetings came to a quick end.

Three days later, Moody's response came in the form of an e-mailed report. Its title said it all: *SIVs: An Oasis of Calm in the Sub-Prime Maelstrom*. Despite the fact that SIV-lites had invested 96 percent of their assets in mortgage bonds, Moody's declared that it expected ratings to "remain stable." A few weeks later, S&P's response arrived in Gordian Knot inboxes: "SIV ratings are weathering the current market disruptions," the report said. The analysts may have been sincere, but it was a laughably optimistic assessment.

Friday, July 27, 2007, is notable for two events in the timeline of the credit crisis. It is the day that the final CDO constructed from subprime bonds reached the market—a deal structured by Citigroup that was packed full of pieces of other unsold Citi CDOs. In a bracing bit of cynicism, it was called Bonifacius, after an ancient general sometimes called "the last of the Romans."[21]

The other notable event that day involved IKB. The Rhineland conduit, a living, breathing subprime-buying android, had expanded to the point of having sold more than $19 billion in IOUs. The umbilical cord that connected Rhineland to IKB had also grown, to the extent that other banks had also promised to repay the IOUs along with the Dusseldorf bank. Other banks were also providing the "enhancement" that was supposed to further protect IOU investors from any loss. One of these providers was Deutsche Bank, and it had grown alarmed about the deterioration in Rhineland's portfolio of subprime bonds and CDOs.

Deutsche knew the android was about to start drawing heavily on the umbilical cord, sucking in cash and additional enhancement, or capital, from the banks that had agreed to provide it. IKB would be on the hook for about 50 percent of that. The problem was that while the rest of the syndicate of banks connected to the umbilical cord were large and able to withstand the impending hemorrhage, IKB did not have the cash to spare, and Deutsche, which had extended loans to IKB, was worried about the Dusseldorf bank's going into bankruptcy. So that Friday, Deutsche's chief executive, Josef Ackermann, called the top German banking regulator and kicked off a frantic weekend in which money from the German government and other German banks was poured into IKB to prop it up. Ortseifen was fired, the first stage of his disgrace that would lead to a suspended prison sentence for fraud. The events of that hectic weekend in Dusseldorf heralded the start of the implosion of the shadow banking system. Hate-to-lose investors such as Mike Smith and the money market funds suddenly fled. In accordance with preordained android mechanisms, umbilical cords pulsed with billions of dollars of cash required to pay them back over a period of weeks. Rhineland and other bank-sponsored conduits were consolidated, as accountants had urged for years. Citigroup bought back its $25 billion of CDO-backed IOUs. It also had to consolidate some $80 billion worth of its SIVs.

More spectacular was the demise of the recent crop of umbilical-free androids. In the previous few months, Morgan Stanley and Barclays had been efficient in ensuring that their creations grew to their maximum possible size, in order to shift the maximum amount of subprime bonds from their balance sheets. By the end of August, Cheyne Finance, Golden Key, and Mainsail were all in trouble and were forced to sell assets. King County, Washington, owned IOUs issued by all three of them, and in Cheyne's case the collapse was so rapid that the county lost 40 percent of the money that Mike Smith had invested in this toxic structure, leading to a class-action fraud complaint against Morgan Stanley and the ratings agencies. Ed Cahill, the Barclays banker notorious for pushing SIV-lite structures to the limit, abruptly left the bank.

There was one android that was mostly clear of this mayhem. Sigma, created by Partridge-Hicks and Sossidis, which had reached $57 billion in size by July 2007, lost its short-term IOU investors at the same time as all the others did. But the protections painstakingly built in by its makers saved it from immediate destruction. The IOU investors were replaced by repo lenders at big banks, and medium-term bond-holders. But despite Partridge-Hicks's and Sossidis's protestations that "we have no subprime and no shit," it was only a temporary stay of execution.

The shutdown of the IOU market (or asset-backed commercial paper) that August was accompanied by a brutal revaluation by the ratings agencies. Thousands of CDOs and subprime bonds were downgraded. The abrupt realization that cash was better than near cash led to hundreds of billions of CDOs and subprime bonds being dumped in the market. At this point the long-term view of credit risk started to become irrelevant, as it was swamped by a flurry of decisions about uncertainty over a period of days, until the market could barely function. Now it was time to worry about the creators of the CDO boom and their big counterparties: the world's biggest financial institutions themselves. They were heading for catastrophe.

CHAPTER EIGHT

Massive Collateral Damage

The market-based system depends on price transparency to maintain the confidence of all parties, but that was undermined by the flood of complex, toxic assets no one could value. Smart firms like Goldman used their trading prowess to their advantage, creating price information that helped them extract huge collateral payments from counterparties like AIG. When plummeting market prices started eroding bank balance sheets, some investors realized that many big banks weren't properly capitalized and started betting on their collapse. Regulators were helpless as disaster loomed.

"Sorry to Bother You on Vacation . . ."

On July 26, 2007, the day before IKB hit the rocks, Andy Davilman, a Goldman Sachs salesman, sent a foreboding e-mail to a client. "Sorry to bother you on vacation. Margin call coming your way. Want to give you a heads up." The client was AIG Financial Products, and that e-mail was the opening salvo of what would become a life-or-death struggle between two financial heavyweights that led to one of the biggest bailouts in history.

Months before that e-mail was sent, Dan Sparks had used the radar system of derivatives to rebuild his mortgage department from the inside out, hidden from the view of Wall Street or even Goldman clients. Pete Ostrem, rooted in the old system of warehousing billions of mortgages in order to run a CDO factory, left in May, two days after Sparks handed his warehouse over to traders Dave Lehman, Michael

Swenson, and Josh Birnbaum with the order to "shut it all down." If you bought a CDO from Goldman that spring, you probably were unwittingly betting against traders like Josh Birnbaum, who had pushed Sparks to let him max out "the big short" that was already making John Paulson a billionaire. By late July the short positions were very big—some $4 billion in both single-name mortgage bonds and the ABX index.

In the last week of July, Ostrem's legacy CDO warehouse had lost the firm $230 million, but Birnbaum and his fellow traders had more than compensated for that with their short positions, which made $373 million. "Tells you what might be happening to people who don't have the big short," Goldman CFO David Viniar e-mailed to Goldman's president, Gary Cohn, on July 25.[1] Say, for example, to Goldman's biggest super-senior credit default swap counterparty, AIGFP.

Aside from a handful of CDOs such as Abacus, where AIGFP had taken on the super-senior risk directly with Sparks's desk, most of the AIGFP default swaps were done to hedge the underlying slices of super-senior deals owned by European banks. These Goldman clients bought a combined package of CDO and default swap hedge in order to exploit the Basel bank speed limits, with Goldman acting as middleman. The trader-conduit here was Ram Sundaram, and his job looked easy. All he had to do was take in protection payments from AIGFP and pay out slightly less money to the European banks, keeping the difference as profit. Since he wasn't in the mortgage department, it wasn't his responsibility to determine what the underlying subprime-linked CDOs were worth for collateral purposes. That job fell to Sparks and his traders, who up until July would send in monthly quotes for Sundaram, quotes that Cassano had recently told his bosses were "largely stable."

They were about to quickly become very unstable. Goldman risk manager Craig Broderick had seen the implications of Sparks's CDO price-slashing. There were hundreds of trades where the pricing used by Goldman's mortgage desk fed into the collateral plumbing the firm used to manage its credit exposure. That meant Goldman would be sending out margin calls. "We need to take a shot at determining our most vulnerable clients . . . this is getting lots of 30th floor attention right now," Broderick told colleagues in an e-mail, warning them that senior management was watching their moves closely.

Under pressure from Broderick, Sundaram requested that Sparks's team provide "actionable bids"—the price at which they would actually buy the super-senior CDOs underlying AIGFP's default swaps. While Goldman may insist that its pricing was independently verified by internal controllers, Sparks's traders, whose "marks" were a key input into the price calculations, were massively short and wanted to see prices as low as possible. The quotes received by Sundaram suggested that AIGFP's CDOs, which had flatlined at 100 percent ever since issue, were suddenly worth only 80 or 90 percent of their face value. (In the market world, remember, a plunge in value and a default are barely distinguishable.) If AIG were to suddenly go bust, then according to its own calculations, Goldman would have a $2 billion hole in its books. It was Broderick's job to minimize the chances of that happening, and the systems he had in place required Sundaram to go and get collateral from AIGFP.

Late on the afternoon of July 27, the same Friday that Deutsche Bank tipped off its regulator about problems at IKB, AIGFP received Goldman's demand for $1.8 billion in collateral. This was bad news for several reasons—the most pressing being that AIGFP couldn't come up with that much cash. On a conference call the following Monday with staff, Forster was shocked to hear that despite having hundreds of billions in bonds and derivatives, the firm only had $2 billion in cash on hand.

While IKB's bailout by the German government and other banks played out in the financial news headlines, Forster, Frost, and the others assigned by Cassano to handle the issue deliberated on how they could say no to Goldman's demands. Remember how the layers of CDOs operate. A Cayman Islands robot corporation owned a $1 billion worth of subprime bonds and raised money from investors by offering them risky or less risky floors in a virtual apartment block. As subprime bonds got hit by a wave of U.S. foreclosures, the effect on the CDO was as if a flood had swamped the building. AIGFP was in effect earning some danger money by occupying the topmost floors of the building. The question was: Had the flood reached AIGFP's level yet, and had it done any damage?

The answer depended on whom you asked . . . and believed. On August 1, during a conference call with Sundaram, Forster's colleague, Tom Athan, would recount how he heard the Goldman trader become increasingly agitated as he demanded that $1.8 billion.[2] "This has gone to the highest levels," Sundaram told them. "This is a test case."[3] Athan's answer was that of an insurance underwriter—Goldman had to prove that a loss had actually taken place before it could be paid. (That was what the "default" in credit default swap meant.) Sundaram's rebuttal was that its contracts with AIGFP were not insurance. If there were a default—if the flood damaged AIGFP's floor of the "building"—AIGFP would have to pay Goldman. But that was not the only mechanism in play here. The contracts were also derivatives, with rules that specified that the market was to provide a daily estimate of the damage, and AIGFP had to post collateral to cover the estimate. And the market was now showing damage.

But what was "the market"? AIGFP argued that super-senior slices of CDOs seldom traded. It was as if the lower floors of the "building" were rented to short-term tenants who were constantly making judgments about flood risk—these slices traded all the time—but the upper floors had a long-standing tenant: AIGFP. Here, there was no market, only the actuarial valuations that said *this* floor was perfectly safe. On the call, Sundaram insisted on "firm actionable bids." And he had a bid: the mortgage desk's fire sale price. In essence, Goldman was telling AIGFP that *it* was the market and AIGFP should pay up.

There was one other part of this stand-off that troubled AIGFP. During its banner year of writing super-senior swaps in 2005, it had taken on exposure to over 20 banks. All of them were entitled to use market prices and request collateral, just as Goldman was doing now. But here was what perplexed Forster and his colleagues: Goldman's prices were much lower than everyone else's. Goldman has since defended its valuations by listing trades that fed into its state-of-the-art pricing radar system.[4] But these disclosures don't completely dispel the concern that counterparties, including AIGFP, expressed in 2007: that the investment bank was exploiting its pricing power as a market-maker in order to obtain cash.

Realizing that they were getting nowhere with Sundaram, Forster and the others decided to involve their boss. Cassano would phone his old contact, Michael Sherwood, and try to patch things up. And so, on August 8, Goldman apparently blinked. Sherwood apologized to Cassano for the abrupt change in valuation, and the discrepancy with what other dealers were quoting.[5] Cassano remembers Sherwood telling him, "We haven't covered ourselves in glory."[6] While not budging on Goldman's valuation, Sherwood agreed to accept just $450 million in collateral. Relieved, Cassano and Forster went on vacation, while Broderick's risk management system required Goldman's derivatives desk to start buying default swap protection on AIG to cover the shortfall in collateral that the firm's prices said AIGFP still owed them.

Cracks in the Street

AIGFP's staff could only speculate, but Goldman, like the four other Wall Street securities firms, had a good reason to get in as much cash as possible that August. None more so than the smallest of the bunch, Bear Stearns, which had spooked the market with its CDO hedge fund fiasco in June.

On Friday, August 3, Mike Macchiaroli, associate director at the SEC's Trading and Markets division in Washington, D.C., was concerned. Over the previous decade, the "broker-dealers" that this veteran regulator had known since the 1970s had transformed themselves beyond recognition, spawning a web of affiliates—some regulated, some outside anyone's jurisdiction. Using derivatives and securitization, these firms were competing directly with the traditional banks in the post–Glass-Steagall world. That Friday rumors were flying that Bear Stearns was concealing big problems, and that its management was in turmoil. Macchiaroli phoned a colleague, Matt Eichner, at home that evening. "What the heck is going on there?" he said. "I'm really worried about Bear Stearns. This is a disaster waiting to happen. Get those people in on Sunday!" A call from the SEC went out to Bear Stearns, as Macchiaroli and Eichner booked flights to New York.

Bear Stearns had built up a $400 billion balance sheet with the help of repo, a $2 trillion market in short-term borrowing in which assets it wanted to own were pledged as collateral.[7] On the other side of that deal were money market mutual funds, such as Fidelity's $120 billion Cash Reserves Fund. In would come a $500 million loan to Bear, repayable in a few months. Bear would buy $500 million worth of equities or mortgage bonds with the money and pledge them with Fidelity. Normally, Bear could keep re-borrowing every few months and re-pledging the assets, continuing to own them with the help of repo lenders such as Fidelity. But on that fateful Friday in August, these lenders were worried about the mortgage market, to which Bear Stearns was heavily exposed. Unlike a standard commercial bank, Bear Stearns had no central bank standing behind it, ready to take up the slack if repo lenders pulled out.

As he greeted Macchiaroli and Eichner at Bear Stearns's offices on Madison Avenue that Sunday afternoon, Bear Stearns's CFO, Sam Molinaro, Jr., was not taken in by Macchiaroli's attempts at levity. "This is a formal meeting," he had warned colleagues. "There is stuff going on and we've got to respect their need to know." That same morning, he had attended a board meeting in which Warren Spector, Bear Stearns's co-president, was fired, taking the fall for the firm's CDO hedge fund disaster.

Reassuring his SEC visitors that the high-level management shakeup was not a sign of worse things to come, Molinaro fielded questions about Bear Stearns's numbers. *What's your capital? How are earnings? What's the liquidity situation?* Then Macchiaroli and Eichner zeroed in on their big worry: a loss in confidence that could force a fire-sale. *Are there illiquid assets that are going to have to be sold to raise money?*

They knew that taking losses in a forced sale would force Bear to take a huge hit to its capital. At that point, Bear Stearns was balancing its $400 billion balance sheet on a capital sliver of just $12 billion—a leverage ratio of 33 times. From the outside, Bear Stearns looked like a powerful, thriving investment bank with 13,000 employees. But Macchiaroli felt uneasy. If shareholders lost confidence, and the likes of Fidelity pulled the plug, Bear would be sucked down the drain. And lacking the Fed's ability to lend Bear money, he knew there was nothing the SEC could do about it. Looking back on the meeting today, the participants agree that Bear should either have chosen to raise capital or been forced to raise it by the SEC. But it seems that wasn't discussed.

Returning to Washington that evening, Macchiaroli and Eichner phoned their SEC colleagues. "They're confident they're going to weather the storm," they reported. "But we'll have to keep a close watch on them."

In the short term, Bear Stearns managed to quash the rumors and keep operating, and Molinaro was vindicated. But he noticed troubling signs all the same. In the absence of a central bank or the Federal Deposit Insurance Corporation (FDIC) protecting their interests, Bear Stearns's repo lenders had to look after themselves. They started requesting bigger "haircuts," or additional collateral covering their loans. And they drastically reduced the timescale of the loans, from six months to periods as short as overnight. Like cartoon characters running manically on the spot, Molinaro's treasury team would have to phone each day and renew the repo agreements. Each day they would have to speak to clearing banks—such as J.P. Morgan—that provided huge temporary credit lines every morning while the overnight agreements were renegotiated.

As veterans in their fields, both Macchiaroli and Molinaro knew how things used to work when securities markets became troubled and dysfunctional in this way. In October 1987, when the stock market crashed, New York Fed president Gerald Corrigan opened a spigot of government money for the big commercial banks on Wall Street and told them to lend to the securities firms across the Glass-Steagall divide. It worked, and the market bounced back. That pipeline was still supposed to be there in August 2007, but Molinaro and his counterparts at other investment banks noticed it wasn't working properly.

The world had changed. Using their phalanxes of SPV robots, securities firms had become massive lenders to American consumers, usurping the traditional role of the banks. The commercial banks had gotten into the securities business, sponsoring SIVs and conduits to hold the same mortgage and credit card bonds and CDOs that the likes of Bear Stearns manufactured. These financial androids issued IOUs to support their debt, closing the consumer finance loop by attracting money funds like Fidelity. After the near-meltdown of IKB, that market disappeared virtually overnight, and the banks—Citigroup, HSBC, Dresdner Bank, ABN AMRO, and others—suddenly had to buy back the assets to prevent their stricken androids from collapse. On August 8, the European Central Bank opened the liquidity floodgates for its charges, followed by the Fed. By September, the U.S. Treasury entered the android support business itself, trying to marshal banks into supporting an LTCM-style industry bailout of SIVs called the Master Liquidity Enhancement Conduit, or MLEC. As their own creations, the SIV androids, sucked the Fed and ECB pipeline dry, the commercial banks were unwilling or unable to support the balance sheets of firms like Bear Stearns.

Was it risk management or something more ruthless? According to a former senior SEC official, "I could sit here and tell a credible story that J.P. Morgan and the other clearing banks were doing what any rational bank would do to protect its own equity. But I could also tell you a story that says the securities firms had become competitors in a way that wasn't the case under Glass-Steagall, and when a situation came about where they could determine who lived or died, the banks did what capitalists are supposed to do."

No commercial bank looked more ruthless than J.P. Morgan, which, having steered clear of SIVs, appeared to torpedo the Treasury's MLEC initiative. The giant bank likes to insist that it was a steadfast "good citizen" when it came to helping Wall Street through the crisis. However, according to a senior fund manager involved in the discussions, "Some of the players were along for the ride to shoot a hole in the bottom of the boat—they just didn't want it to work. To say I was suspicious of J.P. Morgan's enthusiasm for the project would be polite."

In this tough environment, the most aggressive Wall Street securities firm of all was not going to roll over and accept the situation. As kingpin of the credit derivatives market, Goldman Sachs had its own ways of keeping the cash flowing in.

Children Driving Lamborghinis

At Goldman, the financial quarter that closed the end of August 2007 was a very good one for the mortgage division, as well as for the firm as a whole. Although the net gain was offset by a write-down on residential loans and Ostrem's CDO portfolio, the short positions led by Birnbaum made over $2 billion. With the firm using the subprime derivatives radar system as aggressively as it did, Sherwood's collateral concession was only a stay of execution for AIGFP. The inability to get its pricing recognized by AIGFP—and the shortfall in the collateral it felt it was owed—was more than just an affront to Goldman. As part of what its CFO David Viniar referred to as "liquidity pre-funding," Goldman needed its collateral machine to run perfectly.[8] In September, Sherwood and Cassano met to formalize a protocol for handling CDO margin calls, which required their staffs to again discuss the thorny issue of pricing. Forster led the discussions on AIGFP's side, while Sparks was brought in to present Goldman's case.

First, Sparks offered to sell AIGFP the underlying bonds it had written protection on, at a discount. He would then rip up the default swap. "You say it's at par," Sparks told Forster. "We think the price is 95 and you have to put up one unit of margin. But we will trade in this market, so if you think our price is too low, we'll sell it to you at the price."

But Forster had no interest in buying a CDO, even at a 5 percent discount. "We don't want to take any more risk right now," he told Sparks, who countered by offering an incentive for AIGFP to accept Goldman's lower price. "If the market really is 5 points higher than where we say it is, you can go and sell it." But Forster did not want to fall into the trap of helping Goldman establish a traded price that would bolster its remaining collateral demands. He rejected Sparks's proposal.

There was an obvious way to break this impasse: credit default swap documentation calls for third-party dealers to provide an independent price if counterparties disagree. But Goldman didn't trust the motives of third parties, fearing they might provide inflated prices that supported AIGFP's case. Broderick pointed out that banks such as Société Générale or UBS didn't want to acknowledge write-downs on *their* CDO portfolios. "A lot of the misinformation on prices in the market is not due to firms' legitimately being unable to get good prices," he argued. "Rather, it is because they are unwilling to accept the price information because it is too painful."

Meanwhile, the banks that had made those optimistic valuations of super-senior CDOs—the ones that had buoyed AIGFP in its battle with Goldman—were getting pummeled by the market. In tandem with its battle against AIGFP, Goldman had been in a collateral war with Morgan Stanley, where a proprietary trader named Howie Hubler had sold $16 billion of protection on super-senior CDOs at the end of 2006. Here, Goldman was unwittingly assisted by Deutsche Bank's Greg Lippmann, who together with his firm's CDO group, had bought $4 billion of the protection Hubler offered. While Goldman's aggressive campaign to extract collateral from counterparties may have been driven by the need for liquidity that it couldn't obtain from commercial banks or the Fed, such a justification didn't apply to Deutsche Bank, which had ready access to ECB funding in Frankfurt. But Lippmann, whom Deutsche assigned additional responsibilities for valuations in summer 2007, was under pressure to realize profits on his proprietary short position in order to protect the German bank from subprime losses elsewhere. As recounted by author Michael Lewis in his book *The Big Short*, Lippmann took a hard line with Morgan Stanley and eventually enlisted the help of senior Deutsche staff to demand $2 billion in collateral that Hubler had refused to pay.[9] That prompted Morgan Stanley senior management to examine Hubler's positions and finally accept Lippmann's pricing, leading to an announcement to investors on November 7.[10]

Forever cocky, Lippmann (who would pocket a $50 million bonus for his efforts in 2007) spun Hubler's blow-up as a cautionary tale akin to keeping kids away from matches. He describes Hubler as someone who wasn't grown-up enough to play with new derivatives without adult supervision. "You have a situation where people always traded very small sizes and nothing ever blew up. It's like people were always driving golf carts on a very straight road. Because of derivatives—*voilà*—you can trade enormous sizes, so it's as if that golf cart was suddenly replaced with a Ferrari. Now, we have this fast car—Let's go! But immediately after getting in the car, the road changed from a very straight road to a very winding road."[11] But Lippmann was not merely a passive observer of Hubler's driving skills—he also helped force him off the road.

If Morgan Stanley wasn't enough of a data point to show to AIGFP, there was Merrill Lynch, which in late October disclosed a $6 billion loss in super-senior CDOs and fired its chief executive, Stan O'Neal.[12] A few days later, Citigroup and UBS also revealed nasty secrets about their CDO positions and fired senior executives in turn.[13] These developments worried Andrew Forster, who saw Merrill now providing lower valuations on its super-senior positions with his firm. Bowing to this shifting consensus, AIGFP upped the collateral it handed over to Goldman, to a total of $1.5 billion.

It wasn't enough. At the end of November, Sherwood phoned Cassano with an ominous message: "We think the market's going our way." Two days later came Goldman's margin call for an additional $2 billion. Worse still, an accountant working for AIG's auditors,

PricewaterhouseCoopers (PWC), Tim Ryan, had learned of the market prices that Goldman was providing in its collateral calls (it may have been a coincidence, but PWC was Goldman's auditor too). Ryan now insisted that this was a market "data point" that should be used to revalue AIGFP's CDO portfolio.

Cassano participated in a conference call with stock analysts on December 5 to discuss AIG's earnings for the third quarter. In the call, he joked about the pessimism in market pricing. "Credit is not going to completely disappear. It's the second oldest profession—somebody needed to borrow money for the oldest profession." Quizzed by analysts about the margin calls, Cassano made light of his counterparties for trying to exploit market turmoil by using low-ball valuations to raid AIG's cash pile. While he did not mention Goldman, the target of his mockery was easy to guess. "The market's kind of screwed up . . . We say to them, 'Well, we don't agree with your numbers.' And they go, 'Oh,' and they go away . . . it's like a drive-by in a way."[14]

Two days later, Cassano made a last-ditch effort to save his career: he wrote to Goldman, boldly demanding the return of the $1.5 billion that AIGFP had posted. Two weeks later, he made the same demand in an e-mail to Sherwood.

Goldman's financial controller, Brian Lee, studied the spreadsheets detailing the AIG CDO trades carefully. "This is a total drag on our time," Sparks complained to him. "We just want to get the right collateral so we can go and do our jobs." But Lee felt the firm's reputation was at stake if it couldn't get a market price for the AIGFP swaps that justified its collateral calls. Lee declared that Goldman had to come up with a credible price. Since the CDO market was virtually frozen, Goldman would have to create some facts on the ground. It was what Lee called a *trade spot*, executing trades in order to get a handle on what things are worth, or, as he explained to Sparks, "You're going to have to sell some of your portfolio to demonstrate where the price actually is."

Hitting Their Mark

Over in London, Yusuf Alireza was oblivious to the Goldman-AIGFP death match. A handsome, gregarious man with a clipped black beard, Alireza had rapidly ascended the ranks of investment banking greatness to become head of European sales at Goldman Sachs. Alireza had good reason to feel jaded about Sparks's mortgage products. At the start of 2007, Alireza had deployed his European salespeople for Sparks's benefit, using them to sell exposure to super-senior CDOs such as Fabrice Tourre's Abacus 2007 AC-1 trade to clients like ABN AMRO. By October, the CDOs had performed so badly that Alireza e-mailed Sparks, reminding him to recognize the efforts of his salespeople because these blown-up clients were no longer accepting their phone calls. He wrote in the e-mail, "Dan. Real bad feeling across European sales about some of the trades we did with clients. The damage this has done to our franchise has been significant. Aggregate loss for our clients on just these 5 trades alone is 1bln+."[15] Having been burned badly, these banking clients were unlikely to buy Goldman mortgage products again. But as he scanned the price quotes e-mailed out by Sparks's traders, Alireza saw how he could help another breed of client—hedge funds—exploit the market disruption. As he liked to tell colleagues, the trick was to "get new clients into the opportunity quickly."

David Gorton was one of the big success stories of London's ten-year financial boom. Following a stellar career trading interest rate swaps for J.P. Morgan, he and two colleagues had set up a hedge fund called London Diversified Fund Management (LDFM). Having started out making some astute bets in the wake of the 1998 LTCM crisis, Gorton built up his main hedge fund—the London Diversified Fund—to $3.4 billion. Alireza, who had known Gorton for years, felt he had just the kind of deal the hedge fund manager was looking for.[16] Alireza proposed buying and selling default swaps linked to pieces of subprime CDOs, or what was known as a correlation trade. The prices came from Goldman's mortgage desk in New York—Alireza produced some graphs that showed how cheap the Goldman price was compared with the actuarial estimates of their value. Gorton took the bait. While the precise details of the transaction remain unclear, the timing and sheer cheapness of the deal being offered suggest that what Alireza innocently saw as a good opportunity for his client, Gorton, was none other than a trade spot cooked up by Lee and Sparks to justify the low CDO valuations being shown to AIGFP.

As soon as these trades went through at the start of 2008, Sparks called Cassano. "Joe, we have some data points for you. We did these trades on CDOs very similar to yours." At this point, AIG's auditors, PWC, were receiving all the collateral communications from Goldman. The unconvincing stance of Cassano in demanding his collateral back, combined with the compelling evidence that Goldman was trading in a market Cassano claimed was "screwed up," alarmed PWC's Ryan so much that he argued to AIG's board that the company had a "material weakness" in its accounts. As the gatekeeper between AIG and its share-holders, this volte-face by PWC required it to make its concerns public. This had devastating consequences for Cassano, and Sparks now detected defeat in his adversary's voice. After talking to Cassano again about the collateral payments, Sparks told colleagues, "That was ugly."

AIGFP's defeat proved just how powerful the "derivatization of credit" (as Sherwood called it) had become. By trading with hedge fund clients, Goldman could refute the actuarial dismissal of markets as "screwed up" and enforce its collateral agreements. Which doesn't mean LDFM did well on the deal. While most of the trades Alireza sold to Gorton were successful, a small number went against him in 2008. The London hedge fund lost $400 million on its correlation trades with Goldman and other dealers and froze investor redemptions that November.

Dinallo's Dilemma

The headquarters of the New York State insurance department are only a couple of blocks from the New York Fed in lower Manhattan's Financial District. The regulator's status as a state agency lent a certain dowdiness to the building: the security guards were a few pounds heavier than their lean New York Fed counterparts and didn't sport the marksmanship badges that backed up the Fed's undercurrent of manly power.

The department's chief, Eric Dinallo, had been appointed in January 2007 by Governor Eliot Spitzer. Looking and sounding the part of a tough New York lawyer, Dinallo had inherited a team that handled day-to-day supervision of the industry, led by a gruff Irish American deputy named Mike Moriarty. Their work combined protection of property and casualty (P&C) and life insurance consumers on the one side with maintaining the solvency of insurers, including AIG's New York–based subsidiaries, on the other. It wasn't a sexy beat. Every week, press releases bearing Dinallo's name went out, warning New Yorkers about, say, the quirks of rental car policies or flood insurance scams.

When the subprime crisis hit, Dinallo was initially thankful that it had passed New York's insurance department by—and AIG in particular. But by January 2008, he was no longer sanguine. Moriarty explained to him that an obscure but troubling issue had cropped up in a corner of AIG's sprawling $1 trillion empire. It sprang from a kind of complacency that comes to certain insurers and pension funds that have the luxury of owning stocks and bonds for long periods of time in order to back policies and retirement plans.

Sure, you have to protect policyholders who trust you with their money, which is why you bought the assets on their behalf in the first place. But who's to stop you from earning a little extra cash with those assets before the policyholders need them? With twelve separate U.S. life insurance subsidiaries, AIG had a lot of policyholder assets to play with—some $76 billion—that were managed by a special department called the global investment group. This department found it could earn extra money for shareholders by providing a service to Wall Street called *securities lending*.

Traders at banks and hedge funds like to borrow stocks and bonds (for a fee) in order to sell them short. In other words, they speculate against falls in price, then buy the securities back again and return them to their rightful owners. Some pension funds and insurers object to short selling and refuse to lend their securities out, but most were happy to comply in return for a few points in fees.[17]

In the mid-2000s, Win Neuger, who ran the global investment group for AIG, had the bright idea of taking this notion further. Normally, securities lenders park the cash collateral received for lent securities in the safest possible Treasury bills or government bonds so that they can redeem the loans quickly, if necessary. But with $76 billion to play with, Neuger spotted a way of making extra money for AIG. He ventured into the valley of subprime robots, buying the triple-*A* slices of New Century or Option One mortgage bonds.

That worked very well until about July of 2007, when those markets froze. Margin calls meant that the traders needed their cash. That shouldn't have been a problem if AIG had been able to sell the mortgage bonds it owned and repay the securities lenders, but from that summer on, it could only sell them at a loss. Through its greed in squeezing out some additional "rent" from its policyholders, AIG had transformed its life insurance companies into something resembling Bear Stearns. Securities lending was similar to repo lending, which in turn was similar to money market funds accepting IOUs from SIV androids. That was a strange pickle for an insurance company to be in. As regulator of AIG's New York insurance companies, Moriarty was quietly pushing AIG to wind down the portfolio without suffering a loss.[18]

That was trouble enough for Dinallo, but now something else came at him. This problem had begun in an obscure sector of the market, where the insurance companies had names like MBIA (Municipal Bond Insurance Association), ACA, and Ambac, and provided a unique service. Since the 1970s, these companies had specialized in the insurance of municipal bonds, an intensely political business in which policyholders were small towns and districts across America. In return for a premium, bonds that financed museums, sewers, and schools would be wrapped with the insurer's triple-A credit rating, lowering the interest payments. These monolines, as they were called, had an incestuous relationship with the credit ratings agencies, whose triple-A seal of approval was essential to their business model. The business was dependent on the actuarial world at every step, like a traditional insurance company pooling the risks of fires or unexpected death. The ratings agencies checking the municipal bonds, the monolines writing insurance policies on them, and the ratings agencies finally issuing triple-A ratings that reassured buyers that the monolines could pay out on bond insurance— it all depended on the idea of credit being held for the long term in a portfolio where diversified risks supposedly balanced out and justified the magical triple-A rating.

Then the monolines began insuring securitized bonds issued by banks. In 2006, Ambac earned $1 billion in revenues and paid its chief executive $11 million. By the summer of 2007, Ambac and MBIA had insured nearly $400 billion of mortgage bonds and CDOs, displacing much of their traditional municipal activity.

Despite the Wall Street–style revenues and perks, even as the subprime crisis was brewing early in 2007, all appeared well in the actuarial world. One of the first items waiting in Dinallo's in-box when he became superintendent was a request from MBIA to reduce its capital needed to pay claims by $1 billion and pay that money to its shareholders. With a twinge of trepidation, Dinallo told MBIA to cut its dividend to $500 million.

Six months later, it was obvious that the monolines were in trouble, when Ambac and MBIA both reported billions in unexpected CDO-related losses and fired their chief executives.[19] At this point the monolines were struggling to retain their triple-A ratings. (They would ultimately be downgraded in June 2008, and by November 2010, Ambac filed for bankruptcy.) "Why did we ever let them do this?" Dinallo asked his grizzled deputy.

The dealers buying all that monoline insurance were motivated by the same reasons that drove Goldman to hedge its CDOs with AIGFP. In order for its illusion of fully hedged efficiency to work, the market-based world had to keep one foot in the actuarial world. So it was that Merrill Lynch, a securities firm based firmly in the market world whose leverage of 30 to 1 was seen as risky, could pile on additional risk by purchasing insurance from monolines whose leverage of over 100 to 1 justified a triple-A rating.

As with Goldman and AIGFP, the important thing for the banks was that the hedges had to work, had to pay off. If the insurance company found a way of wriggling out, then the whole system fell apart. MBIA, Ambac, and the others had obliged, setting up special subsidiaries called *transformers* that traded default swaps with the banks. That gave those banks the kind of market protection that trumped the actuarial view, allowing dealers to suck cash out of the monolines, like Goldman was doing with AIG.

As a former Wall Street lawyer, Dinallo realized why the banks had been so keen to do business with the monolines. "The banks are saying, 'I have a supercharged insurance policy—an insurance policy, plus all these acceleration bells and whistles.' But is this really an insurance policy?" This time he answered the question himself. "We could have had these written straight up as insurance policies, but Wall Street wanted it done by CDS. We were trying to be user friendly, believe it or not. Why did we let this happen?"

New York's insurance regulator, seeing his charges in mortal danger, encouraged them to fight back and resist the dealers' demands. Dinallo saw default swaps as a dangerous innovation that had fooled the insurance industry. Now, the humble municipalities that depended on bond insurance needed his protection. The devil's derivative needed to be put back in its box. Throughout 2008 and 2009, the big banks would write down tens of billions apiece in monoline protection as it became increasingly obvious how worthless it was.

Dinallo didn't yet know that the two problems on his radar screen—securities lending and default swaps—were connected within AIG. (AIGFP had already written more default swap protection than Ambac and MBIA combined.) As collateral flowed out of AIGFP into the hands of Goldman and others, the parent company had to make up the difference. But meanwhile, with the encouragement of Dinallo and other state insurance supervisors, AIG's life subsidiaries were also calling on the parent company to compensate them for selling mortgage bonds at a loss as the securities lending program wound down.

AIG senior management was now caught in a pincer movement between insurance regulators and investment banks. Dinallo liked to tell people that AIG's New York insurance subsidiaries were protected by what he called a *moat of solvency*: highly cautious actuarial rules requiring hefty buffers of capital that could not be touched by the parent company. That was the idea, at least, until Win Neuger's global investment group reached across the "moat" and lent out the subsidiaries' assets in return for mortgage bonds. However, it was not Dinallo's job to regulate AIG itself—that was the responsibility of the U.S. Office of Thrift Supervision (OTS). AIGFP's strategy of using default swaps to take on an additional $500 billion of CDO credit risk had been waved through by the OTS supervisors, and it barely featured in ratings agency calculations. S&P, for example, referred to the triple-A rating of the CDOs in calculating AIG's double-A rating. Oddly enough, the legal rights of Goldman and other counterparties depended on this actuarial view, in addition to the market prices used to compute margin calls. If S&P or Moody's were to downgrade AIG to a single-A rating, $13 billion of additional collateral would immediately become payable.

In February 2008, AIG was finally forced by PWC to admit a "material weakness" in its accounting and restated its numbers. The ratings agencies then declared that the giant had a "negative outlook." Cassano resigned in March (although he stayed on for six months as a consultant, with a $1 million per month retainer), and by May, AIG had fired its chief executive and was raising $12.5 billion from shareholders in order to pay margin calls. Seeing that Goldman's collateral calls were sucking the life out of the company, Sparks was finding it painful to talk to AIGFP. "This is a very hard thing," he said to colleagues. "You don't want to be the one making that call."

Too Much to Bear

Ever since he and a fellow SEC examiner had visited Bear Stearns's Madison Avenue office the previous August, Mike Macchiaroli had been haunted by the feeling that the Wall Street's smallest, least-diversified securities firm was vulnerable to a run-on-the-bank by its repo lenders, but he was powerless to prevent the disaster he suspected was increasingly likely. Despite the SEC's increased reviews of Bear's activities, he feared the worst as the subprime malaise deepened.

At the end of January 2008, Macchiaroli exclaimed to Matt Eichner, "I'm worried that this firm is going to fail on me!" He and Eichner immediately flew to New York to meet with Molinaro. The Bear Stearns CFO had become used to the SEC's reviews and didn't think the meeting was out of the ordinary. "Everything's fine," he told his visitors, fully believing his own words. "We're liquid. We're going to make money." In December, Bear had reported its first ever quarterly loss, and a disbelieving Macchiaroli shot back, "And how are you going to make money? There's no private client business here—you can't make money. How can you carry this overhead?" Molinaro offered soothing reassurances—"We'll be all right," he said. As Macchiaroli left the meeting, he had a sudden flash of doubt. Half-joking, he asked a final question: "Sam—you aren't going to fail on me, are you?" Molinaro laughed it off as a wisecrack, say people who attended the meeting. "Ha ha," he said. "That's funny."

Six weeks later, Bear Stearns was dead. In mid-March, repo counterparties apologetically told Molinaro, "I know we've been lending you money against mortgage collateral for years, but we're not rolling today. We're out." Within days, the firm was taken over by J.P. Morgan, which used the Fed money pipeline to prop up Bear Stearns's balance sheet. The real story was not so much how J.P. Morgan scooped up a consumer finance competitor, but rather how the New York Fed ended up owning $30 billion of Bear's most toxic assets, including New Century's NCHET mortgage robots and chains of hotels. Just like its favorite bank, Citigroup, which deployed financial innovation to keep things off its balance sheet, the New York Fed created its own robo corporation, called Maiden Lane I, to maintain the official line that it didn't undertake risky lending, but the pretense was wafer-thin. Equally thin was the pretense that traditional securities firms like Goldman or Lehman were not part of the commercial banking system—after Bear went down, the New York Fed effectively opened its discount window to those firms for the first time. Over the next fourteen months, the Federal Reserve would make loans against collateral of $8.9 trillion to investment banks, including the U.S. securities trading subsidiaries of foreign banks such as Barclays.[20] From that point on, it was an open secret within government circles that the craziness in banking and housing (including Fannie Mae and Freddie Mac) was soon going to become a massive problem for taxpayers.

Capital Punishment

On the fortieth floor of a Manhattan skyscraper, John Paulson was doing some important calculations. In 2007, he had stayed with his short subprime default swap positions as the androids toppled and collapsed all the way down to zero. That earned his investors $15 billion, and almost $4 billion for him. Toward the end of the year, he began making the connection between the triple-B layer of subprime mortgage androids and the junior debt of mortgage banks.

The clues were to be found in the herds of bond-issuing androids clustered around the biggest U.S. mortgage originators. Paulson knew which banks were the worst originators and were likely to run into problems as a result. Better still, credit default swaps on the debt of banks like Lehman, Countrywide, IndyMac, and Washington Mutual could be bought cheaply in 2007. Although the return on capital would be smaller, these anti-bank bets (a description Paulson hates) would make him more money than his subprime mortgage trade.

Paulson was surprised that the U.K. bank Abbey (part of Spain's Santander), announced in April 2008 that it would no longer be offering 100 percent loan-to-value (LTV) self-certified mortgages. "That blew me away," he recalls.[21] Liar loans with no money down? Mortgages that risky had not been available in the United States since January 2007, which told Paulson that the United Kingdom's housing market was following the disastrous path of the U.S. housing market, but with a fifteen-month lag.

Paulson's vulture eyes landed on Britain just as the Royal Bank of Scotland (RBS) was asking shareholders for $24 billion in additional capital. On April 22, equity analysts gathered in London's Bishopsgate for a presentation by RBS board members, led by chief executive Sir Fred Goodwin and chairman Sir Tom McKillop. Nicknamed "Fred the Shred" because of his abrasive management style, Goodwin had been knighted for "services to banking," but during the time lag between Britain's housing market's catching up with America's, RBS shareholders and regulators had allowed Goodwin's megalomania to let rip. In January, they let RBS consummate a €72 billion takeover of Dutch bank ABN AMRO (split with two other European banks). Next came the nasty surprises: $12 billion in write-downs from America, where the British and Dutch had both bought regional banks and trading firms, and gone headlong into subprime and CDOs.

Among the analysts in the audience that day was Simon Samuels from Citigroup. He asked about leverage, and the RBS finance director, Guy Whittaker, answered, "I think a number of you rightly estimated ratios of about 1.5, 1.4 [percent] toward the end of last year." The number that Whittaker was referring to was the equity-to-asset ratio that was used by U.S. banking analysts and regulators to judge bank solvency. Crucially, this ratio strips out something called *goodwill*, or the value a company places on acquisitions. In other words, if you took out what RBS thought ABN was worth based on an inflated price, then the merged bank was leveraged some sixty or seventy times.

Paulson couldn't believe what he was hearing. If RBS were a U.S. bank, a leverage ratio under 2 percent would have forced the FDIC to shut it down immediately. Even a well-run bank in a benign economy could not be trusted to protect its depositors with sixty times leverage. RBS, on the other hand, faced headwinds from thousands of mortgage borrowers exposed to the United Kingdom's inflated housing market, as well as its foolhardy U.S. ventures. "This bank is weak," Paulson laughed to himself. "Basel has created delusions!"

He knew RBS had a balance sheet larger than the U.K. economy, measured by GDP. Negligent British regulators had set this bank up to fail, in much the same way that U.S. regulators had set up the subprime fiasco. Paulson swooped in; he borrowed 144 million shares of the bank, or 0.87 percent of RBS equity, selling it short in the hope of profiting from an impending meltdown. He looked around for other over-leveraged British banks and made similar short equity bets: 0.95 percent of Halifax Bank of Scotland (HBOS) and 1.18 percent of Barclays.[22] He staked almost $2 billion in shorting British bank equities.

For its regulator, the Financial Services Authority, RBS was Britain's Citigroup. One former senior FSA manager, Oliver Page, commented about the firm. "I thought RBS was one of the better-run banks. Fred the Shred just got things done. They weren't one of the banks that I got annoyed with because they wouldn't do a proper stress test."[23] Yet, having declared in its annual report that its 99-day-in-100 value at risk (VAR) was $90 million at the end of February 2008, why was RBS reporting a trading book loss of $12 billion just a month later? As with UBS, Merrill Lynch, and Citigroup, the British bank exposed once again the truth that—Goldman excepted—risk managers trusted by regulators were lackeys of powerful executives, under instructions to manipulate the statistics. Within the FSA that spring, the bank examiner responsible for RBS, Clive Adamson, was overheard saying in a fit of exasperation that the bank's Basel-approved disclosures were "a pack of lies," and was reproved by his more politically correct colleagues. (The FSA insists that this account of its machinations is "inaccurate," and in June 2010 threatened me with criminal prosecution for attempting to write about its supervision of RBS.)

Nothing's Free, Not Even in a Free Fall

By the summer of 2008, everyone knew the flood was here, and there was little high ground left. Many players in this free-for-all market were going to get very wet, if not drowned. In June, Lehman Brothers had to write down its portfolio and raise $6 billion in capital, while depending on the Fed's lending facility to support its balance sheet. The SEC's Macchiaroli, who was still supposed to be regulating Lehman, felt underqualified to question the optimistic valuations the firm was using for its real estate assets. He and the Fed just had to hope that Lehman could find a buyer—a savior—before it collapsed. In London, FSA officials, who like Macchiaroli had no ability to prop up their charges, were already talking to the U.K. Treasury about plans for bailing out the big U.K. banks. A former Treasury minister, Kitty Ussher, recalls a briefing in July outlining bailout plans for banks whose names were replaced with animals or planets to preserve secrecy. They knew what was coming.

Regulators in the United States were now playing a desperate game of catch-up, scrambling to do what little they could, even if that meant keeping investors in the dark. Lehman Brothers's chief executive, Dick Fuld, panicked by David Einhorn's famous short-selling campaign against his firm, persuaded the SEC to restrict short selling of large financial firms. A couple of months after Fannie Mae and Freddie Mac raised shareholder capital, Congress gave the Treasury Department new powers to take over the imploding mortgage behemoths. Those powers came not a moment too soon: Fannie and Freddie were placed in conservatorship by the Treasury Department in early September, stripping away once and for all the private sector fig leaf of what had always been a massive government housing subsidy scheme.

Life—and Death—on Planet Derivative

By 2008, the traditional world of banking that had held sway for hundreds of years had been overthrown by the market system. Not only did bank share prices reflect changes in investor confidence from one day to the next, but so did the default swap markets. Thus, as the prices of bank shares declined, John Paulson received margin payments on his short bets. Meanwhile, as default swap spreads on bank-subordinated debt drifted upward, he was steadily receiving collateral thanks to his buying of protection. For sellers of such protection, cash was flowing out the door. On August 7, 2008, RBS paid $840 million to

Goldman Sachs in order to close out its super-senior default swap position in the Abacus CDO, which it had inherited from ABN AMRO. Goldman Sachs then turned around and paid that money to Paulson.[24]

For Paulson and the small number of winners that summer, the stars—and numbers—were aligned as never before. Some laud these geniuses for making "the greatest trade ever," but Eric Dinallo thought that the tools they used—default swaps—were infernal machines sucking the financial system dry. In August 2008, he left his office on Liberty Street and walked the few blocks to the fortresslike New York Fed. He had spent the past few months helping the stricken monolines get out of their underwater default swap commitments to the banks. Now he felt it was time to go further. He believed that since the default swap market had depended on insurers, it should be regulated like the insurance industry.

Meeting with Dinallo that day were a group of senior New York Fed officials, including Theo Lubke, who ran a department called market infrastructure.[25] Dinallo went through his argument, showing how default swaps had undermined the actuarial approach to credit insurance. He told them, "It is clear that there is some percentage of this market that is indistinguishable from an insurance transaction. We can bring clarity, transparency, and safety to a portion of it." He proposed that his department regulate any default swaps in which the buyer had an "insurable interest" in the bond it wanted protection on. No longer would collateral have to be posted.

Lubke frowned as he listened to Dinallo's pitch. Who was *he* to lecture the New York Fed about market safety, when his department had allowed the monolines to bankrupt themselves by selling tens of billions of subprime protection? Lubke gently chided Dinallo, reminding him how the market approach to credit worked. "There's a way to manage the risk of buying and selling protection of CDSs—by collecting collateral on the mark-to-market exposure. If I'm posting mark-to-market collateral on a position, you're protected against me from a default."

Echoing AIGFP's argument against Goldman, Dinallo responded that market prices shouldn't determine whether money changed hands. He recalls telling Lubke, "When you have insurance, and your car is wrecked or your house is burned down, you need to produce the revenues to the insurance company—it's what an adjustor does. This is all so basic. It scares me a bit that these are, apparently, revelatory conversations."

Lubke remained unconvinced. "So you propose there is no collateral posted? But you've got this huge exposure to me as you get more and more in-the-money, and this is what happened with the financial guarantors," he said, referring pointedly to the monolines. "It's a question of where you balance out these various risks between liquidity and credit, and where you put the protections in place."

Dinallo reminded the New York Fed officials that since the passage of a key law in 2000, default swaps were unregulated in the United States, and he believed insurance law could—and should—close that loophole. "I'm slightly riled that we don't have much of an argument under law," he told Lubke. "I could read the insurance law to you—it's as clear as a bell."

One of Lubke's colleagues attempted to end the meeting on a conciliatory note. "Please be part of a holistic solution," he urged Dinallo. "Please be reasonable in your interpretation and your outlook—you should be able to understand the needs of the market."

But what exactly were the needs of the market when the entire financial system was hurtling toward the rocks? Serving under New York Fed chairman Tim Geithner, Lubke had defended the mark-to-market and collateral system of default swaps. The New York Fed had pushed the dealers to improve their back-office paperwork for credit derivatives, and their efforts had removed some of the operational risks in the system. After two decades of cheering on over-the-counter derivatives innovation, it couldn't backtrack now.

Before the collateral plumbing systems were built, fluctuating derivative exposures were equivalent to unsecured debt. If a company was approaching insolvency, derivatives counterparties were simply considered to be just another form of creditor, part of a long pecking order of lenders that would jockey for position in order to best protect themselves. The collateral that you received via a derivative was not your property—just because a ten-year swap moved in your favor after two years didn't mean that it would always be profitable. Because of this ambiguity, a bankruptcy judge might demand that the collateral be returned, ordering the swap counterparty to queue up along with other creditors. In 2005, after prompting from dealers, Congress quietly passed a key amendment to the U.S. bankruptcy code as part of a bill focused on tightening up the rules for personal bankruptcy.[26] Under the amendment, derivatives and repo collateral were "carved out" from Chapter 11 protections. That meant derivative contracts on which you had received collateral could be closed down in the event of counterparty default, allowing you to walk off with the collateral already posted.

With little debate, corporate bankruptcy had been cleaved into two separate planets. On planet Earth, bankruptcy judges continued to freeze creditor claims and work out the fairest solution in full view at a measured pace. On "planet Derivative," the moment bankruptcy was declared, collateral could be seized in secret and disposed of before a judge even had time to put on his robes.

"A Dynamic There That's Quite Vicious . . ."

A week after Fannie and Freddie became wards of the state, the New York Fed was in exhausting talks, trying to help Lehman find a buyer, while it was also anticipating the imminent downgrading of AIG, which had posted still more collateral to Goldman, for a total of nearly $7 billion. All told, to all the banks it had deals with, AIGFP had paid out nearly $18 billion in margin.

In early September 2008, Geithner and his lieutenants felt reassured by the rules on planet Derivative as they saw the bankruptcy of Lehman Brothers tumbling toward them. They believed that over-the-counter derivatives, as a network of bilateral, privately negotiated agreements, had built-in incentives for people to protect themselves. For example, if dealers anticipated a default, they could redirect (or *novate*) derivatives away from a troubled counterparty, thereby retrieving collateral without having to wait for bankruptcy proceedings. And just as Goldman did with AIG, they could buy default swaps as an extra failsafe against a collateral shortfall. Sure, Bear Stearns was troublesome because counterparty confidence evaporated suddenly, but in Lehman's case, the market had had time to prepare. The aggressive free market self-interest of traders kept things safe without regulatory intervention.

Indeed, from the narrow perspective of those who dwelled on planet Derivative, the bankruptcy of Lehman Brothers on September 15 was an unremarkable event. As Geithner's lieutenants predicted, the industry coped with it, conducting a "credit event auction" and ensuring that default swaps linked to Lehman paid out smoothly, while Britain's Barclays Bank grabbed Lehman's U.S. brokerage business at a lucrative discount. It was only if you jumped off planet Derivative and back onto planet Earth that you saw the chaos and devastation caused by Lehman's collapse. On planet Earth, getting eight and a half cents on the dollar was a disaster for investors across the world. On planet Earth was the Reserve Primary Fund, whose holding of Lehman IOUs caused it to "break the buck," triggering a run on money market mutual funds. Clearly, the New York Fed's view of what was an efficient free market was too narrow.

In fact, it took only twenty-four hours for this regulatory confidence to evaporate. The trouble had been brewing a week before Lehman's bankruptcy—New York Fed officials had learned that Moody's and Standard & Poor's were about to downgrade AIG to a single-A rating, which would trigger a payment of $13 billion of additional default swap collateral. They knew this was going to be cataclysmic. The end was near.

According to Moody's eighty years of statistics, a single-A company may have been riskier than a double-A but was still a pretty safe bet.[27] On average, fewer than one in one thousand such companies defaulted in a given year. On planet Derivative, however, things were different. While AIG might be OK in the long term, in the short term it had run out of cash. If Goldman and the other default swap counterparties didn't receive their $13 billion, they had the contractual right to put the company straight into bankruptcy.

In a meeting with Moody's that week, the New York Fed staff tried to understand why the ratings agency was downgrading AIG. Surely, these guardians of the actuarial view of credit had a long-term explanation for their thinking? They did not. The New York Fed was dismayed to learn that Moody's was merely holding a mirror to the market approach. "The current volatility in AIG's stock price and borrowing spreads have made it more difficult to address the company's immediate liquidity and capital needs through traditional capital market issuance," was what Moody's impending announcement said.[28]

The New York Fed officials were stunned when they read this.[29] When considering the risk of default, didn't Moody's believe that AIG's diverse, global empire of well-capitalized insurance subsidiaries balanced out the stricken AIGFP, irrespective of what markets thought? In other words, the Fed argued, a downgrade was unnecessary because the underlying strength of the company would, in time, prevail. "The dynamic is unclear," one of the Fed officials said to Moody's. "How much is your view really based on fundamental assessment of liquidity viability, and how much do you factor in market perception?"

"We're focused on fundamental assessment," Moody's analysts replied. "You might say that," responded the Fed. "But you also say that the company needs to raise some capital, and the market is telling you that it can't raise the capital; then that justifies your downgrade. There's a dynamic there that's quite vicious."

Although its pleas to hold off on the downgrade were ignored, the New York Fed did persuade Moody's to add a sentence to its report that held out a slim branch of hope. Since the Fed was feverishly trying to persuade Wall Street firms to come up with emergency cash (just as it had done for LTCM ten years earlier), Moody's agreed to add this bit of equivocation to its AIG death sentence: "However, the company may be able to address these needs through alternative means."

But by the time the downgrade announcement was made (S&P also downgraded AIG the same day), Lehman had filed for bankruptcy, and Wall Street was not going to cough up all the money AIG desperately needed. This was money that Wall Street itself expected as part of its great collateral plumbing system. In fact, AIGFP's collateral payments were propping up the capital strength of a dozen European banks. A day after Lehman's bankruptcy was filed, the New York Fed set up an $85 billion loan fund to save AIG.

The Snake Is Eating Its Tail

In light of the global meltdown set off by AIG's plunge, an obvious question repeatedly asked is, Why couldn't Wall Street and the European banks forgo the additional collateral that a downgraded AIG was obliged to pay them? The answer is that they could have done that, but at the price of triggering an AIG default. Goldman, sitting at the heart of the super-senior swap deals and CDO pricing mechanism, like a spider at the center of its web, had hedged against that outcome, using default swaps written on AIG itself. On planet Derivative, Goldman had its bases covered. There was only one scenario that scared Goldman—if AIG was prevented from defaulting by the government and was also prevented from making default swap collateral payments. According to a senior official at the firm, "Through the aggregate of our collateral and our CDS, we were fully protected against the default. What we were not protected against was not receiving full payment from AIG and not being able to trigger default."

Eric Dinallo was hated on Wall Street precisely because he could bring about this feared outcome for counterparties of monolines, using his powers as New York insurance superintendent.[30] But with AIG, the Fed was powerless to change the derivatives-imposed market reality. When U.S. Treasury secretary Hank Paulson and New York Fed president Tim Geithner pumped $85 billion of government money into AIG on September 16, they weren't bailing out AIG's thousands of small investors; they were bailing out the big players from planet Derivative.

And the government's AIG bailout was a bust because, as Dinallo already knew, the "healthy" bits of the firm, the parts that sold life insurance (which were supposed to be truly protected), had already been plundered. By lending out their assets to Wall Street and reinvesting the cash collateral in mortgage bonds, AIG had turned itself into another Bear Stearns. Dinallo's deputy, Mike Moriarty, had quietly been pushing AIG to reduce this exposure by $18 billion, but fear over a default swap–triggered bankruptcy prompted Wall Street to demand $24 billion in additional cash during the last two weeks of September 2008. The U.S. Treasury and New York Fed were desperate to avoid having AIG be forced to sell its distressed mortgage bonds at a loss, so they pumped in another $50 billion of government bailout money. By this time, even Goldman was looking for shelter from this raging storm. Toward the end of the month, Goldman Sachs and Morgan Stanley got new equity investments and became bank holding companies. Making the Fed the primary regulator and taking the SEC out of the picture, the switch formalized their status as banks that were, in the cruelly paradoxical phrase of that season, "too big to fail."

A month later, the New York Fed created a pair of financial androids. Maiden Lane II would buy the distressed mortgage bonds from AIG's securities lending program. Maiden Lane III would do what Goldman's Dan Sparks had suggested nine months earlier: buy the underlying CDOs behind the AIGFP deals and tear up the default swap contracts with the two dozen or so counterparty banks. Leading negotiations on the New York Fed's behalf was the same bank examiner whose deference toward Wall Street had been noted by fellow regulators a few years earlier, Sarah Dahlgren. Rejecting advice to impose "haircuts" on the payments of taxpayer money, the New York Fed agreed to pay Goldman and other counterparties one hundred cents on the dollar. (The Swiss bank UBS offered to accept a 2 percent haircut, but the offer was declined.) Continuing the sleight-of-hand strategy it had used to "save" Bear Stearns, the Fed quietly added billions more in mortgage bonds and CDOs to its balance sheet.

That was one of the chilling, fundamental lessons of 2008: when confronted with hair-trigger mechanisms refined during a decade of financial innovation, the market approach to credit—the idea that it was more efficient to connect borrowers and investors via trading desks—couldn't survive without massive government assistance. Even Goldman and Morgan Stanley, the two remaining securities firms supposedly supporting their balance sheets purely through market confidence, had been forced to turn themselves into banks, basically hiding behind the skirts of the U.S. government. It turned out that rational self-interest, the bedrock of the free market since Adam Smith, didn't make things safer. It made them much more dangerous. Arbitrage—the process whereby discrepancies between similar assets could be profitably exploited by self-interested traders—stopped working. Flexibility and secrecy, two of the greatest "weapons" in the arsenal of derivatives dealers, were now turned against them, and they were unable to agree on pricing, making quants with their PhDs irrelevant. What had been measurable risk became immeasurable uncertainty. By pouring hundreds of billions of dollars into the system, governments quenched the wildfire of uncertainty and propped up planet Derivative.

Just Throw a TARP over the Bodies

October was a cruel month, as each day brought ever-more-harrowing headlines, and many observers openly questioned whether free market capitalism would survive. Consider just the first two weeks of the month. The U.S. Treasury tried to introduce a Troubled Asset Relief Program (TARP), but Congress failed to pass the emergency legislation on September 29. The markets had a heart attack when that vote was cast: the Dow fell 770 points, and, just as important, the confidence of banks to lend to one another, even for short periods, had evaporated. The world economy was now in free fall. Sigma, the last independent "shadow bank," went bankrupt on October 2, killed by a J.P. Morgan margin call.[31] On October 3, Congress passed a revised TARP bill that made $700 billion of taxpayer funds available to prop up the system and permitted the government to directly invest in troubled banks. The contagion had spread worldwide. On October 6, Wells Fargo scooped up troubled Wachovia while Germany, Belgium, and Holland announced bailouts for some of the "too big to fail" banks (including the pioneering CDO investor LB Kiel, by now part of a larger institution called HSH Nordbank). On October 8, the Federal Reserve and international central banks imposed coordinated emergency interest rate cuts, hoping to restart the frozen interbank lending markets. The next day, Iceland's biggest banks collapsed and were nationalized. October 12 saw Britain's Lloyds Banking Group (which had just taken over the insolvent Halifax Bank of Scotland) and Royal Bank of Scotland receiving an emergency bailout from the U.K. government, and RBS CEO Sir Fred Goodwin was fired. On October 14, the U.S. government announced that it would inject $250 billion of TARP capital into U.S. banks. Finally, this measure tamped down the panic swirling around U.S. lenders, although Citigroup and Bank of America (choking on Merrill Lynch) required a further bailout in December 2008.

And so it went—down and down, as trillions of dollars in value were vaporized from the Dow. Accounts of the 2008 global financial crisis now read like a series of increasingly large and desperate merger and acquisition deals, all of them ultimately propped up by the government. In other words, paid for by taxpayers.

The notion underpinning this approach by regulatory agencies in the United States and Europe was that confidence in banking is rooted in confidence in bank equity, which, as a hostage against poor governance, supports a tower of balance sheet leverage above it. If confidence in Merrill Lynch is faltering, you can solve the problem by joining it to, say, Bank of America. However, the governance mechanism underlying private sector confidence in bank equity had been fatally undermined by the fall of 2008. Regulators initially hoped that they could seize banks and "shoot the hostage"—punish investors for lax governance. But the tricks of financial innovation and regulatory arbitrage meant that these investors held them hostage instead. That's how they made themselves "too big to fail."

In the United States, the only regulator courageous enough to stick to the principles of the free market after Lehman collapsed was the FDIC's Sheila Bair, who seized Washington Mutual bank, sold its deposits to J.P. Morgan, and punished debt holders along with shareholders. For what she described as a "textbook play," Bair was hammered by Geithner for not being a "team player."

Other regulators wanted to follow Bair's lead and punish investors who had pumped capital into irresponsible banks, but they couldn't do it because the banks were all too interlinked. By October 2008, the question of bank shares' having any value was a moot point. What decided the question were the rules of planet Derivative. Any attempt to "haircut" the value of the sliver of subordinated debt holding up big banks would count as a "credit event" for default swaps. Even though a tiny sliver of capital was at stake, the effect in the derivative market would be the same as putting the entire bank into bankruptcy. As a former U.K. Treasury official put it, "You've got this game of chicken. Do you punish the subdebt holder? If you're trying to stabilize financial markets, do you bankrupt a bank to do it?"

The upshot was that the governments of America, Britain, and other countries injected billions of equity into their biggest banks—such as RBS and Citigroup—as well as guaranteeing their debt. And yes, any investor or creditor not on the same level as the government got a free ride—all the hedges constructed by the bankers continued to function, and the bonus culture supported by the hedging continued to function. It was politically embarrassing, for example, when Merrill

Lynch and Citigroup, which together lost $54 billion and received government bailouts of $55 billion, paid out bonuses of $9 billion.[32] A year later, with the government guarantees still supporting the system, nearly all the banks started reporting record profits.

But something had changed. Even the most promarket regulators no longer believed in unfettered over-the-counter derivatives markets; from November 2008 onward, the New York Fed's regulators would start calling for default swaps to be traded on an exchange.

The era of unrestricted financial innovation had come crashing to a halt. The men who loved to win had lost—big.

Epilogue

"During your act you made bank notes float down from the ceiling . . . Today, when I came to check the till, there was nothing in it but a lot of strips of paper."

"Oh dear, dear, dear!" exclaimed the professor. "Don't tell me people thought those notes were real?"

—Mikhail Bulgakov, *The Master and Margarita*

Kicking Some High-Priced Ass

On July 15, 2010, it seemed that the lords of high finance had finally been humbled and hobbled. The U.S. Senate had just passed the Dodd-Frank bill, the country's biggest overhaul of financial regulation since the Great Depression. For the first time, hidden derivatives markets would be regulated, consumers would get government protection against sharp practices by lenders, and giant banks that had benefited from the "too big to fail" safety net would be reined in. The new so-called Volcker Rule (named after the former Fed chairman) required banks to spin off internal hedge funds, private equity desks, and part of their derivatives businesses. And all this despite one of the most expensive lobbying assaults ever launched on Capitol Hill. As Barney Frank, chairman of the House Financial Services Committee and a coarchitect of the bill, put it, "Public opinion kicked big money's ass." The previous day, the mightiest Wall Street firm, Goldman Sachs, agreed to pay a $550 million fine to the Securities and Exchange Commission (SEC), to settle a claim that it had defrauded clients by creating "designed to fail" securities just before the subprime bubble burst in 2007. The besieged giant, which initially disputed the allegations, acknowledged its "mistake" and pledged to reform its working practices.

Over in London—which in the run-up to the meltdown had outstripped Wall Street as the global center for markets in debt, foreign exchange, and derivatives—even more radical plans were being mooted. In 2009, Lord Turner, the newly appointed chairman of Britain's financial watchdog, the Financial Services Authority (FSA), lambasted bankers for their "socially useless" activity. In June 2010, the recently formed coalition government announced that a commission would examine breaking up Britain's megabanks, prompting Barclays to threaten to move its investment banking operations out of the country. A tax on banking bonuses imposed by the previous government was set to bring in $3.7 billion in revenues, while similar taxes were in the works in France, Germany, and Switzerland. Meanwhile, in Switzerland, the Basel Committee for Banking Supervision, of which the United States was a member, was preparing a new rule book for banks around the world.

But how much has really changed? Has the world been set on a new path that will avoid a repeat of the financial disasters of the past few years? On the contrary. The big banks have only gotten bigger, and the regulatory changes—while in some cases positive—haven't been nearly enough to cure the global financial system of its dysfunctions.

Unchastened Banks

Of the mighty financial institutions that, in their avarice, almost bankrupted the world, only Lehman Brothers is gone. Some of the most ineptly run institutions—Royal Bank of Scotland, AIG, and Citigroup—received huge bailouts and are currently at differing stages of repaying taxpayers. Other firms, such as J.P. Morgan Chase, BNP Paribas, Deutsche Bank, and Barclays, have returned to robust health under private shareholder ownership. Not only were these giants subtly propped up by government guarantees and central bank actions that have made the liability side of their balance sheets cheap to support, but they also gorged themselves on the healthy parts of stricken competitors such as Lehman. While small American banks continue to fail at a rate of about three per week (according to the FDIC), the six biggest U.S. banks—with $9 trillion of assets—now exploit their government backing to increase their dominance.

The big banks are already regaining their swagger. As they did when the New York Fed first learned about VAR in the early 1990s, the multinationals continue to argue that bigger really is better.[1] They say that in order to keep growing in new markets, their clients need global banks that can follow them, providing bundles of services, from currency trading to M&A. The lie that bigger is better (and smarter) now stands exposed as one of the biggest governance flaws ever in the regulatory system. Shareholders and bonus-receiving bankers enjoyed the upside during the credit boom, and taxpayers became responsible for the downside in 2008. Defenders of the bank conglomerates point out that smaller banks, such as America's IndyMac or Britain's Northern Rock, also failed and cost taxpayers. But failures at that scale could be contained, while the failure of RBS or Citigroup could not. The large banks were able to play a game of chicken with governments, a stratagem that wasn't an option for their smaller peers.

Despite a populist backlash, the giants emerged largely intact from the Dodd-Frank bill. Although legislation gave federal regulators new powers to seize and break up rogue conglomerates like AIG or Lehman Brothers, the track record of the New York Fed, OCC, and SEC in kowtowing to megabanks does not bode well. Elsewhere, the idea of curtailing or breaking up bank conglomerates is not even on the table. In Germany and France, for example, so-called universal banking remains the favored model, and reform efforts have focused on "outside" threats, such as credit default swaps or hedge funds. In Japan and Canada, where the banking systems largely escaped the crisis, people ask why they should fix something that isn't broken.

Even the most obvious, rudimentary fix to global banking, a revision of the discredited Basel bank capital rules, has been lobbied down to questionable relevance. An improvement to the most egregious part of Basel II, the rules for trading books, was postponed to the end of 2011, while a new leverage ratio will have to wait until 2018. In the United Kingdom and Switzerland, where large banks have balance sheets measured in multiples of national GDP, curtailing megabanks may seem like too much of a sacrifice. Consider that in the United

Kingdom, the taxes paid on City of London bonuses in early 2010 wiped £10 billion off the country's national debt.[2]

With such taxpaying muscle—and with their old friend, the captured regulator—the large banks are likely to not just survive but thrive. They will patiently lobby against new rule making, waiting until the economy rebounds. Even if the United States and the United Kingdom do curtail their banks, other countries will encourage their national champions to rush into the breach. It also remains to be seen whether shareholders and their board-level representatives are capable of restraining bankers who promise too much. In late 2010, Deutsche Bank's CEO was promising a return on shareholder equity of 25 percent. Given the leverage that such performance requires, one suspects that megabanks still pose a clear and present threat to the financial system.

Derivatives Still (Mostly) Unbound

One of the big lies being told by bankers and their cheerleaders is that the 2008 crisis was caused simply by "poor risk-management" by a few institutions, such as AIG and Lehman Brothers. But 2008 proved that the over-the-counter (OTC) derivatives system was the problem—the huge incentives to take risks and then hedge them, the opacity in pricing, the contagion of collateralization, the uncertainty about the web of counterparties. After all, one of the biggest drivers behind banks using CDSs—themselves a destabilizing influence from 2007 on—was to hedge counterparty risk from other derivatives already on their books. The problem was multiplied by the shadowy repo market, where hedge funds and the brokerage desks of banks lent each other money to hold assets for short periods, pledging and repledging the collateral that they might dump at the first whiff of panic, adding to volatility.

During 2009 and early 2010, as the Dodd-Frank bill was being shaped and debated, a suggestion that came up repeatedly was, Why not force derivatives onto exchanges, which had functioned smoothly throughout the crisis—and where transparency and clear rules make it far harder for dealers to take advantage of their customers. Almost immediately, a strong counterargument was deployed on behalf of the banks by those very customers—in particular, nonfinancial corporations.

Ever since the 1990s, the big selling point of OTC derivatives was their flexibility. An end user of derivatives, such as Boeing or McDonald's, might forecast some foreign currency income or expenditure on a specific date in the future, for example, and buy a hedging contract from a bank tailored to that date. The big exchanges, such as the Chicago Mercantile Exchange or London's Liffe, standardize their derivatives to mature on fixed dates (such as the end of the month or quarter) to ensure that they get traded in sufficient numbers. Backing away from a confrontation with bread-and-butter corporations, Congress focused instead on the other big advantage of exchanges: the way in which a *clearing house,* or central counterparty, stands behind all its transactions with customers

The final bill decreed that most OTC derivatives would have to be routed via these new hubs. Similar plans were afoot in 2010 in Europe, coordinated by the European Commission. But would this make the world a safer place? The New York Fed, an early champion of the idea, hoped that the banks it regulated would gravitate toward a single central counterparty that would be rock solid. However, by the time the bill was signed by President Obama, it was obvious that an archipelago of central counterparties would appear instead. Some were based in the United States, some in Europe; some focusing on certain types of derivatives like CDSs, and some more catholic. The big derivatives dealers publicly welcomed the idea of transferring their contracts to the new creations—which seemed surprising until one noticed that the leading contenders were dealer owned, and that loopholes existed for "nonstandardized" derivatives to be traded bilaterally, as before. It looked like a ruse to keep "business as usual," with the added benefit that regulators would automatically treat the central counterparty as too big to fail and bail it out if it encountered problems. With nonfinancial corporate customers already complaining about collateral requirements imposed by the new entities, the pressure was already there for central counterparties to compete by demanding less collateral and hence operate on a smaller capital base—bringing us all closer to the day when a central derivatives counterparty would face its first solvency crisis.

And what about the repo market, which, as much as OTC derivatives, allowed Lehman and Bear Stearns to gorge on leverage before turning themselves into ticking bombs? Dodd-Frank was silent on that, which was good news for hedge funds, but scary tidings for everyone else.

Buyers Beware

This book has looked at many situations in which cautious, hate-to-lose investors bought unfamiliar products from innovative, love-to-win bankers and ended up regretting it. On the whole, those products were not the basic kinds of securities or derivatives (which are not the same thing as simple) that banks traded directly with each other and clients, such as hedge funds or nonfinancial corporations. They were structured products: bond or cashlike investments that pooled assets and layered them using the robot corporation mechanism of securitization, combined with derivatives.

Bankers will argue that to suggest that only thieves and fools participated in such markets is trafficking in calumny, and that most investors who bought these products were happy with their results. They also argue that structured products allowed corporations around the world to raise capital, and millions of Americans to take out cheap mortgages. Sounding an almost altruistic, utopian note, the bankers insist that while basic derivatives were like computer chips, structured products were intended to be innovative tools, such as Apple's iPhone, that deployed new technology seamlessly for customers and made their lives—and portfolios—the better for it.

But the crash of 2008 makes that defense laughable. Those cheap mortgages were a trick: over 50 percent of subprime mortgages issued in 2006 and 2007 were in default by the summer of 2010, and some $6 trillion of America's housing wealth vanished. The issuance of private-label residential mortgage-backed securities (mortgage bonds not guaranteed by the U.S. government) declined by 96 percent over the same period, while CDOs plunged by 99 percent. The market was moribund. And investors were far from happy: as of mid-2010, 220 subprime-related civil lawsuits had been filed in the United States alone. By November 2010, even the New York Fed (as the owner of the Maiden Lane androids) was considering joining legal proceedings against the originators of failed mortgage bonds. When taken together with regulatory claims such as the SEC's lawsuit against Goldman, that investor unrest shows the hollowness of the bankers' argument. After all, if structured products were really like the iPhone, why did Goldman and other banks respond to investor complaints by insisting that their clients were "sophisticated" and therefore didn't deserve a refund? The "sophisticated" label, which dates back to the 1933 Securities Act that exempted issuers of securities from filing prospectuses where the buyers were either large institutions or rich individuals, became a badge of idiocy during the run-up to the crisis.

The financial reforms of 2010 did offer some hope on this front. The big three ratings agencies, Moody's, Standard & Poor's, and Fitch, had been shamed in the crisis, with over 60 percent of their triple-A-rated CDOs suffering downgrades. The Dodd-Frank bill contained two important measures. The first was to remove the hard-coding of ratings into U.S. financial regulation (that allowed hate-to-lose investors to grow dependent on structured product ratings in the first place), pushing them to finally start doing their own due diligence. Second, the bill withdrew the crucial legal shield that gave the agencies the protection of the First Amendment to the U.S. Constitution—the same right to free-speech protections that journalists enjoy. This was becoming moot anyway, as judges handling subprime-related civil lawsuits recognized the absurdity of granting free-speech protection to raters whose profits depended on selling triple-A ratings to the banks creating structured products. Another Dodd-Frank measure, mirrored in European Union legislation, required issuers of mortgage bonds to keep "skin in the game"—to retain 5 percent of the amount issued on their own balance sheets as an incentive to underwrite responsibly.

Alas, all these worthy moves were mostly a distraction. Structured financial products, and their attendant dysfunctions, aren't going away. Governments were no more likely to abolish the structured mortgage products market than turkeys are to vote for Thanksgiving. The reason is that in the United States, and to some degree in Europe too, securitization has largely replaced banking as the means of financing consumer lending (not just mortgages, but credit cards and auto loans too). From 2008 on, the U.S. government worked to underpin securitization, from the trillions of dollars in guarantees provided by Fannie

Mae and Freddie Mac, to a host of special programs such as the Term Asset-backed Lending Facility (TALF) and the Public-Private Investment Program (PPIP). And to replace investors who had abandoned the market, the Federal Reserve bought over $1 trillion of mortgage bonds, while in Europe, banks securitized nearly $500 billion of loans in 2009, which they promptly pledged as collateral to the European Central Bank. On both sides of the Atlantic, securitization of consumer loans has been quasi-nationalized.

There is a private sector structured products market today, but it exists away from housing finance and flourishes in the world of retail investments. In this world, the old tradition of love-to-win traders crafting derivatives into psychologically appealing packages for hate-to-lose investors lives on, including so-called exchange traded funds (ETFs), guaranteed bonds, and indexed annuities. As with subprime, the uncertainties from overexploiting customers or misjudging derivative trades are big and unknowable, but the profits are too juicy to pass up for the banks that control these markets. The structured product utopians—with their iPhone analogies and the staggering profits that corrupt everyone—are here to stay.

Governments as Financial Risk Factors

In the decade before the meltdown, while bankers were busy inventing new products, reaping bountiful bonuses, and winning awards, the government officials responsible for national balance sheets were mostly silent. Protecting the taxpayer from financial instability was an important part of their jobs. The problem was, What did that entail?

In October 2002, a former UBS Warburg investment banker named James Sassoon was appointed to a civil service post in the U.K. Treasury, Britain's most prestigious government department. As part of the program for improving government efficiency by measuring the performance of its bureaucrats, Sassoon was assigned a set of performance targets. "One of the first things I was given was my objectives, one of which was, maintain financial stability," he recalls.[3]

But a question soon nagged at Sassoon: how would the U.K. Treasury define success? "I thought to myself, 'Here I am, I've arrived. I am one cog in this great system. How can I be assessed at the end of the year on how much I contributed to whether we have or haven't maintained financial stability?'" He quickly learned that, according to the rules, responsibility was shared by his department, the Bank of England, and the FSA. The idea was that in monthly "tripartite meetings," over civilized cups of English tea, the various officials from these institutions would keep Britain's financial system safe.

Sassoon left the Treasury in 2005, with the global economy booming and Britain's chancellor, Gordon Brown, claiming to have permanently "locked in" financial stability. In May 2010, having been raised to the peerage by the newly elected prime minister, David Cameron, Lord Sassoon returned to his old department as a government minister. While he'd been away, the government's role in the financial world had been turned on its head. In the United Kingdom, the United States, and elsewhere, the silent government officials had failed in their most sacred duty. A vicious recession had whipsawed Britain's economy, and government bailouts of the banking system had increased the country's debt ratio to its highest level since the Second World War. Sassoon's department now was the not-so-proud owner of a majority stake in Britain's two biggest banks while propping up their balance sheets with guarantees of over half a trillion dollars.

The great crisis put even more problems—and responsibilities—on the backs of government regulatory agencies. They first got their hands dirty—that is, crossed over from regulator to coconspirator—as they desperately tried to save the stricken financial system, but by 2010 they were seen as part of the problem as well. Everyone knew government shouldn't be up to its eyeballs in private sector activity; what is even more disturbing now is that it is obvious that governments can't afford to keep propping up the system. And they can't afford to stop.

After the banking crisis was tamped down, and the markets were swamped by newly printed money, the next challenge came not from the financial sector, but from a spendthrift nation on Europe's fringe: Greece, a country that for a decade had fiddled the books in plain sight, with the eager assistance of investment banks. In July 2003, my account of Goldman Sachs's use of swaps to help the Greek government conceal some $3 billion of its debt languished in the pages of an industry trade magazine.[4] The head of Greece's debt management office wrote a huffy letter to the editor who had published my article, insisting that the transaction was "based on prudent debt management rather than accounting concerns," and concluding, "It is hard to see why this merits cover-story treatment."

Over the following six years, Greece continued to borrow and conceal its debt position, bestowing largesse on its public sector workforce, until the shocking scale of the deception became apparent following an election at the end of 2009. The bond market began to take notice when thrifty Germany, the biggest country in the euro currency zone, started muttering that Greece's profligacy was damaging the euro's hard-won credibility. Early in 2010 the story that I had written in 2003 was belatedly picked up and subsequently broke across the world's financial pages. The Goldman deal (which was restructured and securitized after my original article) exposed the complicity of the European single currency's watchdogs in allowing things to get so out of hand. By April 2010, Greece's debt was at junk levels, and a rescue package was put together by Brussels and the International Monetary Fund (IMF). Despite the rescue, the taint of dishonesty in Europe's accounts was impossible to clean up that easily. Contagion spread to other heavily indebted EU countries—particularly Spain, Portugal, Ireland, and Italy—and echoing the battle in 2008 between Goldman and AIG, a fight between the market and actuarial views emerged as the role of CDSs in hedging or speculating against sovereign default became hotly debated. In June 2010, the members of the euro currency overrode German distaste for bailing out profligate neighbors, and agreed to set up a $500 billion European Financial Stability Facility to prop up ailing members. Together with a plan to "stress test" EU banks (following in the footsteps of the United States, which had performed a similar exercise a year before), the measures only temporarily arrested the contagion. By the end of 2010, Ireland was forced into using the new facility, with Portugal anticipated to follow suit.

The creeping malaise caused by too much debt was never going to be easy to fix. What was clear by the end of summer 2010 was that a crisis forged in the workshops of investment bank financial innovators had metamorphosed into a crisis all too familiar to economic historians. As Carmen Reinhart and Kenneth Rogoff point out in their book, *This Time Is Different*, there is a clear pattern to the credit booms that have bankrupted banks and nation states over the past eight centuries.[5]

What was different in 2010 was the global scale of the problem, and how regulators in the world's developed countries, led by the United States and Britain, were ill suited to handle the burden of their failed consumer finance and banking systems. Ben Bernanke's Federal Reserve, which, despite its stark failures in preventing the bubble and the subsequent bust, emerged stronger than ever from the Dodd-Frank reforms and (as of August 2010) ready to print trillions more dollars to keep America out of a second recession. In other words, "bad business as usual."

Ultimately, in the world of paper currency, where does the buck stop? Who is going to bail out the government the next time the bills come due? Starting in 2009, America's biggest creditor, China, started voicing concerns about its creditworthiness. After all, with its off–balance sheet surprises (a trillion here or there), was America that much better than Greece? The lesson of history is clear: faced with such debts, either Americans themselves (via their tax burden, their subsidized homes, or their benefits) will lose out, or their dollar-owning creditors will—in a big way. What started out as an arcane twist of high finance—derivatives—has now corrupted the entire financial world, and has set a hellish trap for taxpayers and their representatives that offers no way out.

Appendix

A timeline of some significant historical events referred to in the book, and episodes involving the book's key characters.

1973	Fischer Black, Myron Scholes, and Robert Merton publish seminal papers on option pricing
1974	Robert Merton publishes paper using option theory to link debt and equity
1986	Start of S&L crisis
1987	Oldrich Vasicek publishes working paper applying Merton's work to credit portfolios
	Federal Reserve protects Wall Street securities firms from October stock market crash by ensuring that banks lend
1988	Basel I bank capital accord agreed
	Nick Sossidis and Stephen Partridge-Hicks set up Alpha Finance for Citibank
1994	VAR models protect commercial banks from market turmoil
1995	Barings Bank almost bankrupted by Nick Leeson's rogue trading
	Sossidis and Partridge-Hicks set up Sigma
1996	Basel Committee agrees to incorporate VAR-based trading book rules into bank capital accord
	Citibank launches Centauri SIV
	Moody's binomial expansion technique CDO rating model published
1997	J.P. Morgan launches BISTRO synthetic CDO
	Emerging market debt crisis begins
1998	U.S. Financial Accounting Standards Board (FASB) introduces fair value accounting for derivatives
	AIG Financial Products sells super-senior protection on BISTRO to J.P. Morgan
	LTCM nearly collapses and is bailed out by consortium of major banks
	Basel Committee announces plans for a new capital accord (Basel II)
	Basel Committee agrees on "specific risk" rule for credit risk in the trading book

1999	Oka Usi forms risk finance group at Barclays to create arbitrage CDOs
	Gramm-Leach-Bliley Act passes Congress, effectively ending Glass-Steagall
	David Li publishes Gaussian copula working paper at J.P. Morgan
2000	U.K. Financial Services and Markets Act leads to creation of FSA
	Commodity Futures Modernization Act (CFMA) excludes over-the-counter derivatives from securities and futures regulation
	Peter Hancock leaves J.P. Morgan; merger with Chase Manhattan announced in December
	J.P. Morgan's Antonio Polverino establishes relationship with Poste Italiane's Massimo Catasta
	(December) Goldman Sachs transacts its first swap with Greece designed to conceal the country's debt ratio
	Anshu Jain and Rajeev Misra gain senior management roles at Deutsche Bank
2001	Single-tranche synthetic CDOs pitched by J.P. Morgan, Deutsche, and other dealers to European investors
	Oka Usi leaves Barclays; his CDOs are subsequently substituted into one another
	Dirk Röthig joins IKB
	(December) Enron bankruptcy
2002	LB Kiel purchases North Street 4 CDO from UBS
	Andrea Vella creates Mayu synthetic CDO at J.P. Morgan
	(July) WorldCom bankruptcy; CDO investors experience losses
	IKB creates the Rhineland conduit
2003	Daniel Sparks appointed head of Goldman Sachs mortgage trading
	Dealers launch corporate credit derivatives indexes
	Gordian Knot finalizes post-LTCM improvements to Sigma
2004	(January) Moody's publishes SIV "recipe book"
	Basel Committee initiates trading book review
	International Accounting Standards Board (IASB) introduces derivatives fair value accounting globally
	(April) Poste Italiane reports a €104 million interest rate derivatives loss and sues J.P. Morgan
	(June) Daniel Sparks visits IKB in Dusseldorf; Goldman issues Abacus 2004 AC-1
	The SEC agrees to supervise U.S. securities firms at holding company level, applying the Basel II standards
	(October) HSH Nordbank (formerly LB Kiel) sues Barclays bank over Corvus CDO
2005	(February) Greg Lippmann meets Steve Kasoff of Elliott Associates and discusses shorting subprime via a CDO
	(March) Federal Reserve sets up Large Financial Institutions (LFI) committee in response to complaints about lack of access to information; New York Fed criticized over lack of supervision of Citigroup
	(May) GM and Ford downgraded; J.P. Morgan suffers losses in CDO correlation trading

	(June) Under Lippmann's leadership, Wall Street firms agree on standardized subprime default swap (ABCDS) contract
	John Paulson enters first short subprime trade with Bear Stearns
	Cheyne SIV launched by Morgan Stanley
	(December) Lippmann initiates his own proprietary bet against subprime
	AIG Financial Products formally stops insuring super-senior subprime CDOs
2006	(January) ABX family of indexes launched
	Ameriquest settles predatory lending investigation
	John Paulson's credit opportunities fund raises $1 billion to short subprime
	(May) AIGFP super-senior subprime positions reach $80 billion
	Magnetar Capital launches Constellation fund to go long and short tranches of ABS CDO
	(July) Case-Shiller U.S. house price index reaches peak
	(October) Deutsche Bank's Coriolanus synthetic CDO sold to Bank Thai
	ABN AMRO launches constant proportional debt obligation (CPDO) product
	Option One and other smaller subprime lenders begin experiencing problems
	(November) ABX BBB index suffers decline; Goldman mortgage desk experiences ten days of losses
	(December) Goldman Sachs CFO David Viniar instructs Sparks to reduce risk
2007	(January) Fabrice Tourre introduces Paulson & Co. to ACA to discuss Abacus 2007 AC-1
	(February) More subprime lenders fail; Sparks warns management about problems
	(March) Ben Bernanke describes subprime crisis as "contained"
	(April) Abacus 2007 AC-1 deal closes and is bought by IKB
	(May) Goldman mortgage department makes second-quarter loss as the firm's CDO warehouse written down
	(June) Bear Stearns freezes CDO hedge funds and begins liquidating them
	(July) Ratings agencies start mass downgrades of mortgage bonds and CDOs
	Sossidis and Partridge-Hicks warn ratings agencies about impending SIV problems
	IKB loses access to credit and requires bailout by German government and banks
	Goldman sends AIGFP its first margin call
	(August) SEC visits Bear Stearns in response to rumors about liquidity problems
	European Central Bank (ECB) announces emergency liquidity for banks as ABCP markets freeze
	(September) U.S. Treasury announces MLEC initiative to rescue SIVs
	(October) King County, WA, discloses SIV exposure
	Merrill Lynch reports $6 billion of super-senior CDO losses and fires Stan O'Neal
	(November) Citigroup discloses $55 billion of subprime exposure and fires Chuck Prince
	Morgan Stanley discloses proprietary trading CDO losses
	Goldman Sachs reports record annual trading revenues of $31 billion; Dan Sparks, Josh Birnbaum, and other Goldman mortgage traders receive bonuses of $15–$20 million each

PWC auditors express concern about implications of Goldman margin calls for AIG's accounts; AIGFP chief Joseph Cassano concedes that if Goldman is right, AIG has lost $5 billion

(December) AIG investor conference during which Cassano dismisses low-ball margin calls as "drive-bys"

Goldman pitches distressed CDO trades to London hedge funds, creating prices to justify AIG margin calls

John Paulson reports $20 billion in revenues from his "big short" on subprime

Greg Lippmann receives $50 million bonus from Deutsche Bank

Royal Bank of Scotland closes takeover of ABN AMRO

2008	(January) New York Insurance Department announces efforts to recapitalize monolines

(February) HSH Nordbank files lawsuit against UBS over North Street 4 deal

AIG publicly reveals that its auditor, PWC, has identified a "material weakness" in its CDO valuations and reports $11 billion of super-senior writedowns

SEC's Macchiaroli makes a return visit to Bear Stearns

UBS reports full-year CDO writedowns of $18.7 billion

(March) Bear Stearns suffers a loss in counterparty confidence and is taken over by J.P. Morgan, with losses backstopped by the New York Fed

Cassano resigns as CEO of AIGFP but stays on as consultant

Dan Sparks decides to retire from Goldman but agrees to stay on until August

(April) Royal Bank of Scotland carries out £12 billion rights issue

Bloomberg story on U.K. banks exiting 100 percent LTV mortgage market prompts Paulson to take short positions on U.K. bank stocks

(June) Lehman Brothers writes down part of its portfolio and raises $6 billion additional capital

(August) Congress gives U.S. Treasury new powers to take over mortgage agencies

Lehman Brothers tries to raise capital from Korea Development Bank, but talks go nowhere

(September 8) Fannie Mae and Freddie Mac placed into conservatorship by Treasury

(September 12) Counterparties lose confidence in Lehman, prompting a weekend of attempted deal making at the New York Fed

Credit ratings agencies warn of imminent downgrade of AIG; New York Fed holds discussions concurrent with Lehman talks

(September 14) U.K. government declines to facilitate takeover of Lehman by Barclays; Bank of America takes over Merrill Lynch

(September 15) Lehman files for bankruptcy

(September 16) New York Fed provides an emergency $85 billion loan facility to save AIG from bankruptcy triggered by collateral calls, and appoints a new CEO at AIG

Reserve Primary Fund, invested in Lehman, "breaks the buck," forcing the Fed to support money market funds

(September 24) Goldman Sachs and Morgan Stanley receive new equity investments and become bank holding companies, formalizing their "too big to fail" status

FDIC seizes Washington Mutual

(September 29) Congress fails to pass TARP, and the Dow falls 770 points

(October 3) Revised TARP bill passes Congress

(October 6) Wells Fargo acquires Wachovia

Germany, Belgium, and The Netherlands announce bailouts for problem banks

(October 8) Federal Reserve and international central banks impose coordinated emergency interest rate cuts

(October 10) OIS-Libor spread peaks at 364 basis points: interbank lending has broken down

(October 12) Royal Bank of Scotland receives emergency bailout from U.K. government, and CEO Sir Fred Goodwin is ousted

(October 14) U.S. government announces injection of $250 billion of TARP capital into U.S. banks

New York Fed creates two special companies to buy AIGFP-related CDOs and securities lending-related mortgage bonds, paying counterparties such as Goldman 100 percent of market value

(October 3) Avoiding the need for U.K. government funds, Barclays raises £7 billion of capital from Middle Eastern investors

(November) President Obama elected; Geithner tapped as Treasury Secretary

HSH Nordbank receives German government bailout

(December) Irish government bails out banks

Citigroup receives an additional $20 billion TARP bailout and $300 billion of debt guarantees from the U.S. government

2009   (January) U.K. government announces additional bailout of Royal Bank of Scotland and other banks

President Obama inaugurated

(April) Case-Shiller house price index reaches a trough

2010   (May) Greece is frozen out of bond markets, leading to an EU and IMF bailout

(July) Goldman pays $550 million to settle SEC lawsuit over Abacus 2007 AC-1

Dodd-Frank bill signed into law

(September) Basel III banking rules finalized

(October) "Robo-signing" foreclosure scandal leads to wave of lawsuits against banks

(November) Market confidence in Ireland evaporates, leading to an IMF/EU bailout in December

Notes

Chapter One

1. According to the Bank for International Settlements (Triennial Central Bank Surveys, December 2007 and September 2010), the global turnover in currency forwards outstripped spot transactions in 1995 and today is twice the size of the spot market.

2. See the Bank for International Settlements report, OTC derivatives market activity for the second half of 2008 (May 2009).

3. Daniel Defoe, *An Essay upon Projects* (London, 1697).

4. Standard & Poor's and Fitch both restrict themselves to capital letters in their ratings along with plus or minus signs, while Moody's includes lowercase letters and numbers. Thus an S&P or Fitch *BB–* rating is equivalent to a Moody's *Ba3* rating.

5. As calculated by John Hull in his book *Options, Futures and Other Derivatives* (Upper Saddle River, NJ: Prentice Hall, 2007).

6. See United States Office of the Comptroller of the Currency, bank call reports, fourth quarter 2000. (See OCC Quarterly Reports on Bank Trading and Derivatives Activities, http://www.occ.treas.gov/topics/capital-markets/financial-markets/trading/derivatives/derivatives-quarterly-report.html.) The capital ratio was computed using J.P. Morgan's U.S.–regulated bank subsidiary, which had less than half of the bank's total derivatives exposure measured at holding-company level.

7. Nicholas Dunbar, "Revealed: Goldman Sachs' Mega-Deal for Greece," *Risk*, July 2003, 20.

8. For example, see *Report by Eurostat on the Revision of Greek Government Debt and Deficit Figures*, November 22, 2004, http://epp.eurostat.ec.europa.eu/cache/ity_public/Greece/en/Greece-en.pdf.

9. Serious attempts to reform Greek pensions in 2007–2008 led to massive strikes and riots in Athens. By 2010, Greece was locked out of the credit markets and was forced to depend on emergency loans from the International Monetary Fund and the EU.

10. Addressing Parliament in December 2005, Greece's finance minister George Alogoskoufis said, "Our efforts to restore fiscal transparency have revealed . . . the detrimental swap agreements of 2001, which under a complicated structure of 12 different contracts led to the vanishing of €2.8 billion of debt. These swap agreements had a direct cost of €500 million in transaction fees and an indirect cost of €1 billion. They will cost the budget €400 million annually until 2019," from a transcript of a public Greek parliamentary proceeding cited in news reports at the time. In March 2010, my old *Risk* story from 2003 became the source of renewed interest in the Goldman–Greece swap deal; see Dunbar, "Revealed."

11. See Nicholas Dunbar, "The Battle over Loan Accounting," *Risk*, July 2001, 26.

12. Interview for *Risk* article, 2001.

13. The story of Enron has been told in detail in a number of books; for example, see Bethany McLean and Peter Elkind, *The Smartest Guys in the Room: The Amazing Rise and Scandalous Fall of Enron* (New York: Portfolio, 2003).

14. Quoted in the testimony of Robert Roach, chief investigator, U.S. Senate Permanent Subcommittee on Investigations, *The Role of the Financial Institutions in Enron's Collapse*, July 23, 2002.

15. Interview by author, 2002.

16. Citigroup had provided hidden financing to Enron similar to that provided by Chase, with the difference that the credit risk was transferred to investors via a default swap. Although Citi was fined $48 million by the SEC, it didn't lose money on the CDS.

Chapter Two

1. This is an important technical point. Most large commercial banks are not supported directly by shareholders, but are owned by holding companies that raise equity. Bank regulators are reassured by the ability of holding companies to inject additional capital into troubled bank subsidiaries, but if the holding company has other commitments, such as a trading business, then there is less reassurance.

2. This instinct may have deep biological roots because evolution has hardwired us to connect ambiguity with danger: scans demonstrate that a region of the brain called the amygdala, associated with emotions, becomes active when subjects are faced with uncertainty. For example, see Dan Ariely, *Predictably Irrational: The Hidden Forces That Shape Our Decisions* (New York: HarperCollins, 2008).

3. E. Gerald Corrigan, speech to New York State Bankers Association, January 1992.

4. This is discussed in detail in Ian Hacking, *The Emergence of Probability: A Philosophical Study of Early Ideas About Probability, Induction and Statistical Inference* (Cambridge: Cambridge University Press, 1984).

5. For example, a $100 investment in the S&P 500 index might have a 99 percent one-day VAR of $3 using the past decade of daily data, and a required capital cushion of $25 (using the BIS 1996 scaling factors). Having to borrow $125 for every $100 invested increases interest payments on the borrowing by 25 percent, reducing the breakeven profitability and hence acting as a disincentive to take such a position.

6. Nitpickers will point out that the economics Nobel Prize was not actually established by the inventor of dynamite but was rather an add-on created by the Swedish central bank in his memory.

7. Robert C. Merton, *Continuous-Time Finance* (Cambridge, MA: Blackwell, 1990), chap. 14.

8. After our meeting, Taleb wrote up his views as an article, "How the Ought Became the Is," which I published in a Black-Scholes twenty-fifth anniversary supplement for the trade magazine *Futures & Options World* in July 1998.

9. See Nassim Taleb and Pablo Triana, "Bystanders to This Financial Crime Were Many," *Financial Times*, December 8, 2008.

10. For example, see the report *Improving Counterparty Risk Management Practices* published in June 1999 by an industry working group chaired by Gerald Corrigan.

11. See the remarks by Goldman's then head of firmwide risk, Bob Litzenberger, in Nicholas Dunbar, *Inventing Money: The Story of Long-Term Capital Management and the Legends Behind It* (Chichester: Wiley, 2000), 203.

12. The BIS actually further liberalized the VAR-based capital rules in 1998, introducing a so-called specific risk amendment that a Federal Reserve official described in 2009 as "the kiss of death."

13. For example, see the chapter on consumer credit in Richard H. Thaler and Cass R. Sunstein, *Nudge: Improving Decisions About Health, Wealth, and Happiness* (New Haven, CT: Yale University Press, 2008).

14. The products are normally sold to intermediaries such as small banks or insurance companies before passing into the hands of the consumer.

15. An edited version of my interview with Sartori di Borgoricco was published in "The Key to Successful Client Solutions," *Risk*, October 2004, 53.

16. For example, consider this quote by Ford CEO Alan Mulally: "That's what strategy is all about—a point of view about the future and then making decisions based on that," in Bill Vlasic, "Ford's Bet: It's a Small World After All," *New York Times*, January 9, 2010.

17. Frank Partnoy, *Infectious Greed: How Deceit and Risk Corrupted the Financial Markets* (New York: Times Books, 2003), provides an excellent summary of the scandal and its aftermath.

18. A claim was filed in London's High Court in 2004. As of the time of writing, the legal dispute between Poste Italiane and J.P. Morgan had not been resolved.

Chapter Three

1. Following complaints by Deutsche Bank, the European Commission in Brussels would rule in 2002 that this state guarantee had to be withdrawn.

2. The source material for the case studies in this chapter is a mixture of interviews, published articles, and court documents. BPI's version of events is given in its London High Court claim against Barclays (Queen's Bench, Commercial Division, 2006, 129). Barclays settled with BPI after a one-day public hearing in February 2010.

3. For an excellent high-level account of Bob Diamond's rise to power at Barclays, see Martin Vander Weyer, *Falling Eagle: The Decline of Barclays Bank* (London: Weidenfeld, 2000).

4. Usi used this example in an interview for *Derivatives Strategy* magazine, June 1997.

5. Note that we ignore any mention of time, or the time value of money, in this example, which is the equivalent of setting the risk-free interest rate to zero.

6. One might argue that since the market values the loans at $800 million, the bank ought to write down the value of the equity investment to zero. However, accounting rules for loan books don't require such recognitions to take place.

7. After de Moivre's death, the refinement of mortality calculations was continued in London by Richard Price, friend of Thomas Bayes and Benjamin Franklin, and founding actuary of the Equitable Life Assurance Society.

8. Arturo Cifuentes and Gerard O'Connor, "The Binomial Expansion Method Applied to CBO/CLO Analysis," Moody's Investors Service special report, December 13, 1996.

9. Ibid.

10. For a detailed account of the invention of BISTRO, see Gillian Tett, *Fool's Gold: How the Bold Dream of a Small Tribe at J.P. Morgan Was Corrupted by Wall Street Greed and Unleashed a Catastrophe* (New York: Free Press, 2009).

11. Harry Markowitz, "Portfolio Selection," *Journal of Finance* 7, no.1. (1952): 77–91.

12. Markowitz and his followers initially demanded extraordinary skills from their hypothetical investors. They were envisaged as gifted beings who could frame their beliefs about potential investments in the form of detailed probability distributions, including the correlations between investments. In a footnote to his paper, Markowitz said, "This paper does not consider the difficult question of how investors do (or should) form their probability beliefs." Since then, analysts have typically assumed that beliefs are formed purely from historical statistics.

13. Richard H. Thaler and Cass R. Sunstein, *Nudge: Improving Decisions About Health, Wealth, and Happiness* (New Haven, CT: Yale University Press, 2008).

14. Barclays issued an emerging market CDO structured by Usi's group named RF Alts Finance in January 2000.

15. E-mail evidence presented at Banca Popolare di Intra and Barclays Bank PLC, transcript of High Court Hearing, February 9, 2010; and witness statement of Stefano Silocchi quoted in Barclays' pre-trial argument to the High Court.

16. Excerpt from Barclays' Policies and Procedures Manual, as presented at Banca Popolare di Intra and Barclays Bank PLC, transcript of High Court Hearing, February 9, 2010.

17. See Banca Popolare di Intra and Barclays Bank PLC, Defense and Counterclaim (High Court of Justice, London, 2006). I have attempted to combine both sides' versions of events in these paragraphs.

18. Barclays Capital North America internal audit document of July 2001, quoted in the BPI versus Barclays court hearing in February 2010.

19. Usi no longer works with credit derivatives or CDOs, and instead has carved out a career investing in renewable energy and carbon projects.

20. Halblaub gave an interview about his experience with Barclays in Duncan Wood, "HSH Takes a Long-Term View," *Risk*, January 2005.

21. For background about the lawsuit, see Nicholas Dunbar, "Barclays Fights CDO Lawsuit," *Risk*, October 2004, 12.

Chapter Four

1. Quoted in the write-up for *Risk*'s Lifetime Achievement Award to Bill Winters (*Risk*, January 2005, 18).

2. See the write-up for *Risk*'s House of the Year Award to J.P. Morgan (*Risk*, January 2002, 46).

3. Robert C. Merton, "On the Pricing of Corporate Debt: The Risk Structure of Interest Rates," *Journal of Finance* 29, no. 2 (1974): 449–470.

4. Roughly speaking, the correlation parameter is equivalent to *beta* in Sharpe's capital asset pricing model (CAPM).

5. David X. Li, "On Default Correlation: A Copula Function Approach" (working paper, RiskMetrics Group, 1999).

6. It was not an unreasonable argument. In 2008, structured products with a money-back guarantee based on a single issuer—Lehman Brothers—defaulted, losing money for consumers in the United States, Germany, and Hong Kong.

7. "Another area where Deutsche has shown innovation . . . is in structuring bespoke tranches of CDOs . . . Deutsche has executed $15 billion of deals in the U.S., Europe, Japan, and Asia this year, leading industry insiders to state that Deutsche's mono-tranche business is now bigger than J.P. Morgan's," from *Risk*'s Credit Derivatives House of the Year Award to Deutsche Bank (*Risk*, January 2003).

8. Some people familiar with the transaction argue that Deutsche Bank could have readily purchased default swap protection on Enron and the telecom credits from dealer counterparties if it wanted to. However, in the case of Enron, when REPON-16 closed, the energy company was already frozen out of the market in unsecured borrowing, and default swaps on its debt were barely trading.

9. See "Deutsche Bank Credit Team Gets a Spanish Lesson," *Risk*, December 2002, 12.

10. See "*Risk* Manager of the Year: Richard Evans, Deutsche Bank," *Risk*, January 2004, 21.

11. See Nicholas Dunbar, "Seduced by CDOs," *Risk*, September 2004, 38–44.

12. Letter from S&P to Alesco Preferred Funding I Ltd., September 2003 (Federal Court of New York, Southern District). Among issuers, Fitch had a reputation for being slightly cheaper than its two competitors.

13. According to the Securities Industry and Financial Markets Association (SIFMA); see www.sifma.org/research/statistics.aspx.

14. According to the Triennial Central Bank surveys published by the Bank for International Settlements in 2004 and 2007, respectively; see www.bis.org.

15. See press release "Fitch Affirms Mayu B.V.'s and Programma Dinamico S.P.A.'s Notes," August 13, 2004.

16. The dealers agreed on rules for the composition and calculation of these indexes and set themselves up as shareholders in unlisted companies that administered them.

17. Wolfgang Schmidt and Ian Ward, "Pricing and Hedging Basket Credit Derivatives," *Risk*, January 2002, 115–118.

Chapter Five

1. Between 1986 and 1995, 1,043 depositary institutions were closed by U.S. bank regulators at a cost of $145.7 billion. See *Grant's Interest Rate Observer*, February 5, 2010, 11.

2. *Other advanced countries* are defined as member nations of the Organisation for Economic Co-operation & Development (OECD).

3. Alan Greenspan, speech to the Annual Financial Markets Conference of the Federal Reserve Bank of Atlanta, Miami Beach, Florida, February 27, 1998.

4. Bank of England conference on credit risk modeling and the regulatory implications, London, September 21–22, 1998.

5. The 1,043 thrifts that U.S. taxpayers bailed out between 1986 and 1995 experienced an average loss rate of 28.1 percent on total assets of $519 billion, from *Grant's Interest Rate Observer*, February 5, 2010.

6. Presentation to Bank of England conference, September 1998.

7. Andrew Hickman and H. Ugur Koyluoglu, "Reconcilable Differences," *Risk*, October 1998, 56.

8. Michael Gordy, "A Comparative Anatomy of Credit Risk Models," *Journal of Banking and Finance* 24, no. 1/2 (2000): 119–149.

9. William J. McDonough, keynote address to Bank of England conference, September 1998.

10. Nicholas Dunbar, "The Accord Is Dead—Long Live the Accord," *Risk*, October 1998, 9.

11. For more details, see Nicholas Dunbar, *Inventing Money: The Story of Long-Term Capital Management and the Legends Behind It* (Chichester: Wiley, 2000), chap. 8.

12. My source for what follows is a former member of the team who no longer works for the Fed and has requested anonymity. Mac Alfriend has confirmed the veracity of the source but declines to comment personally on the Richmond Fed's relationship with Bank of America.

13. The rule specified a holding period of two weeks, or ten working days. In practice, banks were allowed to compute one-day VAR and scale it up to the required holding period using a capital multiplier.

14. As we will see further on, Basel rules loosened the definition of "shareholder" to include so-called hybrid or Tier 1 capital with some debt-like characteristics: for example, preferred stock.

15. According to Bank of America's financial statements, trading assets increased from $38 billion in 1999 to $64 billion at the end of 2002, while balance sheet loans declined.

16. In 2008, the EBK was merged into a new Swiss financial regulator, FINMA.

17. William Perraudin, interview by author, May 2009.

18. FSA Annual Report, 2001–2002, 48.

19. The Commodity Futures Modernization Act, 2000. This law exempted over-the-counter derivatives from the scope of the Commodities and Exchanges Act and

preempted state level anti-gambling restrictions. Then-Treasury secretary Lawrence Summers and Alan Greenspan were instrumental in steering this industry-friendly bill through Congress over the objections of Commodity Futures Trade Commission (CFTC) chairwoman Brooksley Born, who was forced to resign.

20. Michael Macchiaroli, interview by author, January 2001.

21. Bob Litzenberger, interview by author, December 2000.

22. The measure of bank capitalization is not exact because I am using a figure for all banks, not just VAR-approved banks (which account for the vast majority of derivatives exposures).

23. See http://www.federalreserve.gov/boarddocs/Press/Enforcement/2003/20030728/attachment.pdf.

24. In 2004, Citigroup paid $5 billion to settle class action suits relating to the scandal.

25. Author interviews with Petros Sabatacakis, December 2000 and February 2010.

26. Interview by author, September 2009.

27. See www.fcic.gov/hearings/pdfs/2005_FRBNY_Draft_Close_Out_Report.pdf.

28. Basel Committee newsletter no. 3, June 2004.

29. Joint letter from European Banking Federation, Institute of International Finance, International Swaps & Derivatives Association, London Investment Banking Association, and the Bond Market Association to the Basel Committee, December 9, 2004.

30. Paul Sharma, interview by author, November 2005.

31. "The Application of Basel II to Trading Activities and Double Default Effects," Basel Committee, July 2005.

Chapter Six

1. Its full name was North Street Reference Linked Notes, 2002-4 Limited.

2. Here, one is in acronym city: the androids are officially called REMICs (real estate mortgage investment conduits), and the bonds they issued were initially called CMOs (collateralized mortgage obligations) but are now universally known as RMBS (residential mortgage-backed securities). When we say *mortgage android* we mean REMIC, and by *mortgage bond* we mean RMBS.

3. Sheila Bair, interview by author, August 2009.

4. Why were the 15 percent mortgages typical during the early 1980s not equally suicidal? The difference is that the early 1980s were a period of high inflation, which eroded the value of debts, making the "real" interest rate paid on such mortgages relatively affordable.

5. One might ask whether any proof exists that securitization cheapens mortgage borrowing for consumers, and the answer is surprisingly little, especially after fees are taken into account. Over the years, industry lobbyists and consultants have produced reams of documents claiming benefits for securitization, but one of the few academic studies before the subprime mortgage crisis (Steven Todd, "The Effect of Securitization on Consumer Mortgage Costs," *Real Estate Economics* 29, no. 1 [2001]) found no such evidence.

6. Greg Lippmann, interview by author, June 2008.

7. Note that up until 2008, Goldman Sachs published annual accounts with a November year-end.

8. Agreeing to Goldman's collateral provisions was not the only mistake Cassano made. The default swap contracts permitted substitution of old mortgage bonds with new ones in the underlying CDOs, which meant that despite its claims to have restricted exposure to 2005 vintages of subprime, AIGFP ended up being exposed to the more toxic later vintages too.

9. In April 2005, a Deutsche Bank press release listed Lippmann as "Global Head of CDO and ABS Correlation Trading and Head of North American ABS Trading and Syndicate." In a conference bio published in early 2006, Egol described himself as "responsible for structured product correlation trading." In the wake of the financial crisis, both Deutsche Bank and Lippmann himself have attempted to downplay his involvement in CDOs.

10. John Paulson, interview by author, July 2009.

11. Its official name is the Markit ABX.HE, after the company that owns and compiles the index using prices provided by dealers. Four series of ABX were created: the 06-1, the 06-2, the 07-1, and finally the 07-2.

12. See the trending reports by Clayton Services Inc. released by the Financial Crisis Inquiry Commission and the accompanying testimony delivered by Clayton executives in September 2010 (www.fcic.gov).

13. See Bank Thai operating results for the nine-month period ending September 30, 2007 (http://www.bankthai.co.th/website/upload/content/000000000010791/documents/Operating_9m_e50.pdf). The prospectus of Coriolanus Series 39 is available from the Irish Stock Exchange (www.ise.ie). After losing over $200 million in CDO investments, Bank Thai was purchased by Malaysia's CIMB Bank in January 2009.

14. See Exhibits 17–18 in the 900 pages of Goldman e-mails and documents relating to mortgages released by the U.S. Senate Permanent Subcommittee on Investigations (PSI) in the summer of 2010. Also, by the end of November 2006, the price of the ABX 06-1 BBB index fell to 98 versus its initial par value of 100, and never recovered. With a $6 billion long position in the index, this implies a mark-to-market loss of around $120 million.

15. See e-mail from David Viniar to Tom Montag, Senate PSI disclosures, Exhibit 3.

16. I have reconstructed Birnbaum's remark from his own words used in his 2007 annual performance review, disclosed by the U.S. Senate.

17. Remember that CDO investors would look at credit ratings as a guide to risk, rather than as a guide to price. If the price was lower, the yield or default swap premium that subprime bonds paid was higher, which looked like a "good deal" for the same risk to the investors.

18. See e-mails between Ostrem and Goldman traders in Senate PSI disclosures, exhibits 89, 94, and 97.

19. A key bone of contention was the meaning of VAR numbers. As subprime began to melt down, the VAR of the mortgage traders' positions rose with the increased volatility. That signal caused the risk managers to order a reduction in positions, even though these positions were short bets that would ultimately prove highly profitable for Goldman.

20. See the Senate PSI disclosures, Exhibit 163. Goldman sources point out that these trading book disclosures do not reflect the aggregate exposure of the entire mortgage department.

21. From an e-mail dated January 2007 and released by Goldman Sachs, summer 2010.

Chapter Seven

1. Doug Extine, interview by author, October 2009.

2. See "King County, Washington: Asset-Backed Commercial Paper Analysis" report by PFM Asset Management LLC, October 10, 2007. A number of other U.S. municipal cash funds invested in ABCP, including those in Arizona, Colorado, Louisiana, and Maryland.

3. See the New York Fed paper on shadow banking by Zoltan Pozsar, Tobias Adrian, Adam Ashcraft, and Hayley Boesky, July 2010. If tax-exempt and "enhanced" cash funds are included, the figure rises to $3 trillion. When European repo is included, some estimates put the figures as high as $7 trillion.

4. Stephen Partridge-Hicks and Nick Sossidis, interview by author, September 2008 and January 2009.

5. Delaware is the base of such a large number of financial androids that the fact ought to be celebrated on its car license plates.

6. Fees are calculated as a percentage of spread that reflects the trading risk to the market maker. Higher-risk tranches of CDOs or ABSs pay a higher spread, so the dealing costs are higher.

7. See Nicholas Dunbar, "The Great German Structured Credit Experiment," *Risk*, February 2004, 16–18.

8. In 2003, a Morgan Stanley quant named Peter Cotton submitted a technical paper to *Risk* questioning the Gaussian copula, but it was rejected by anonymous referees.

9. This was admitted by Barclays in a December 2008 London High Court filing. CRSM's case against Barclays, relating to this CDO squared, was dismissed by London's High Court in March 2011.

10. Awarded by *Risk* magazine, January 2007.

11. Author interview with former ABN AMRO quant, December 2008.

12. Securities and Exchange Commission, Report of investigation pursuant to Section 21(a) of the Securities Exchange Act of 1934; Moody's Investor Service Inc.

13. In most of its trades, Magnetar did not short the same CDOs in which it was long equity, but used careful analysis to pick similar deals where there was a lot of overlap between the underlying mortgage bonds.

14. Author interview with Dave Snyderman and Magnetar staff, August 2009.

15. According to the UBS shareholder report on CDO write-downs published in April 2008, "UBS did not take mark-to-market losses on warehouse positions if it was believed that the probability of securitization was 90% or better" (Shareholder Report, p. 23, www.ubs.com).

16. See *SEC v. Tzolov and Butler*, Southern District Court of New York, September 2008. Following a brief spell as a fugitive, Tzolov was recaptured by the FBI and in July 2009 pleaded guilty to the charges.

17. Conversation with unnamed broker cited in Securities and Exchange Commission (SEC) complaint against Ralph Cioffi and Matthew Tannin, June 2008.

18. Author interview with unnamed former Fed official. The Federal Reserve Board press office declined to comment.

19. Transcript of phone call released by the Financial Crisis Inquiry Commission, July 2010.

20. Internal memo obtained by the *Washington Post,* December 2009.

21. Bonifacius would undergo liquidation (a type of CDO default event) in January 2008.

Chapter Eight

1. See Exhibit 26 in the documents released by the Senate Permanent Subcommittee on Investigations (PSI), 2010.

2. E-mail from Tom Athan to Andrew Forster, August 2, 2007.

3. Goldman Sachs declined to make Sundaram available to comment.

4. For example, see http://www2.goldmansachs.com/our-firm/on-the-issues/responses-fcic.html.

5. Testimony of Joseph Cassano to the Financial Crisis Inquiry Commission, July 2010.

6. Sherwood says he has no recollection of saying this.

7. Federal Reserve Bank of New York. *Tri-Party Repo Infrastructure Reform* (New York: Federal Reserve Bank of New York, 2010): www.newyorkfed.org.

8. For example, see the Goldman Sachs 10-K filing for 2006.

9. Michael Lewis, *The Big Short: Inside the Doomsday Machine* (New York: W.W. Norton, 2010).

10. On December 21, 2007, Morgan Stanley reported full-year losses on super-senior CDOs of $9.4 billion.

11. Interview by author, June 2008.

12. Merrill Lynch would report full-year CDO losses of $20 billion in January 2008.

13. UBS's cumulative CDO losses rose to $38 billion by April 2008.

14. Thomson Street Events transcript of AIG investor meeting, December 5, 2007.

15. Senate PSI disclosure.

16. Former LDFM employee, interview by author, 2009.

17. An example of such a refusal is Germany's Raiffeisen und Volksbanken (R+V) Versicherung, a mutually owned insurer with assets of €28 billion, which told *Life & Pensions* magazine in January 2009 that "R+V has not done it and will not do it," on the grounds that securities lending was detrimental to its own interests; see Aaron Woolner, "Collateral Damage," *Life & Pensions,* February 2009.

18. Some pension funds that discovered their asset managers engaging in such activity during the crisis were forced to sell at a loss and initiated court proceedings afterward (for example, *BP North American Pension Fund v. Northern Trust,* U.S. District Court of Northern Illinois, which later settled out of court). By early 2009, many large U.S. pension funds had terminated their securities lending programs.

19. At the time of writing, both Ambac and MBIA were defending class action lawsuits brought by shareholders alleging that the monolines had deceived them about their CDO exposures.

20. See the Primary Dealer Credit Facility disclosures made by the Federal Reserve in December 2010, http://www.federalreserve.gov/newsevents/redform_pdcf.htm.

21. John Paulson, interview by author, July 2009.

22. These figures were disclosed by Paulson & Co. in August 2008 following the imposition of short-selling rules by the FSA.

23. Interview by author, March 2010.

24. See the SEC's complaint against Goldman Sachs and Fabrice Tourre, April 2010, http://www.sec.gov/litigation/complaints/2010/comp-pr2010-59.pdf.

25. Dinallo confirmed that this meeting took place. I have reconstructed the conversation from interviews with Dinallo and New York Fed officials.

26. The Bankruptcy Abuse Prevention and Consumer Protection Act (BAPCPA).

27. Corporate default and recovery rates, 1920–2008, Moody's Investors Service, www.moodys.com.

28. "Moody's Downgrades AIG Senior to A2," Moody's Investors Service press release, September 15, 2008.

29. I have reconstructed this conversation from conversations with New York Fed officials.

30. Dinallo could call the bluff of monoline default swap counterparties threatening to use collateral triggers, because under New York law he was the designated administrator of insolvent insurance companies, which gave him the power to determine who got paid and when. Other U.S. state insurance regulators had similar powers. By contrast, AIG's holding company was not an insurer.

31. Of the $57 billion in debt that Sigma had outstanding in June 2007, all but $6 billion had been paid back by October 2008.

32. See the report by New York attorney general Andrew Cuomo, *No Rhyme or Reason: The "Heads I Win, Tails You Lose" Bank Bonus Culture*, 2009, http://www.ag.ny.gov/media_center/2009/july/pdfs/Bonus%20Report%20Final%207.30.09.pdf.

Epilogue

1. For example, see the report *Global Banks—Too Big to Fail?*, published by J.P. Morgan Chase in February 2010, www.jpmorgan.com.

2. See U.K. Office of Budget Responsibility prebudget report, June 2010, http://budgetresponsibility.independent.gov.uk/index.html.

3. James Sassoon, interview by author, November 2009.

4. Nicholas Dunbar, "Revealed: Goldman Sachs' Mega-Deal for Greece," *Risk*, July 2003, 20.

5. Carmen M. Reinhart and Kenneth S. Rogoff, *This Time Is Different: Eight Centuries of Financial Folly* (Princeton, NJ: Princeton University Press, 2009).

Index

fair value
    Goldman's pricing of credit deriva-
        tives and, 24
    CDO pricing and, 101
fair value accounting
    description of, 13
    FASB on use for derivatives, 53, 251
    Fed examiners on trading business
        and, 138
    IASB on use for derivatives, 53, 253
Fannie Mae, 117, 145, 146–147, 225,
    228, 231, 245–246, 254
Fastow, Andy, 25
Federal Deposit Insurance Corporation
    (FDIC), 117, 122, 146, 179–180,
    213, 226, 241, 255
Federal Deposit Insurance Corpora-
    tion (FDIC) Improvement Act of
    1991, 117
Federal Open Markets Committee
    (FOMC), 201
Federal Reserve
    as central bank, 122–123
    commercial bank lending by, 27–28
    emergency interest rate cuts and, 255
    interest rates and, 4
    Large Financial Institutions (LFIs)
        committee of, 136, 252
    as regulator of banks, 27–29, 30,
        32, 44–45, 80, 115–116, 119–121,
        122–123, 124, 129, 133–136, 219,
        234–235, 238, 241, 243
    Volcker's 8 percent rule and,
        119, 129
Federal Reserve Bank of New York. *See*
    New York Fed
Fermat, Pierre de, 64
Fidelity, 189, 211–212
fiduciaries, fund managers as, 79
Fimalac, 102
Financial Accounting Standards Board
    (FASB), 23–24, 109, 251
Financial Crisis Inquiry Commission,
    137
Financial Industry Regulatory Authority
    (FINRA), 88

Financial Services and Markets Act,
    United Kingdom, 252
Financial Services Authority (FSA),
    United Kingdom, 121, 129, 130,
    131, 140, 141, 189, 227, 228, 240,
    247, 252
First Amendment, 245
First Boston, 149
First Franklin, 166
Fisher, Peter, 27, 29, 30–31, 32, 33, 43,
    44, 121, 124, 126, 216, 241
Fitch Ratings, 10, 11, 70, 73, 74, 75, 76,
    82, 101, 102–105, 148, 185, 189,
    195, 196, 245, 253
Foot, Michael, 121
Ford Motor Company, 112–113, 151, 252
foreign exchange markets, 3
Forster, Andrew, 160, 202, 209, 210,
    211, 214–215, 216
forward contracts, 2–3, 4, 25, 38
Frank, Barney, 239
Freddie Mac, 52, 117, 145, 146–147,
    151, 225, 228, 231, 246, 254
Fremont Investment and Loan, 173
Frost, Alan, 202, 209
Fuld, Dick, 228
futures exchanges, 37–38

Gasvoda, Kevin, 150, 156, 161, 165,
    168–169, 170, 171, 172, 173
Gaussian copula, 90, 92, 93–94, 101,
    103–104, 106, 108, 109, 110, 112,
    128, 156, 192, 252
Gaussian distribution curve, 64, 91
Geithner, Timothy, 134, 230, 231,
    234, 255
General Electric, 8, 178
General Motors (GM), 111–113, 252
Germany
    bank bailouts in, 205, 209, 248,
        253, 255
    CDO sales in, 95
    credit derivative investment from, 152
    Greek bailout and, 22
GFI, 110
Gibson Greetings, 50

federal role in guarantees of, 145–147

Goldman Sachs and, 149–150, 151, 156–158, 165–166, 168–176, 207–208, 218, 252, 253

representations and warranties for protection in, 168

securitizations of, 67, 145, 146

mortgage markets

chain of specialists in, 148

liar loans in, 147, 161, 166, 226

NINJAs (borrowers with No Income, No Job, No Assets) in, 161, 196

Morton, Andy, xiii

Municipal Bond Insurance Association (MBIA), 221, 222–223

naive diversification, 72

NationsBank, 119

National Westminster Bank, 119

NCHET (New Century Home Equity Trust) residential mortgage-backed securities, 144–145, 147–148, 151–152, 154, 163, 225

negative basis trades, 132

Nerva CDO, 75, 79, 82

net capital rule, 33

netting of derivatives contracts, 45

Netherlands, bank bailouts by, 255

Neuger, Win, 220

New Century Financial Corporation, 145, 147–148, 150, 151, 153–154, 173, 194, 220, 225

New York Fed (Federal Reserve Bank of New York)

AIG's problems and, 254, 255

Barclays' risk finance group and, 80

Bear Stearns' losses and, 254

commercial bank lending by, 27

Citigroup supervision by, 137–138, 252

Geithner's career at, 134

Lehman Brothers' problems and, 254

value at risk (VAR) models and, 134, 241

New York State Insurance Department, and monolines, 221, 222, 223, 234, 254

NINJA (borrowers with No Income, No Job, No Assets) loans, 161, 196

1998 market risk amendment, 123, 124–125, 126, 131–132, 134

1996 market risk amendment, 34

no-arbitrage rule, 38, 39, 41, 42–43

normal distribution, 64

Northern Rock, 241

North Street CDOs, 144–145, 149, 150, 151, 152, 193, 252, 254

notional portfolios, 167–168

Nudge (Sunstein and Thaler), 72

NYSE Liffe, 243

Obama, Barack, 243, 255

Ocwen Financial Corporation, 148

Office of the Comptroller of the Currency (OCC), 122, 123, 135, 136, 241

Office of Thrift Supervision (OTS), 122, 159, 223

OIS-Libor spread, 255

Oliver Wyman, 120, 121

O'Neal, Stan, 216, 253

Option One Mortgage Corporation, 220, 253

Ortseifen, Stefan, 184–185, 187

Ostrem, Pete, 150–151, 156–157, 159, 162, 170, 171, 173, 174, 207, 208, 214

over-the-counter (OTC) derivatives, 5, 41, 252

Page, Oliver, 140, 141, 227

Pallieres, Bertrand des, 110

Palma, Justo, 99

Paribas, 42, 47

Partridge-Hicks, Stephen, 182–183, 188–190, 192, 194, 195, 203–204, 206, 251, 253

Paulson, Hank, 234

Paulson, John, 162–163, 166–167, 172, 174, 175, 208, 225–226, 228, 253, 254

Acknowledgments

Someone who fits Amartya Sen's description of a rational fool would be fairly close to a psychopath. The economic world is full of these psychopaths: they are corporations. Corporations don't have emotions . . . they have PR departments that make up accounts of the company's motivations to fit a situation . . . Yet we not only survive but prosper in a world where they exist, because there are mechanisms that force them to be open and honest about their own motivation.

—J. Storrs Hall, *Beyond AI*

This book is the culmination of a fourteen-year career as a financial journalist. Although I began to think about writing it late in 2007, the book's origins go back to around 2000, after the publication of my first book, *Inventing Money*. I came to know well the large corporations of finance—the global investment banks—and saw at close hand how effectively they deflected calls for reform after the Long-Term Capital Management crisis emasculated their regulators.

I saw the power of the bank lobbying machine and its hold over editors and publishers. I realized for myself the role that journalists needed to play in forcing these corporations to be open and honest. In a series of stories published between 2002 and 2005, I attempted to put my theory into practice. Although I didn't know it at the time, those articles were the germ of what became this book. I would like to thank Matthew Crabbe of Incisive Media for his support during this period. Thanks are also due to the loyal staff of *Life & Pensions* magazine for many rewarding discussions between 2005 and 2009.

It would be impossible to list all the people who helped me during the book's formative decade. In my roles as writer, editor, and publisher, I was lucky to have virtually unfettered access to the derivatives industry during the peak phase of its growth. Although I now argue that certain business practices of this industry and its fellow travellers were morally indefensible, it would be ungracious of me not to thank the many decent individuals within financial institutions and regulatory bodies who generously shared their time and insights.

In writing the book over the past two years, I have drawn on my existing contacts and made many new ones. Many of those who helped me in my research are bound by confidentiality agreements, and I have agreed not to cite them as sources or quote them by name in the book. Such agreements are essential, since some large organizations do not take kindly to being forced to be accountable, for example the U.K.'s Financial Services Authority, whose delightfully named Accountability department sent me the following message in response to a fact-checking query:

> To the extent that the information you intend to publish was originally received by the FSA in the course of carrying out our supervisory functions, it will be "confidential information" for the purposes of the confidentiality regime set up under section 348 of the Financial Services and Markets Act 2000 ("FSMA") . . . You should be aware that the unauthorised disclosure of confidential information is a criminal offence (see section 352 FSMA).

The contacts whom it is safe to publicly thank would include Sheila Bair, Clive Briault, Andrew Cross, Eric Dinallo, Peter Fisher, Michael Gibson, Michael Gordy, Patricia Jackson, Greg Lippmann, Ben Logan, Anthony Neuberger, Stephen Partridge-Hicks, Ernest Patrikis, John Paulson, William Perraudin, James Sassoon, Nick Sossidis, Ron Tanemura, Axel Tillmann, Paul Tucker, Adair Turner, Kitty Ussher, and Tom Wilde. Any errors in the book are my responsibility alone.

Special thanks are due to Hugo Dixon and his team at Reuters Breakingviews. I first worked for Hugo in 2001, when his company was a start-up. Over the years, I have learned a lot about the interface between financial news and comment through my work for Hugo. It was particularly helpful to use Breakingviews as a sounding board while conceiving and writing this book.

I am grateful to my agent Peter Tallack for first taking an interest in the project and working with me throughout, and to Christy Fletcher for finding a good home for this book at Harvard Business Review Press. Thanks are also due to my Harvard editors: Jacqueline Murphy, for shepherding the book from proposal to second-draft manuscript; Justin Fox, for ably guiding the book to publication; and Bob Roe, for his invaluable hands-on development work. I am also grateful to the rest of the Harvard team, particularly Kevin Evers and Allison Peter.

My deepest gratitude of all goes to my wife, Teresa Chick, without whose support this project would not have been possible.

—La Adrada, London, New York 2008–2011

About the Author

Nicholas Dunbar grew up in London and trained as a physicist at Manchester, Cambridge, and Harvard universities. He was inspired to become a financial journalist by university friends who took their mathematical skills from academia onto the trading floors of investment banks.

From 1998 until 2009, Dunbar was technical editor of *Risk* magazine, a specialist derivatives publication. In 2005, he launched *Life & Pensions*, a sister publication to *Risk* aimed at the insurance and pensions industry.

During this time, Dunbar wrote a series of exclusive stories on derivatives blowups, which cemented his reputation as an investigative journalist, and in 2007 he won the State Street award for institutional financial journalism. He has also written a column called Risky Finance for the authoritative financial commentary service Reuters Breakingviews.

In 1999, Dunbar wrote his first book, *Inventing Money: The Story of Long-Term Capital Management and the Legends Behind It* (Wiley, 2000). *The Devil's Derivatives* is his second book. For further information visit www.nickdunbar.net.